# WRITERS
# READING WRITERS

Robert Hollander. Photo courtesy of Denise Applewhite,
Office of Communications, Princeton University.

# WRITERS
# READING WRITERS

## Intertextual Studies
## in Medieval and
## Early Modern Literature

in Honor of Robert Hollander

Edited by
Janet Levarie Smarr

**DELAWARE**

Newark: University of Delaware Press

Associated University Presses
2010 Eastpark Boulevard
Cranbury, NJ 08512

The paper used in this publication meets the requirements of the American National Standard for Permanence of Paper for Printed Library Materials Z39.48–1984.

Library of Congress Cataloging-in-Publication Data

Writers reading writers : intertextual studies in medieval and early modern literature in honor of Robert Hollander / edited by Janet Levarie Smarr.
    p. cm.
    Includes bibliographical references and index.
    ISBN-13: 978-0-87413-976-1 (alk. paper)
    ISBN-10: 0-87413-976-7 (alk. paper)
    1. Literature—History and criticism. I. Hollander, Robert, 1933- II. Smarr, Janet Levarie, 1949-
    PN36.H63W75 2007
    809—dc22
                                                2006035602

PRINTED IN THE UNITED STATES OF AMERICA

"Vagliami 'l lungo studio e' l grande amore
che m'ha fatto cercar lo tuo volume"

[Let my long study and great love avail
that made me delve so deep into your volume]
—Dante, *Inferno*, 2.83–84

# Contents

8 CONTENTS

# Introduction

JANET LEVARIE SMARR
AND ALBERT J. RIVERO

ROBERT HOLLANDER'S REPUTATION AS A SCHOLAR IN DANTE AND Boccaccio studies is well known both in Europe and in the United States. He served several terms as the elected President of the American Dante Society; received the gold medal of the City of Florence and the International Nicola Zingarelli Prize in recognition of his scholarship on Dante; and Certaldo made him an honorary citizen in similar recognition of his work on Boccaccio. Hollander's scholarship has won support from the Guggenheim, Fulbright, NEH, and Rockefeller Foundations, and has resulted in the publication of nearly two dozen books, written or edited, plus more than eighty articles.

Professor Hollander's influence on students is similarly powerful and widespread. He taught at Princeton University for forty years, mentoring several generations of new scholars. This volume—and the enthusiastic alacrity with which its contributors agreed to participate—is a testament to his long career of admired teaching by students of his from across the decades. It is typical of Hollander that the contributors include his past undergraduate as well as graduate students. Professor Hollander took students at every level just as seriously, brought to them all his passion for the study of great texts and offered them the tools for their own analytical and reflective work. As a result, not only have Hollander's doctoral students gone on to teach and publish internationally, but undergraduates in his Dante courses have repeatedly won essay prizes for their papers, and students in his other comparative literature courses have gone on to a lifetime of serious reading. It is not surprising, therefore, to find among the volumes edited by

Hollander on one hand a sixteenth-century commentary on Dante and on the other hand volume two of a three-volume anthology of *Western Literature*. It was Hollander, in fact, who first established the "great books" course at Princeton that became the core of the undergraduate comparative literature program. His students are now professors and researchers in the fields of Romance Languages, English, and Comparative Literature. Beyond his attention to our work in his courses, he has continued generously to mentor and assist us in our careers.

How can we, as the diverse offspring of this shared "father," describe the inheritance we have from him? Certainly he has communicated methods and standards of scholarship. Often these were conveyed more by example and by his warmly twinkling smile than by precept; however, they can be at least partly articulated. Like a medieval text surrounded by marginal glosses, his own books are notorious for giving at least as much space to footnotes as to the main body of critical text. Those notes convey his respect for the work of scholars who have gone before him, and his sense of obligation to read and cite their contributions to his topic of research. Working on writers whose texts have received commentary for six hundred years, Hollander has never been content to look only at modern critical discussions, but has frequently mined the forgotten nuggets of insight buried in the scholarship of previous centuries. This concern to leave no stone unturned led to his avant-garde technological project of making Dante commentaries available via computer networks even before the ubiquitous World Wide Web. The imperative, both scientific and moral, to read everything ever written on one's topic can be daunting to students working on a writer such as Dante, about whom more has been written than perhaps any other poet ever; and obviously some limitations apply. Nonetheless, the general principle of seeking out and giving respectful consideration to others' work in the field has been an honored model.

This attention to the ideas of others is closely connected to Hollander's encouraging attention to his students' ideas. In his lectures and precepts, he would often point out when a certain idea had come from one of his former students. He would mention that student's name and usually share some memory of that particular student. There was no greater honor than when one of us made a comment in one of his classes and he would stop, write it and our name in his book, and let us know that that comment would now be part of his future lectures on the subject. He has frequently given credit and drawn notice to students' work in his written essays or conference papers; sometimes he has published jointly with them. His treating his students—even undergraduates —as already contributing members of a scholarly endeavor has provided a wonderful introduction for many of us to the communal as well as individual nature of the scholarly life. Hollander's wide network of scholar-friends indicates the lasting quality of these relationships.

Working on literature that has remained a productive site for scholarly discussion and literary inspiration for six centuries, Hollander has learned to take a long-term view, forward in time as well as back through history. As president of the American Dante Society, he launched a series of *lectura Dantis* conceived as the gradual publication of a volume on each canto of the *Commedia*, an endeavor projected—even at a pace of improbable rapidity— to take at least a century to complete. Similarly his Princeton Faculty Dante Seminar, meeting once a month to discuss a canto at a time, began in 1983 and fulfilled its anticipated continuation through 2001. His Center for Electronic Texts in the Humanities, launched as a pilot project in 1988, had the open-ended aim of creating an ongoing bibliography of machine-readable texts in the humanities; obviously developments of the Internet and electronic publishing have replaced this original endeavor, but they have also demonstrated the rightness of its foresight.

Hollander's classes have always been intended to provoke explorative thought rather than to transmit an established wisdom. This holds true not only for seminar discussions: even a polished lecture on *Don Quixote*, for example, laid out opposing approaches to the text and let students ponder the arguments on both sides. One particular reminiscence from thirty-nine years ago, of the young assistant professor giving a lecture on Beckett to over one hundred freshmen in Burt Sonnenfeld's European literature course, is typical, suggesting that Hollander's pedagogical mastery was there from the very beginning. According to one of those freshmen who has since become a professor, what was wonderful, after Sonnenfeld's pyrotechnics, was Hollander's tone of quiet whimsy that managed somehow to convey at the same time both great seriousness and wonder. Indeed that combination of seriousness and wonder, of great erudition conveyed with effortlessness and an on-going curiosity rooted in astonishment, has inspired students to find and pursue their own questions, making use of, but remaining undaunted by, centuries of previous scholarship. Hollander's passion for his own research and his good-humored encouragement of students have welcomed and guided their efforts.

Students in his courses are led to consider both small-scale detail and large-scale patterns. A typical assignment requests students to trace a particular word or word-cluster through its recurring appearances, in the text at hand and also beyond into other texts the writer might have read. The local meanings of the words thus emerge from their multiple relations to wider contexts, and at the same time the local inquiry turns into a perception of broader effects. Students have learned to see, for example, both how Dante may use a phrase from Ovid or Vergil, but also how he may then rework the implications of that phrase from its infernal to its purgatorial and celestial appearances.

Following the traces of specific words or allusions rapidly leads from textual analysis to intertextual reading. Just like the communal nature of scholarship, Hollander's teaching lays open the conversational nature of poetic writing: the way writers are always also readers, responding to texts that have provoked their thought. The move is natural from Dante studies to the studies of the texts he read or of the writers who read his work, and ultimately outward to the whole cultural history that the "great books" courses and comparative literature program have embodied. That is why the former students who have contributed to this volume, even when they are not Dante scholars, have all been working within the framework of its overarching theme: writers reading and responding to other writers.

Intertextual study, the focus of much of Hollander's writing and teaching, has clearly remained a key approach for his former students. Several studies deal explicitly with the complexly mediated nature of such readings: as Chaucer read Ovid through the lens of Dante's uses of that poet (Fumo), or as Boccaccio contemplated Vergil's figure of Manto along with the conspicuous interventions of Dante's Virgil (Hagedorn). Curtius's contribution to Dante studies was a recognition not only of Dante's Latin readings but also of the situatedness of contemporary scholarship that resisted acknowledging their significance; thus Curtius dealt simultaneously with Dante as a reader and with readers of Dante (Richards).

Sometimes writers found through their readings a formal or technical model: as Vasari sought a narrative strategy for discussing the work of artists (McGregor), or as Langland searched for a framework on which to unfurl his vision (Smith). At times some particular detail, such as the names of Actaeon's dogs (Marchesi) or a miracle of medicine in the Greek romances (Robins), inspired an intriguing recontextualization that casts light on the writer's self-image or his concept of human interiority. At other times, the reading directly provoked large questions with which the later writer felt compelled to grapple in turn: as Maggi struggled with the injustices of Boccaccio's Griselda story (Smarr), and as Dante grappled with the risks of human judgment (Seem) or reworked the distressing myth of Philomela's rape and its consequences (Levenstein). All the essays demonstrate the importance of such readings to the later writer's conception and formulation of his own work.

Although many of the essays in this volume—as might be expected—do deal in some way with Dante or Boccaccio, both as readers of earlier material and as the sources and models for later writers, these essays are not exclusively about the two fourteenth-century Italians to whom Hollander has devoted most of his own voluminous research. The essays have been divided into two groups. The first group concerns writers reading ancient texts, including Latin poetry, Greek romances, and the Bible. The second group concerns the reading of what Dante and subsequent Europeans would have considered "the moderns," i.e., medieval and later texts.

"Reading the ancients" treats the uses of the Greek romances, Vergil, Ovid, and the Bible, mostly by Dante, Boccaccio, and Chaucer, but also by Shakespeare. Simone Marchesi describes Dante's shift of personal model, for both the political and poetic self, from Brunetto Latini to Ovid. Like Hollander, Marchesi finds in details of wording and naming the clues to this major shift in the poet's self-imagining. Jessica Levenstein, remembering Professor Hollander's assignments, traces Dante's references to an Ovidian myth and discusses what use he made of it within its new Christianized context. Suzanne Hagedorn similarly traces the references to the sybil from Vergil and other ancient historians into the poetry of Dante and the historicizing prose of Boccaccio. Concerned, like Marchesi, with the writer's search for models, she argues that Boccaccio's increasingly negative portraits of Manto reveal the shifting weight of his self-identification as a writer from the pagan Vergil to the Christian Dante. Lauren Scancarelli Seem turns to Dante's biblical sources for statements about justice, arguing that Dante was caught in a dilemma: displaying the arrogance of judging others, which his religious source texts warn against, yet which his poem requires. Jamie Fumo, like Marchesi and Hagedorn, comes back to the topic of the writer's competing models for his sense of his own authorial function, in this case Chaucer's relation to Ovid both through and against his recognition of Dante's relation to Ovid. Fumo argues that Chaucer identifies himself more closely with the vatic Apollonian image of the poet than critics have commonly acknowledged, but at the same time complicates that vatic image through Apollo's Ovidian identification as a failed lover. William Robins picks up Hollander's technique of close reading and the ability of a word or phrase to evoke its ancient sources in a way that enlightens a much larger issue. His discussion of how Shakespeare in *Pericles* alters his sources in the Greek romances richly broadens into a question about the conception of interiority that emerges from three scenes of lost consciousness. Associable with other essays in this volume that treat the poet's often divided sense of self, this study reveals in the play's main characters a self split between what can be articulated by social authorities and an ineffable core experienced as a transcendence that is both humanly intersubjective and linked to the divine.

"Reading the moderns," while maintaining connections with the previous essays, moves into a wider variety of periods and writers. Earl Jeffrey Richards returns to Dante as the object of Curtius's scholarly work; he shows how Curtius's emphasis on Dante's medieval Latin sources not only opened a new area of Dante studies but also attempted an intervention in the politics of Curtius's time, just as Dante had commented on earlier writers in order to speak about the dangers in his own society. Writers read in part because they are seeking models for themselves and for their writing. Macklin Smith queries whether Langland might have derived some of his ideas, both poetic and conceptual, from Bonaventure's *Lignum vitae*. Although Langland did not know Dante's writings, the two poets shared some common readings and aims. Thus, while taking on an English rather than Italian writer, Smith draws guidance from aspects of Hollander's work: the attention to details combined with attention to the larger structures to which they contribute, and a sensual appreciation of poetry that acknowledges at the same time how this poetry constructs a view of the moral universe. James McGregor similarly suggests that Vasari, for his lives of the painters, found in Dante's and Boccaccio's writings about artists a model that could solve both formal and conceptual problems: how to make such narratives dynamic, and how to reconceptualize the artists' manual craft as an intellectual art. Without denying the importance of classical biographies as one of Vasari's models, McGregor adds the vernacular writing of Dante and Boccaccio as another shaping influence. Boccaccio provides the model again in Janet Smarr's essay on the playwright Carlo Maria Maggi. Smarr suggests that Maggi's play based on the *Decameron*'s famous last story lends support to Hollander's critical reading of the tale's two main characters. Maggi combines Boccaccio with Machiavelli as his sources when he sets two women against each other to demonstrate that both are too extreme. In so doing, Maggi emphasizes the political rather than domestic implications of Boccaccio's tale, making it harder to treat either Griselda or Gualtiero as exemplary. Even Nicholas Rennie's essay, which moves away from Dante and Boccaccio to treat texts much more modern than Hollander has normally written about, takes on the need of Goethe and Leopardi to deal with inherited traditions of cosmology—the same traditions that were so fundamental to Dante's worldview and to the shaping of Dante's poem. When natural cosmology has become a basis for the moral order, what are modern writers to do who seek a foundational image for a serious moral vision yet for whom the ancient science has been overthrown? How are modern writers to treat that outdated cosmology when the art and literature that it inspired remain dear to them? How can they convert the power of those images to convey a new and more unsettling worldview and epistemology?

While Professor Hollander's publications primarily concern medieval literature, he put into place and frequently taught the comparative literature courses at Princeton that introduce students, through judiciously selected examples, to the full sweep of Western literary history. The chosen topic for this volume—

of writers responding to and reworking other writers—extends through the varied fields of Robert Hollander's former students Hollander's own techniques of scholarship and modes of questioning with regard to that long series of readings and responses which is the history of European literature.

# WRITERS
# READING WRITERS

# I
## *Reading the Ancients*

# Distilling Ovid:
## Dante's Exile and Some
## Metamorphic Nomenclature in Hell

SIMONE MARCHESI

WHEN—DIRECTLY AND FOR THE FIRST TIME—DANTE COMMENTS IN *Convivio* I about the circumstances of his banishment from Florence, his literary-autobiographic model of choice seems to be Brunetto Latini. Several correspondences between his predicament and that of his teacher invite such an identification. Brunetto and Dante were both writers of doctrinal prose, the *Convivio* being inspired in part by the same vulgarizing goal as the *Tresor*. Dante must also have realized that, beyond the necessary shift in the balance of political power that allowed his return to Florence, Brunetto was able to reclaim the position of leading intellectual in the city thanks to his work: not by chance, Villani acknowledged him to be the "first teacher in refining the Florentines."[1] With his doctrinal work, the writer of the *Convivio* aimed to pattern his experience on Brunetto's and become the second "maestro" of his former (and, perhaps, also future) fellow citizens. But this model will soon shift, as we will see, from Brunetto to another exiled poet: Ovid.

A hint of the uncanny sense Dante must have felt of reenacting Brunetto's biography in the first years of his exile can be found in *Convivio* I. iii. 4. The option of a return to Florence and a readmission into her cultural life still appears viable, as he declares his love for the city and pleads for a peaceful return:

Poi che fu piacere de li cittadini de la bellissima e famosissima figlia di Roma, Fiorenza, di gittarmi fuori del suo dolce seno—nel quale nato e nutrito fui in fino al colmo de la vita mia, e nel quale,

21

con buona pace di quella, desidero con tutto lo cuore di riposare l'animo stancato e terminare lo tempo che m'è dato ... (*Convivio* I.iii.4)

[Since it was the pleasure of the citizens of the most beautiful and famous daughter of Rome, Florence, to cast me out of her sweet bosom—where I was born and bred up to the pinnacle of my life, and where, with her good will, I desire with all my heart to rest my weary mind and to complete the span of time that is given to me ... ] (Trans. R. Lansing).

Traditionally, scholars (Vasoli for the *Convivio* and Mengaldo for *De vulgari eloquentia*) have glossed this passage with *De vulgari eloquentia* I.vi.3.[2] In so doing, they insist upon a continuity in Dante's thought on the point that a return to Florence might still have seemed possible while he was composing both texts. However, the link that they establish between *De vulgari eloquentia* and *Convivio* I regarding this aspect of Dante's political poetics is not as obvious as it may appear. The phrasing of the Latin treatise suggests that the possibility of a political pardon (and consequent readmission) had actually disappeared sometime during the short span of time separating those two works.[3] The note that the editors append to the passages overlooks two determining elements in the text.

First, the passage from *De vulgari eloquentia* that Mengaldo and Vasoli propose as a gloss for *Convivio* I is not indisputably relevant. In *De vulgari* I.vi.3, Dante draws attention to the fact of his exile rather than to its potential suspension:

Nos autem, cui mundus est patria velut piscibus equor, quanquam Sarnum biberimus ante dentes et Florentiam adeo diligamus ut, quia dileximus, exilium patiamur iniuste ...

[To me, however, the whole world is a homeland, like the sea to fish—though I drank from the Arno before cutting my teeth, and love Florence so much that, because I loved her, I suffer exile unjustly ...] (Trans. S. Botterill).

If he pleads innocence (*exilium patiamur iniuste*) and declares his love for Florence (*Florentiam ... diligamus*), Dante also distances himself from the arguments of those who, through an ill-conceived sense of municipal duty and pride, regard the Florentine dialect as the perfect language. The sentence I have just cited comes as a conclusion to his most stinging attack against the delusions of the advocates of a municipal language:

> "Nam, quicumque tam obscene rationis ut locum sue nationis delitiosissimum credit esse sub sole, hic etiam pre cunctis proprium vulgare licetur, id est maternam locutionem, et per consequens credit ipsum fuisse illud quod fuit Ade" (I.vi.2)

> [For whoever is so misguided as to think that the place of his birth is the most delightful spot under the sun may also believe that his own language—his mother tongue, that is—is pre-eminent among all others; and, as a result, he may believe that his language was also Adam's.]

In keeping with the overall argument of the Latin treatise, Dante's linguistic and poetic horizon is no longer limited to the city—whether Florence or the imaginary and parodic town of *Petramala*. Rather, he projects the intellectual role of the poet-philosopher onto a much broader, world-scale, and potentially universal backdrop:

> [Nos] revolventes et poetarum et aliorum scriptorum volumina, quibus mundus universaliter et membratim describitur, ratiocinantesque in nobis situationes varias mundi locorum et eorum habitudine ad utrunque polum et circulum equatorem, multas esse perpendimus firmiterque censemus et magis nobiles et magis delitiosas et regiones et urbes quam Tusciam et Florentiam, unde sumus oriundus et civis, et plerasque nationes et gentes delectabiliori atque utiliori sermone uti quam Latinos. (I.vi.3)

> [When I turn the pages of the volumes of poets and other writers, by whom the world is described as a whole and in its constituent parts, and when I reflect inwardly on the various locations of places in the world, and their relations to the two poles and the circle at the equator, I am convinced, and firmly maintain, that there are many regions and cities more noble and more delightful than Tuscany and Florence, where I was born and of which I am a citizen, and many nations and peoples who speak a more elegant and practical language than do the Italians.]

The larger intellectual horizon within which Dante moves in *De vulgari* counterbalances his scarcely exclusive affection for

Florence. The poet's homecoming might still be appealing, but the universalistic rhetoric of the treatise makes it seem, at the very least, unnecessary.

Second, the relevant passage with which to gloss *Convivio*'s declaration of love is not the one that has been thus far proposed. At *De vulgari eloquentia* II.vi.4, we find a parallel text that is a much more appropriate "translation" of the sentiment expressed in *Convivio* I than the passage from Book I. As the culminating example of the various levels of syntactical construction, Dante proposes a sentence of his own devising: "Eiecta maxima parte florum de sinu tuo, Florentia, nequicquam Trinacriam Totila secundus adivit." (II.vi.4) [The greater part of your flowers, o Florence, having being snatched from your breast, the second Totila advanced in vain towards Trinacria.] The ablative absolute with which Dante denounces the foolish politics of Charles of Valois and the effects that this political reversal had on his own political career reveals Dante's detachment from the spatial and temporal circumstances of his exile's origins.[4]

When he writes *De vulgari eloquentia* Dante may thus still be in love with his city, but the manner in which he writes about his slim chances of return has radically shifted away from the still-optimistic outlook of *Convivio* I. Not only has the hopeful statement advocating a return to Florence been superseded by a cold, satiric depiction of the city's political predicament; the text of the *De vulgari eloquentia* itself has also replaced that wish with the bitter reality of a factual statement. In the Latin prose, there are no hints of a possible reversal in the course of history. Dante's prospect of homecoming has shifted into a remote syntactical background. On this point, the Latin treatise is engaged in a radically different discourse from its vernacular antecedent.

A significant detail reinforces this impression: not only does Dante's Latin treatise marginalize the model of the fortunate teacher's homecoming; it indicates what will be Brunetto's paradigmatic substitute as well. In fact, the loaded simile linking Dante's notion of home (*patria*) not to Florence but to the whole world has a revealing pedigree. The words we read at the imaginative core of the argument in *De vulgari eloquentia*, "Nos autem, cui mundus est patria velut piscibus equor," derive from Ovid: "Omne solum forti patria est, ut piscibus aequor" (*Fasti* I.493). To be sure, the notion that the magnanimous individual considers the whole world his homeland and the specific language Dante uses *may* still be found in Brunetto's *Tresor* II.84.11: "Toutes terres sont païs au preudome autresi comme la mers as poissons." Nevertheless, Dante's Latinizing word-order ("like to fish the sea," not "like the sea to fish" as Brunetto translates) and the rhythm of his prose (*velut piscibus equor*—the same *cursus planus* as Ovid's hexametric *clausula*) suggest an interest in modeling his stance on the Latin poet rather than on the writer of Old French prose. In Dante's mind, the model of Ovid's exile-without-return infiltrates Brunetto's compellingly successful narrative of reentry into Florence and destabilizes it.[5]

⁂ ⁂ ⁂

For Dante, the model of Brunetto's felicitous cultural and political return will only openly cease to be operative in *Inferno* 14, with the tragic double entendre on the words *a ca'*—a morally no less than sentimentally charged syntagma that suggests to Brunetto his pupil's possible return from exile ("home"= Florence) and to Dante a superior spiritual destination ("home"= Heaven).[6] Yet Brunetto's prominence in Dante's self-portrayal already shows signs of erosion in *De vulgari eloquentia*, when the second model of intellectual in exile peeks through the surface of his identity as a vernacular writer. In spite of its early appearance in Dante's oeuvre, Ovid's model is apparently marginal to his project of self-fashioning. Even in the *Commedia*, Dante's perception and representation of his exile appear to involve few elements of the Ovidian paradigm. *Peregrinus* through almost all the parts of Italy, the Dante we encounter in *Inferno* is still eminently a banished politician in exile, not a relegated poet. His trysts with Ciacco, Farinata, Vanni Fucci, and Brunetto himself, the *loci classici* for a discussion of his banishment from the divided city, are all dominated by the interweaving of politics and exile. In each of them, Dante figures as the party man about to be removed from power and the political scene altogether.[7]

And yet, the trace Ovid left in *De vulgari eloquentia*, however faint, might be worth pursuing. Ovidian poetry and exile will share the stage, in fact, in another episode of *Inferno*, that of the Malebranche in cantos 21 through 23. It is here that the allusion to the Latin poet as an alternate model will once again be activated. As we will see, the intersection of two Ovidian texts, the myth of Actaeon in the *Metamorphoses* and its allusive redeployment in *Tristia* 2, provides the poem with the image substratum for the long episode in the *bolgia* of the barrators. That the classic, even paradigmatic, poet of exile should be evoked at this juncture in the poem's plot is not surprising. It is here that the character of Dante comes face to face with the sin of which he was accused in life, and it is here that he is confronted by a pack of demons for which his poetry establishes a finely allusive, if amused, pedigree. The role that Ovid takes on for the poet of the *Commedia* does not only displace Brunetto's paradigm as a literary, autobiographical model, but it also provides Dante with a new and more richly inflected mythologeme for his poetry of exile.

From the time of the first commentators, the long episode devoted to the pouch of the barrators has drawn significant attention for its potential autobiographical nature.[8] In 1302 Dante was banned from Florence under the (customary and unspecific) accusation of being a *barattiere*—that is, someone who made "fraudulent use and sale of offices and employments of public trust."[9] Professional readers of the poem have often scrutinized the text for clues that might reveal a connection linking the storyline of Dante's extra-textual life and the moment at which the character reaches the place in hell that would, presumably, be his final and eternal destination. Some elements of the narrative in the *bolgia* of the barrators have therefore been interpreted as allusions to the circumstance of his earthly predicament. First, the fear that the Pilgrim shows throughout the episode, an unspecified but dominating element throughout cantos 21–23, has been read as one such allusion.[10] When the soon-to-be-exiled politician comes face to face with his earthly destiny in the frame of eternity, the Pilgrim is for the first and only time in real physical danger. In this light, the *Commedia* has appeared to register a transfer of features from the *auctor* to the *actor*: Dante's biographical danger and fear would be allusively assigned to the character that bears his name in the poem.[11] Similarly, but with a different connotation, the comic tone of *Inferno* 21 and 22 has been considered an indication of the poet's indignant protestation of innocence and of his sarcastic attitude toward a crime and a sin of which he had been unjustly accused.[12]

The autobiographical interpretations of the canto have found support in the suggestive proposal that Dante Gabriele Rossetti advanced in the *nota finale* of his 1826 commentary on *Inferno*. According to Rossetti, the Evil-Claws, the twelve demons that are explicitly called up in *Inferno* 21, bear names that are supposed to evoke those of historical Florentine and Lucchese Black families.[13] In his view, the (comic) devils that guard and persecute the barrators in the bolgia have names that would have been recognized by Dante's first readers. The catalogue on which Rossetti concentrates is given in two dense tercets in the voice of Malacoda:

> "Tra'ti avante, Alichino, e Calcabrina,"
> cominciò elli a dire, "e tu, Cagnazzo;
> e Barbariccia guidi la decina.
>   Libicocco vegn'oltre e Draghignazzo,
> Ciriatto sannuto e Graffiacane
> e Farfarello e Rubicante pazzo"
>
> (*Inferno* 21. 118–23)

> ["Step forward, Alichino, Calabrina,"
> he continued, "and you Cagnazzo,
> and let Barbaricia lead the squad.
>   Let Libicocco come too, and Draghignazzo,
> Ciriatto with his tusks, and Graffiacane,
> Farfarello, and madcap Rubicante."][14]

The names listed here, and the textual pleasure derived from the act of naming itself, appear to Rossetti as indicting—preventively and from a safe distance—the members of the Black party who had been more or less responsible for the poet's exile. Rossetti's argument is triggered by (and develops along a new line) a cursive gloss appended to the episode in the Renaissance: Castelvetro was actually the first to note that the names of ten devils are carefully recorded in *Inferno* 21 and then reprised in canto 22. To account for such an exact record, the poem, speaking *in persona auctoris*, clarifies that Dante had "noted them all when they were chosen (*eletti*)." In the technical term *eletti*—which means "picked," but also "voted into office"—Rossetti finds a confirmation of his political intuition. In *Inferno* 21, the Malebranche work as public servants who, after having been chosen, perform an office; the act of nomination they undergo in the *Commedia* recalls the election of politicians to their posts. The enjoyment that modern readers of the poem derive from the inventive onomastics of the episode is, in this light, distinct from the pleasure that contemporary readers could have drawn from recognizing political personalities caricatured in the devils of the bolgia. As Moore notes, "the whole travesty might have been transparently obvious and irresistibly telling when the names and incidents were fresh in men's minds."[15]

It is on this last detail that I wish to insist here, proposing to see in Dante's playful act of naming a reflection not only of an immediate political concern, but also of the reactivation of a classical poetic paradigm. Following a suggestion of Parodi from the beginning of the twentieth century, I propose to see the naming of the devils as influenced by the episode of Actaeon's death as narrated in the third book of Ovid's *Metamorphoses*.[16] Dante's naming of the devils recuperates Ovid's tour de force with canine onomastics and changes its tone, from tragic to mock-heroic. Taking the argument further than Parodi did, and adding a new element to the chain of Ovidian allusions in the episode, I also propose to consider Ovid's mention of Actaeon as his own mythological double in *Tristia* II as pertinent to Dante's mythography of exile. In *Metamorphoses* III, Ovid had constructed the mythological paradigm of the innocent hero who is unjustly punished; and in the elegy from exile he had applied this paradigm to himself, thus superimposing on the *exemplar* of the myth the poetic *exemplum* of the innocent exile. I argue that Ovid's re-use of the Actaeon myth in his poetry of exile is the missing link—or, to continue the metaphor of my title, the missing ingredient—that may connect the lines of Dante's political and poetic autobiographies of exile. While pleading for a supplement of clemency from Augustus, Ovid writes:

> Cur aliquid vidi? Cur noxia lumina feci?
> Cur imprudenti cognita culpa mihi?
> Inscius Actaeon vidit sine veste Dianam:
> Praeda fuit canibus non minus ille suis.
> (*Tristia* II, 103–6)

[Why did I see that? Why did I make my eyes guilty? Why, imprudent that I was, have I witnessed a fault? Unwillingly did Acteon see Diana naked: not unlike me he became the prey of his own dogs.] (my translation)

By echoing *Metamorphoses* III in an autobiographic context through the nomination of the canine devils that pursue him, Dante appropriates the Ovidian model of the poet in exile. Not unlike the unjustly relegated Ovid, who had cast himself as a new Actaeon, Dante subjects his narrative projection to the threat of the pack of Ovidian devils.

Seeing the canto of the barrators in this light has an essential advantage: it brings together the strain of biographical explanation of the episode and the literary approach to the catalogue of the devils' names. As Rossetti proposed, the cantos that name Dante's alleged persecutors do indeed contain an allusion to Dante's exile, and this allusion does indeed pass through the names of the twelve demons in the canto. Yet the literary construct of Ovid-in-exile functions as the fundamental filter between the infernal plot and Dante's biography. We need not accept Rossetti's hermeneutically strong (but philologically weak) hypothesis, nor its philologically stronger (but hermeneutically weaker) variants by Torraca and Luiso: there need not be a *direct* connection between the devils' names and names in the political history of the Black cities of Florence and Lucca. The connection may exist, but it passes through the overarching allusion to Ovid and the invention of the devils' speaking names. As a text arguably addressed to a double audience, contemporary readers and posterity, the *Commedia* hedges its bets: while it plays with its first public, it also takes advantage of a classical, and perhaps more enduring, paradigm. It redeploys the game of mirrors that Ovid set up between *Tristia* II and *Metamorphoses* III and portrays its protagonist as a potential Ovidian Actaeon. In *Inferno* 21–23, Dante patterns some key elements of the narrative on his classical *exemplar* and treats them—like Ovid—as a paradigm for his own poetic autobiography.

※ ※ ※

Actaeon's episode in *Metamorphoses* III can be divided into two main sections. The first is concerned with the etiology of the character's transformation: a hunting scene, Diana bathing, Actaeon stumbling upon her, the goddess's rage and revenge, the transformation of the hero into a stag. The second part of the story is devoted to the manner of Actaeon's death: his consciousness of the new appearance that has befallen him, the necessary social adjustments in the form of a rhetorical internal debate ("should I return to society or should I stay in the wilderness?"), the lively catalogue of the chasing dogs, his capture and eventual dismemberment. The two phases correspond to the double punishment Diana metes out to the innocently guilty Actaeon: the sibylline words she pronounces right after she has half-instinctively, half-maliciously sprinkled the hunter's face with water, "now you are free to tell / that you have seen me all unrobed—if you can tell," only superficially referred to the inability of animals to communicate; rather, they entailed a secondary menace of death. Indeed, Actaeon will be unable to recount his vision of the naked goddess both because his power of articulating human language is gone and because his death will almost immediately follow his metamorphosis into the timid stag. In his brief mention at the core of *Tristia* II, Ovid is more interested in evoking the first part of the myth; in *Inferno* 21 and 22, Dante subtly evokes the second part.

In *Inferno* 21–23, there are several motifs that may be seen as alluding to the *Metamorphoses*. The first, general element of consonance is the metaphoric, potentially metamorphic, overgrowth of Dante's text. Both the sinners immersed in the pitch and the devils who keep watch over them are caught in an ever-changing flux of metaphors. In a very Ovidian gesture, their verbal nature is incessantly metamorphosized. The fallen angels are—generically—endowed with mixed feral traits: they are *malebranche* (evil-claws, 21.37; implicitly also in 22.41, 137, and 140); the first to appear is an actual mastiff who chases a thief (21.40); the band that approaches, menacing Virgil, is a pack of dogs (21.60). Metaphorically, the devils shift from dogs to cats (22.58), to evil birds (22.96), to hawks (22.132 and 139) and again to hounds (23.18).[17] Singularly, they are a varied group of beasts: Ciriatto is nominally a pig and iconographically a wild boar (22.56); Cagnazzo, who has a muzzle more than a face (22.106), Graffiacane (cat-like), and Draghignazzo (dragon- or snake-like) are likely named after their dominating physical traits. On the other side of the melee, sinners as a group are likened to dolphins (22.19), toads (22.26), and frogs (22.33); Ciampolo is successively an otter (22.36), a mouse (22.58), and a duck (22.130). Such a heightened, allusively Ovidian, fluidity of forms anticipates on the level of poetic signifiers the actual, expressly Ovidian, transformations in the *bolgia* of the thieves. Before affecting the literal reality of the souls, the changed—and ever-changing forms—of the *Metamorphoses* control Dante's language.

A second element in the comedic episode, more strictly pertinent to the tale of Actaeon as it is recounted in *Metamorphoses* III, is Dante's position as unthreatened (as long as unseen) observer. His moving into the field of vision of the Malebranche exposes him to danger. The particular nature of the devils' threat alludes both to the actual risk that the exiled Dante ran of coming within the reach of the Blacks, and to the fable of Actaeon. One will have to wait a little while to see what the grimace with which the devils welcome the Pilgrim meant: the menacing claws and hunting/cooking implements these devils bear are explicit enough to suggest what their specialty is from the beginning of the episode. Displaced onto the guilty Ciampòlo in *Inferno* 22, the threat becomes actual dismemberment. Ciriatto tears into Ciampòlo's flesh (22.57), Libicocco snatches off a portion of muscle from his arm; Dante is afraid that the sinner will be torn to pieces before being able to speak to him: *prima ch'altri 'l disfaccia* ["before I let him have a mangling"] (63).

Finally, and perhaps most importantly, in his detailed and insistent naming of the infernal cohort, Dante echoes and distills Ovid's exercise in precious nomination that takes up half of the Actaeon narrative. Both lists—perhaps uncoincidentally—are arranged in a careful proportion of 1:3. Ovid has thirty-three dogs chase after the metamorphosized Actaeon and three hounds first gnaw into his flesh, for a total of thirty-six names; Dante names twelve devils: eleven minions and, in particular relief, the fraudulent Malacoda. Furthermore, in both catalogues "speaking names" appear that are based on the most salient physical details and the ethical characteristics of the animals or devils that bear them. The roll calls of both texts include verb-noun formations of the type evident in Calcabrina (frost-walker) and Graffiacane (dog-scratcher).[18] On the other hand, Ovid's hounds bear a remarkable chromatic and semantic affinity with the Black devils of *Inferno* 21.29. The *Metamorphoses* lists four names that indicate blackness.[19] Several other names in the Latin poet's list express the idea of speed, in particular that of the winds.[20] They might correspond to the partially enigmatic Dantean Libicocco, which might be named after the wind from Libya in analogy to or in conjunction with the modern-Italian noun *scirocco* (the wind from Syria). The general idea of rapacity common to all the Malebranche, and particularly fitting for Rabicante (*Inferno* 22.40–41) and Farfarello, the evil bird of prey of 22.99, is associated with three of Ovid's names.[21] My insistence on the partial, sometimes remote, and perhaps merely tonal connections between individual names in the Ovidian and Dantean catalogues is not meant to suggest a strict, one-to-one relationship. Dante does not reproduce the roll he read in the *Metamorphoses*. His imitation of the classical example occurs at a sensible distance, and the Ovidian text is adapted in the new context more than adopted.

The connection rests, however, on strong philological ground. Nine cantos earlier, Dante had already reused the allegorized version of the same mythological paradigm in the circle where those who had committed violence against their patrimony were punished. The brief appearance of the squanderers who run through the wood of the suicides near the end of *Inferno* 13 was inspired by the allegorical (Fulgentian and Arnulfian) reading of Actaeon's fable. In this hermeneutic tradition, the young hunter is the emblem of a squanderer who is devoured by his retinue of dogs—that is, his servants or creditors—once his wealth runs out, but is still unable to control his spending. The first allegorical gloss interpreting Actaeon's myth as referring to a profligate is in Fulgentius:

Acteon denique venator Dianam lavantem vidisse dicitur qui in cervum conversus a canibus sui non agnitus eorumque morsibus devoratus est. Anaximenes . . . ait venationem Acteonem dilexisse; qui cum ad maturam pervenisset aetatem, consideratis venationum periculis, id est quasi nudam artis suae rationem videns, timidus factus est. . . . Sed dum periculum venandi fugiret, affectum tamen canum non dimisit, quos inaniter pascendo pene omnem substantiam perdidit; ob hanc rem a canibus suis devoratus esse dicitur.

(*Mitologiarum libri tres* III.3)

[It is said that the hunter Actaeon once saw Diana bathing; he was turned into a stag and was devoured by his dogs, which did not recognize him. Anaximenes . . . says that Actaeon was in love with the sport of hunting and, when he had reached maturity, had become timid because he had realized the dangers involved in hunting—that is, he had seen his craft as if naked. . . . However, even if he avoided the danger of hunting, he did not relinquish his love for dogs, which he kept nurturing and thus dissipated almost all his wealth. For this reason he is said to have been devoured by his dogs.] (my translation)

On a similar note, but stressing the equivalence of midday and midlife, insists also Arnulf:

Acteon de media die Dianam invenit nudam unde mutatus fuit in cervum, et postea a canibus suis dilaceratus. Re vera Acteon venator de media die id est de medio sue etatis vidit Dianam nudam id est consideravit venationem nudam esse id est inutilem. Diana dea venationis bene debet pro venatione poni. Quia venationem tantum abhorruit, fingitur mutatus esse in cervum, qui animalibus ceteris timidior esse perhibetur. Sed cum periculum venandi fugeret affectum tamen canum non dimisit. Quos inaniter pascendo fere omnem substantiam perdidit. Ob hanc ergo causam a canibus suis fuit dilaceratus.

(*Allegoriae super Ovidii Metamorphosin* III.2)[22]

[In the middle of the day, Actaeon stumbled upon Diana naked; he was therefore changed into a stag and then torn to pieces by his dogs. The truth of the matter is that the hunter Actaeon, in the middle of the day—that is in the middle of his life—saw Diana naked—that is, he considered hunting "naked," which is tantamount to useless. . . . Since he despised hunting so much, he is imagined as having been turned into a stag, an animal which is considered more timid than all other animals. However, even if he avoided the danger of hunting, he did not relinquish his affection for the dogs, which he kept nurturing, and thus dissipated almost all his wealth. For this reason, then, he was torn to pieces by his dogs.] (my translation)

Boccaccio's attentive reprise of the Dantesque scene in the novella of Nastagio degli Onesti—himself an exemplary (but not allegorical) potential squanderer for love—works as an intertextual reading of *Inferno* 13 that brings out its Ovidian substratum.[23] It also suggests that Dante's adherence to the traditionally allegorical interpretation of Ovid's story could be perceived by attentive readers. The story of Actaeon, in sum, offered a plot that could yield productive narrative results. All the more so, because Ciampolo's genealogy could work as a further intratextual link between the episode of the squanderers and that of the barrators. Ciampolo is the child of a squanderer suicide: "distruggitor di sé e di sue cose" [destroyer of himself and all his goods] (*Inferno* 22.51), the eternal abode of which is, as per *Inferno* 11.40–45, the dark wood in the circle of violence.

Dante, however, does not seem to consider the narrative potentialities of a classical episode exhausted after a single redeployment: the same material from the *Metamorphoses* which he had used, for its allegorical resonance, to build the *contrapasso* for the profligates, he re-uses in the episode of the Malebranche, this time in its literal form and in the service of a poetic-biographic literary game.[24] Like Ovid before him, Dante recuperates the Actaeon myth and reuses it in a pseudoautobiographic poetic situation; unlike Ovid, who in *Tristia* II used Actaeon in order to stress the fully accidental nature of his mistake (*error*, not *culpa*), Dante is more interested in the agents of Actaeon's death-and-dismemberment. He takes up the formal feature of the catalogue of speaking names that Ovid had used for the pack of Acteon's dogs and produces a similar (and similarly enjoyable) catalogue of demons. To be sure, a different principle of imitation is at work in each episode: the first, a semantic reading of Ovid, focused on the meaning that the myth embodied and the allegorist detected; the second, a stylistic interpretation, is more concerned with the poetic surface of the source-text and with its potential resonances. The difference in method is also one of hermeneutics. In the diabolic rhapsody of *Inferno* 21–23, Ovid's text is no longer traversed by allegory to expose its moral meaning, and Dante's text no longer produces the simple reactivation of that meaning. The barrators have very little to do with the morality of Actaeon's tale, but the precious game Dante plays with the devils' names is reminiscent of Ovid's game with canine onomastics in that same tale. The focus of the poem now lies on the signifiers of Actaeon's episode and the effect that may spring from a reproduction of its poetic and rhetorical arrangement. Now the surface of the poetic text is what matters. Its relevance *qua* poetry is open to become literally—that is, historically—true.

The narrative fiction of the *Commedia* moves beyond a figurative reading of its models and adopts them for their stylistics: it is now poetry, no longer intellectual politics, that can respond to exile and overcome it. In the light of the Ovidian substratum we have explored, Dante's pre-comedic openness to Ovid as a potential antecedent for his self-portrait as an exiled poet acquires new meaning. It well fits with, and is symptomatic of, a larger evolution registered in his intellectual development—namely, his progressively more direct approach to classical texts, less and less dependent on vernacular or allegorical moralizing intermediaries.[25] The choice of the Latin poet instead of Brunetto as the target of a direct allusion both in *De vulgari* and in *Inferno* does not only reflect the incipient re-education that Dante undergoes in the first crucial years of his exile; it also anticipates his impending literary re-conversion away from the investigation into philosophic prose, towards the rediscovery of the classical poetic tradition.

# NOTES

1. See the context of Villani's often-quoted tag at IX.10: Brunetto had been "primo maestro in digrossare i fiorentini, e farli scorti in bene parlare, e in sapere giudicare e reggere la nostra Repubblica secondo la politica." I quote from Giovanni Villani, *Nuova cronica*, ed. Giovanni Porta (Parma: Guanda, 1991), 28.

2. See Dante Alighieri, *Convivio*, in *Opere Minori* I, ii ed. C. Vasoli and D. De Robertis (Milano-Napoli: Ricciardi, 1988), 22. The reference to the *Convivio* is in Mengaldo's gloss at *De vulgari eloquentia* I.vi.3, on page 52.

3. The announcement of *De vulgari eloquentia* as a work, at best, *in fieri* that Dante makes at *Convivio* I.v.10 suggests, and arguably even establishes, the anteriority of this portion of the vernacular treatise.

4. As we know from *Purgatorio* 20.70–78. Charles came to Florence supposedly to bring peace, yet left it in even deeper disarray, and went on to wage war in Sicily only to return with a humiliating, negotiated peace.

5. For a discussion of the Ovidian sources for Dante's poetic representation of his exile, see J. L. Smarr, "Poets of love and exile," in *Dante and Ovid: Essays in intertextuality*, ed. M. U. Sowell (Binghamton, NY: Center for Medieval and Early Renaissance Studies, 1991), 139–51; G. Brugnoli, "Forme ovidiane in Dante," in *Aetates Ovidianae: lettori di Ovidio dall'Antichità al Rinascimento*, ed. I. Gallo and L. Nicastri (Napoli: ESI, 1995), 239–59; M. Picone, "Dante, Ovidio e la poesia dell'esilio," *Rassegna europea di letteratura italiana* 14 (1999), 7–23; and R. Wilson, "Exile and relegation in Dante and Ovid," *Annali d'Italianistica* 20 (2002), 55–72. For further examples of Ovidian interference with Dante's changing self-portrait as a poet, see J. Levenstein, "The Pilgrim, the Poet, and the Cowgirl: Dante's Alter-*Io* in *Purgatorio* XXX–XXXI," *Dante Studies* CXIV (1996), 189–208, and her contribution in the present volume.

6. See the commentary in Robert and Jean Hollander, Dante, *The Inferno* (New York: Anchor Books, 2002), 288.

7. As we know, Dante's intellectual trajectory will reach its end only in the last section of the poem (*Paradiso* 25.1–9), and it is to this passage that one should turn for his new approach to the profession of writer in exile. From Dante's final admission that a reentry into his native city would not rise above the level of mere contingency, start the most recent treatments of Dante's poetics of exile. See, for instance, G. De Marco, "L'Esperienza di Dante *exsul immeritus*," *Annali d'Italianistica*, 20 (2002), 21–54, and G. Raffa, "Dante's Poetics of Exile," *ibidem* , 73–87.

8. Scattered hints can be easily found, thanks to the Dartmouth Dante Project, in Benvenuto and, as a consequence, in Buti (all references to commentators are from the DDP and are to be understood as *ad loc*). A. Chiari, *Letture dantesche* (Firenze: Le Monnier, 1939), 6–39, picks up these signals and develops them (see also his "Nota su la baratteria," *L'Alighieri* XVI, 1975, 85–88); G. Favati, "Il 'jeu di Dante,' " *Cultura Neolatina* XXV (1965), 34–52 insists on this point; see, finally, A. M. Chiavacci Leonardi, *Canto XXI: Introduzione*, in Dante Aligheri, *Commedia* (Milano: Mondadori, 1991), 1:621–27. The strongest reaction is in A. Pagliaro, *La rapsodia dei diavoli*, in *Ulisse: Ricerche semantiche sulla "Divina Commedia,"* 2 vols. (Messina-Firenze: D'Anna, 1967), 1:311–24, in part., 312–13.

9. See the rich commentary by Carroll, *ad Inf.* XXI.118–26. For the documentary evidence of Dante's trial and sentence (and Dante's life in general), see R. Piattoli, *Codice diplomatico Dantesco* (Firenze: Gonnelli, 1950) and, by the same author, *Aggiunte al codice diplomatico dantesco* (Firenze: Olschki, 1969).

10. For the dynamics involved in Pilgrim's reaction to his encounters with sinners through hell as articulated in distinct cycles of fear, pity, and firmness, see *Appendix III* in R. Hollander, *Allegory in Dante's Commedia* (Princeton: Princeton University Press, 1969).

11. See, again, the commentary by Carroll; G. A. Cesareo, "Dante e i diavoli," *Nuova Antologia* LIII (1918), 126–37—in part., 128–31; E. Sanguineti, *Interpretazione di Malebolge* (Firenze: Olschki, 1961), 119–21; A. Roncaglia, "Lectura Dantis: Inferno XXI," *Yearbook of Italian Studies*, 19 (1971), 3–28—in part., 5–6; and C. Kleinhenz, "Deceivers deceived: Devilish doubletalk in *Inferno* 21–23," *Quaderni d'Italianistica* X (1989), 133–56—in part., his reaction to the readings overemphasizing the comical elements of the canto (138–39).

12. On the comical/satirical intention of the episode insist a wide array of commentators: Lana inaugurates the series, by hinting that the text aims to "dare dielettazione al lettore"; Benvenuto follows suit asking himself "si autor quantumqumque abstractus non ridebat quando ista fingebat cum mente"; Tommaseo confirms the hypothesis and develops it; see also the notes in Bosco-Reggio and Chiavacci Leonardi. Among the *Lecturae Dantis* that insist on the comical undercurrent, see L. Pirandello, *Il Canto XXI dell'Inferno*, in *Letture Dantesche a cura di G. Getto* (Firenze: Sansoni, 1955 [1916]), 395–414; L. Spitzer, *The farcical elements in "Inferno" Cantos XXI–XXIII*, in *Romanischen Literatur-Studien* (Tübingen: Niemeyer, 1959 [1944]), 569–93; R. Bacchelli, *Da Dite a Malebolge: la tragedia delle porte chiuse e la farsa dei ponti rotti*, in *Saggi Critici* (Milano: Mondadori, 1962 [1954]), 845–78; D. Conrieri,

"Lettura del canto XXI dell'*Inferno*," *Giornale Storico della Letteratura Italiana* CLVIII (1981), 1–43; and G. Costa, "Il Canto XXII dell'*Inferno*," *L'Alighieri* XXXIX (1998), 47–89. The compact front, however, breaks up when it comes to adjudicating the tone of Dante's text: on this point commentators' assessments range from the maximum of divertissement, proposed by Spitzer with the tag "farcical," to the minimum detected by Pirandello in Dante's bitter "sarcasm" or by Costa in his discovery of a detached (biblical) irony. On sarcasm insists also A. Battistini, "L'arte d'inabissarsi o la retorica della 'tenace pece' (*Inferno*, XXI)," *L'Alighieri* XXXVIII (1997), 73–92, in part. 81–85.

13. Rossetti's argument, while it enjoyed scarce direct hermeneutic success, sparked a series of contributions to the question of Dante's choice of onomastics for the devils: see the commentary by Torraca who reorients the research into Florentine general onomastics, taken up in the balanced note by E. G. Parodi *Lingua e Letteratura* (Venezia: Neri Pozza Editore, 1957), 354–56, who suggests that the devils' names are coined as "nicknames"; see also G. G. Lunardi, "Lucca e i Malebranche," *Giornale Dantesco* XXIX (1926), 68–70; F. P. Luisio, *L'Anziano di Santa Zita*, in *Miscellanea lucchese di studi storici e letterari* (Lucca: Tip. Artigianelli, 1931), 61–75; and, most recently, S. Vazzana, "Il diavolo parla toscano," *L"Alighieri* XXXII (1991), 51–67. For a synthetic account of the question and examples of the diabolic *interpretatio nominis*, see the entries *Alichino, Barbariccia, Cagnazzo, Calcabrina, Ciriatto, Draghignazzo, Farfarello, Graffiacane, Libicocco, Malacoda, Malebranche, Rubicante Scarmiglione* by V. Presta, in the *Enciclopedia dantesca*.

14. Translations from Dante's *Inferno* are by Robert and Jean Hollander.

15. E. Moore, *Dante's personal attitude towards different kinds of sin*, in *Studies in Dante, Second Series* (New York: Haskell, 1968), 210–45, in part., 213–35.

16. See E. G. Parodi, *Il comico nella Divina Commedia*, in *Poesia e storia nella Divina Commedia* (Venezia: Neri Pozza, 1965), 71–134. A strong refutation of Parodi's proposal together with the indication of a different line of antecedents for the catalogue can be found in M. Picone, "Giulleria e poesia nella *Commedia*: una lettura intertestuale di *Inferno* XXI–XXII," *Letture Classensi* XVIII (1988), 11–30, who advances the readings first attempted by Spitzer and Favati.

17. Dante the protagonist will retrospectively evaluate the episode through the lens of a different text: the "favola d'Isopo" (23.4), with its tangled set of zoomorphic characters—frog, mouse, and kite. It is significant, however, that the canine traits established by the Ovidian antecedent will remain dominant in the "imaginata caccia" (23.33): see the most relevant echo in their description as "più crudeli / che 'l cane a quella lievre ch'elli acceffa" [more cruelly/ than the hound that sets his fangs into a hare] (23.17–18). For the implications of the episode for Virgil, the other poet who features in it, see R. Hollander, "Virgil and Dante as Mind-Readers," *Medioevo romanzo* IX (1984), 85–100 and C. J. Ryan, "Virgil and Dante: A study in contrasts," *Italica* 59 (1982), 16–31. Dante's guide might have learned how to protect his charge better by witnessing a micro-Acteon myth played out in the scene of the Anzian di Santa Zita, who is caught in the perverse dynamics of seeing and being torn to pieces

(21.48: the potential gazing on the "Santo Volto" and 52: the actual "addentar con più di cento raffi" [with a hundred hooks and more /they ripped him])—but the poem turns him blind to the Ovidian nature of these dogs. On Dante's continued strategic "revision" of Virgil, see S. Hagedorn's contribution in the present volume.

18. In Ovid, Ichnobates is the one who follows traces (vestigium gradiens, according to Du Cange's Onomasticon), Pamphagos is all-devouring (omnia vorans), Oribasos is a mountain trecker (montem gradiens), Nebrophos a fawn killer (occisor hinnulorum), Pterelas moves its wings (alas agitans), Hylactor is a loud barker (latratu valens), Theridamas defeats beasts (feras vincens), and Oresithropos has been raised on the mountains (in montibus nutritus). The form of their names corresponds to Dante's Alichino (in its etymologic interpretation as "the one who banks on his wings"), Calcabrina (frost walker), Graffiacane (the feline "dog-scratcher"), and Scarmiglione (who roughs up everything). On the Ovidian catalogue, see the interpretations of the hounds' names in W. S. Anderson, Ovid's Metamorphoses: Books 1–5 (Norman, OK: 1996), 359–61.

19. Melampus is the black-footed (pes niger), Asbolos dark as soot (a pilorum colore fuligineo—but see on the opposite side of the spectrum, the white Leucon, candidus), Melaneus the black dog (niger), and Melanchaetes with a black mane (niger coma).

20. Laelaps means whirlwind (a vento procelloso), Dromas the runner (velox, cursorius), Tigris from the river Tigris (with its Strabonian etymology: a celeritate cursus sagittae velocitatem aequantis [Strabo, 11.521]), Aello the storm (procella, turbo), Thoos the fast (velox).

21. Harpya from the genus of the Harpies (quasi sint rapinae), Harpalos the snatcher (rapax, avidus), and perhaps also the voracious Labros (vorax).

22. The texts are cited according to R. Helm's edition F. P. Fulgentii Mitologiarum libri tres (Leipzig: Teubner, 1898) and F. Ghisalberti, Arnolfo d'Orléans; un cultore di Ovidio nel secolo XII (Milano: U. Hoeply 1932). See also Pierre de Bersuire's interpretation in his Ovide moralisé: "Rei autem veritas fuit quod iste fuit quidam nobilis qui canum multitudinem nutriebat, a quibus depauperatus est. Et ideo quia iste semper volebat esse in silvis, ipsum poete mutatum in cervum finxerunt. Qui vero a canibus depauperatus est, fictum est quod eum canes sui comederunt" [The truth of the matter was that this man was a certain nobleman who nurtured a great number of dogs by which he was impoverished. And since he always wanted to be in the woods, the poets depicted him as having been turned into a stag. Since he was one who had been impoverished by his dogs, they imagined that his dogs devoured him.] (Ovidius Moralizatus-Reductorium morale XV.ii.xv). The text is cited according to the edition by J. Engels (Utrecht: Rijkuniversiteit, 1962).

23. On the relevance of the Actaeon's myth for Decameron V.8, see V. Branca, "L'Atteone del Boccaccio fra allegoria cristiana, evemerismo trasfigurante, narrativa esemplare, visualizzazione rinascimentale," Studi sul Boccaccio XXIV (1996), 193–208—unquestionably the best account of the mythographical sources tapped by Boccaccio in the novella, but arguably very little sensitive to Boccaccio's independence from them.

24. For Dante's habit of "diffracting" the narrative material he inherits from classical exemplars, see S. Marchesi, "I doppi di Caronte: diffrazione di un tema virgiliano nella *Commedia*," *Electronic Bulletin of the Dante Society of America*, March 1999.

25. The argument was first advanced by U. Leo, "The unfinished *Convivio* and Dante's rereading of the *Aeneid*," *Mediaeval Studies* 13 (1951), 41–64.

# Philomela, Procne, and the Song of the Penitent in Dante's *Purgatorio*

Jessica Levenstein

> And that deep torture may be call'd a hell
> When more is felt than one hath power to tell.
> —Shakespeare, *The Rape of Lucrece*

As dawn breaks on the valley of the princes at the beginning of *Purgatorio* 9, the sleeping pilgrim dreams that an eagle has snatched him in its talons and carried him to a great height.[1] When he wakes, Dante learns that in his sleep he has been carried by St. Lucy to the door of purgatory, where the penitent souls begin their ascent to the earthly paradise. The poet describes the early hour when the dream and the divine transport take place as "l'ora che comincia i tristi lai / la rondinella presso a la mattina, / forse a memoria de' suo' primi guai" (the hour near the verge of morning, / when the swallow begins her plaintive song, / remembering, perhaps, her woes of long ago [*Purg.* 9.13–15]).[2] The swallow plaintively recalling her past pain alludes to the myth of Philomela. In this story, Philomela's brother-in-law, Tereus, rapes her, slices off her tongue, and imprisons her. In response, Philomela weaves the story of the attack into a tapestry and sends it to her sister, Procne, who frees Philomela, murders Itys, Procne's son with Tereus, and feeds him to his father with Philomela's help. When Tereus learns what the sisters have done, he chases after them, but before he can catch them they are transformed into a swallow and a nightingale, birds whose songs of woe resound forevermore. Dante refers to this story a second time when the pilgrim surveys the third terrace, several cantos after his dream at the door of purgatory. Dante here depicts visions of the wrathful, the first of which shows Procne: "De l'empiezza di lei che mutò forma / ne l'uccel ch'a cantar più si diletta, / ne l'imagine mia apparve l'orma" (Of the impious deed of her whose shape was changed / into the bird that most delights to sing, / a picture formed in my imagination [*Purg.* 17.19–21]). Dante's first day in purgatory proper is thus framed by references to the unfortunate sisters.

As the pilgrim makes his way through the realm of penitence, the sphere of self-examination and transformation, the poet aptly recalls the astonishing story of the two women who, enacting their own form of gruesome justice, spend eternity changed into birds, remorsefully lamenting the sad outcome of their actions. Moreover, the figure of Philomela, who discovers a novel form of expression once the most obvious instrument of communication is literally cut off from her, and whose innovative articulation of her past achieves her release from prison, provides Dante with a fitting example of an innovator who makes use of her art to realize her salvation. I will argue, then, that the sisters' repeated appearance in this part of the poem is revealing for the way it emphasizes the centrality of contrition in the pilgrim's journey and the importance of innovation in the poet's art.

Procne and Philomela appear frequently in Greek works, but these would have been largely unknown to Dante.[3] The many Latin versions of the story, several of which Dante would certainly have encountered, differ from their Greek sources in two significant ways. First, despite Greek literature's association of the swallow with Philomela and the nightingale with Procne, Latin poetry often reverses the identification of the birds, linking Procne with the swallow and Philomela with the nightingale.[4] Second, the Roman retellings of the story generally avoid the tragic tone the tale had in the Greek tradition, usually referring to the story only periphrastically and in passing.[5]

It is not until Ovid's *Metamorphoses*, Dante's source for the myth, that the tale of Philomela and Procne receives a fully rendered Roman treatment.[6] I will review this narrative in some detail, for, as we will see, specific details and phrases are important to Dante's rethinking of this text. In the sixth book of the poem, Ovid relates that out of gratitude for the military assistance provided by Tereus, the king of Thrace, Athens's King Pandion offers him his daughter, Procne, as a wife. The couple moves to Tereus's homeland, where Procne gives birth to Itys. Five years pass and she begs Tereus to fetch Philomela for a visit. When Tereus travels to Pandion's palace in Athens, he conceives an uncontrollable passion for Philomela.[7] His desire transfigures him, enabling the barbarian ("barbarus" [6.515]) to employ sophisticated, convincing rhetoric in his effort to persuade Philomela's father to let her accompany him to Thrace: "facundum faciebat amor" (love made him eloquent [6.469]).[8]

Once Tereus and Philomela set sail from Athens, the king, like a voracious eagle, cannot take his eyes from his sister-in-law: "non aliter quam cum pedibus praedator obuncis / deposuit nido leporem Iovis ales in alto; / nulla fuga est capto, spectat sua praemia raptor" (as when the rapacious bird of Jove has placed in his high nest a hare caught in his hooked talons; the captive has no chance to flee, the captor eyes his prize [6.516–18]). When the ship lands in Thrace, Tereus "Pandione natam / in stabula alta trahit, silvis obscura vetustis" (drags Pandion's daughter to a hut well hidden in the ancient woods [6.520–21]). Secluded in the Thracian forest, Tereus rapes the girl, who helplessly calls to the gods. Philomela "tremit velut agna pavens . . . utque columba suo madefactis sanguine plumis / horret" (trembles like a fearful lamb . . . and quivers like a dove whose wings are splattered with its own blood [6.527–30]). When she gathers her senses, Philomela denounces her rapist, accusing Tereus of confusing natural and familial ties; his violation of Philomela amounts to a violation of order. The distraught girl promises, "si tamen haec superi cernunt, si numina divum / sunt aliquid, si non perierunt omnia mecum, / quandocumque mihi poenas dabis!" (if the gods above discern these things, if there is any divine will at all, if everything has not perished with me, some time or other you will pay dearly for what you have done to me [6.542–44]). While Philomela expresses faith in divine justice, "poenas dabis," her sense of disorder is so extreme that she doubts the very existence of the gods who administer it. Gods or no gods, she attests that she will personally ensure the exposure of her assailant, vowing, "si copia detur, / in populos veniam; si silvis clausa tenebor, / inplebo silvas et conscia saxa movebo" (if I get the chance, I will go to the people; if I am kept shut up in these woods, I will fill them with my story and move even the rocks to an understanding of my tale [6.545–47]). Philomela's only possible retaliation is the narration of her tragic story; a representation of her suffering becomes her sole potential weapon.

Fearing the efficacy of Philomela's narration, Tereus removes the instrument of the enunciation of her tale: her tongue. Even as he cuts it out of Philomela's mouth, however, the tongue struggles to hold onto its verbal aptitude, "nomen patris usque vocantem / luctantemque loqui" (calling again and again on the name of her father and struggling to speak [6.555–56]). Extracted from Philomela's mouth, the tongue quivers on the ground by Philomela's feet and, cleaving to language until the end, it issues a final sound: "inmurmurat" (murmurs [6.558]).[9]

Philomela is left imprisoned and apparently powerless to incriminate her attacker: "os mutum facti caret indice" (a mute mouth cannot reveal what was done [6.574]). Despite her physical lack, she translates her pain into action: "grande doloris / ingenium est, miserisque venit sollertia rebus" (anguish has great genius, and in misery cleverness comes [6.574–75]).[10] Philomela conveys her story to Procne through marks on a tapestry: "stamina barbarica suspendit callida tela / purpureasque notas filis intexuit albis, / indicium sceleris" (she hangs a barbarian web on her loom, and she weaves purple marks on a white cloth, as a sign of the wickedness that was done to her [6.576–78]). The *indicium* that her *os mutum* fails to provide is rendered by the *purpureae notae* woven on her loom. Her shuttle compensates for her missing tongue. Ovid's verses, however, remain silent on just what her shuttle weaves. The *notae* might be letters reporting Tereus's brutality and her confinement, or they might be a pictorial account of the ordeal.[11] In either case, the *notae* tell a story; in one way or another they make a text out of Philomela's *textum*.

Despite Tereus's attempts to thwart her expression, Philomela carries out her threat to him through artistic innovation. The purple marks woven into her tapestry, moreover, function as visual reminders of the bloody violence done to her. They stand as graphic signs of Tereus's brutal crime: the dove whose wings were splattered by its own blood ("columba suo madefactis sanguine plumis" [6.529])—in the simile employed to describe Philomela's fragile state after the rape—now scatters red marks across a white cloth, delineating her predator's assault.[12] At the same time that these splotches represent her victimhood, however, they also facilitate her vengeance on her aggressor. The signs of her text thus fulfill both a narrative and a performative role; they recount her circumstances at the same time that they serve to alter them.[13]

When the queen reads the tapestry, conveyed to her by an attendant, she grasps its meaning immediately and is so stunned that "dolor ora repressit, / verbaque quaerenti satis indignantia linguae / defuerunt" (sorrow blocks her mouth, and, hard as it tries, her tongue cannot find adequate words of indignation [6.583–85]). In contrast to her sister's expressive response to *dolor*, "grande doloris ingenium est," Procne's *dolor* temporarily impedes expression. As if in sympathy for her sister's initial speechlessness, Procne's tongue ceases to function. Procne is unable to find words equal to her profound reaction.

The crisis of expression embodied by Philomela's tonguelessness and represented by Procne's mute response to her sister's message is in fact anticipated earlier in the narrative by Ovid's depiction of Tereus's own misuse of language. He begs Pandion to allow Philomela to visit her sister, but "agit sua vota sub illa" (pushes his own agenda under Procne's name [6.468]). He conceals his true intent behind his newly acquired eloquence. Likewise, when he returns to Procne after he has raped and imprisoned her sister, he "commentaque funera narrat" (tells an invented story of [Philomela's] death [6.565]). He uses words to disguise truth, emptying them of their meaning. In the face of the breakdown of language exemplified by Tereus's deception and the sisters' aphony, Procne and Philomela are compelled to devise an innovative means of expression. Philomela makes *notae*; Procne takes revenge: "poenaeque in imagine tota est" (she is the total embodiment of vengeance [6.586]).

In the midst of the confusion occasioned by a festival of Bacchus, Procne dons a Bacchant's costume, finds her sister in the woods, and transports her back to the palace, declaring, "non est lacrimis hoc . . . agendum, / sed ferro" (this moment calls not for tears, but for the sword [6.611–12]). Although initially filled with the shame that afflicts many Ovidian rape victims, Philomela complies with Procne's injunction, and participates in her sister's plan for reprisal.[14]

At first, Procne cannot decide how she wants to avenge her husband's crimes. A solution presents itself, however, when Itys enters the room. Struck by the boy's resemblance to his father, and aided by Philomela, Procne prepares a grisly meal for Tereus, a pie made of his son's dismembered body. The familial confusion the king created when he raped his wife's sister is taken to a macabre extreme when Tereus unwittingly devours the pie; Itys enters the man who entered Philomela. As Tereus realizes what he has just consumed, Philomela thrusts Itys's head at his devastated father in triumph.

Tereus draws his sword and pursues the sisters, who are transformed into birds as they flee in different directions: "pendebant pennis . . . quarum petit altera silvas, / altera tecta subit" (one of them seeks out the woods, the other climbs to the roof [6.668–69]). Which sister favors the woods and which prefers the roof is not made clear, but while their habitats diverge, their physical appearances coincide: "neque adhuc de pectore caedis / excessere notae, signataque sanguine pluma est" (and even now the signs of slaughter still mark their breasts, and their feathers are smeared with blood [6.669–70]). Like the dove splattered with its own blood in the simile describing Philomela after the rape, the birds bear the marks of the violence in which they have been involved. Indeed, the marked breasts of the metamorphosed sisters function in the same way as Philomela's tapestry does; their *notae* act as autobiographies, graphically representing their past experiences, just as Philomela's *notae* narrate her history. Yet the blood the birds' feathers represent is not their own: they exhibit the signs of their own cruelty and embody their own transgression.

In pursuit of the daughters of Pandion, Tereus, too, turns into a bird, the crested hoopoë. The transformation of the three protagonists conspicuously transpires without the benefit of divine assistance, and the absence of celestial aid emphasizes the episode's pervasive suggestion of atheism.[15] Not only does Philomela put the very existence of the pantheon into doubt when she adds the provisos "si numina divum / sunt aliquid" (6.542–43) and "si deus ullus in illo est" (if there is any god in heaven [6.548]) to her promise of revenge, but Bacchus is the only god named in the story.[16] Philomela's misgivings, in fact, appear to be well-founded: there is no sign of divine justice in the narrative. Rather, the story is a tale of what happens when humans mete out their own justice. The metamorphoses of Tereus, Procne, and Philomela do not, then, imply divine intervention so much as the ratification of the bestiality demonstrated by their behavior in the course of the narrative.[17] Indeed, when Ovid equates Tereus with a ravenous eagle snatching a helpless hare, as he describes the king's lust for Philomela, the poet denotes the beginning of Tereus's bestial transformation. The king's final evolution into a hoopoë merely marks the external manifestation of a process begun long before. Procne and Philomela similarly descend to a subhuman level when they decide to murder and cook Procne's child.[18] Just as the red marks on their breasts speak to the blood they have shed, their very metamorphosis into birds corresponds to the brutality of their actions. In the absence of gods, humans become animals.

In the *Tristia*, Ovid lays bare what he considers the root cause of this move toward animality: love.[19] Indignant that he has been punished for taking love as a theme for his poetry, the poet points out that love pervades every kind of writing, including tragedy. As proof, Ovid marshals examples of tragic stories centrally concerned with the subject of love, among them the tale of Tereus, Procne, and Philomela: "fecit amor subitas volucres cum paelice regem, / quaeque suum luget nunc quoque mater Ityn" (love turned the king with his concubine into birds in flight, and also the mother who still laments her Itys [2.389–90]). While Ovid does not concern himself in the *Tristia* with the metamorphoses themselves, his "fecit amor" economically reveals the extent to which he believes love to be the catalyst for the story's tragic outcome.

Dante would appear to agree with Ovid's assessment of the devastating potential of certain kinds of love; the *Commedia*'s purgatory is constructed around the idea of atoning for the sins engendered by abuses of *amore*. As Virgil explains after the allusion to Procne on the terrace of wrath, all sinners, including those spirits consigned to the middle realm, have sinned through excess, deficiency, or perversion of love:

> 'Né creator né creatura mai,'
>   cominciò el, 'figliuol, fu sanza amore,
>   o natural o d'animo; e tu 'l sai.
> Lo naturale è sempre sanza errore,
>   ma l'altro puote errar per malo obietto
>   o per troppo o per poco di vigore.
> Mentre ch'elli è nel primo ben diretto,
>   e ne' secondi sé stesso misura,
>   esser non può cagion di mal diletto;
> ma quando al mal si torce, o con più cura
>   o con men che non dee corre nel bene,
>   contra 'l fattore adovra sua fattura.'
>                                    (*Purg.* 17.91–96)

['Neither Creator nor His creature, my dear son,
   was ever without love, whether natural
   or of the mind,' he began, 'and this you know.
'The natural is always without error,
   but the other may err either in its chosen goal
   or through excessive or deficient vigor.
'While it is directed to the primal good,
   knowing moderation in its lesser goals,
   it cannot be the cause of wrongful pleasure.
'But when it bends to evil, or pursues the good
with more or less concern than needed,
then the creature works against his Maker.']

According to Dante's guide, the origin of sin is in misused love, and as the *Tristia*'s "fecit amor" makes clear, displays of misdirected and immoderate love subtend the tragic events of the Procne and Philomela episode as well. To borrow Virgil's terms, Tereus's unfettered lust for the wrong sibling, his "[amore] per malo obietto" (*Purg.* 17.95), turns him into a merciless brute. At the same time, the immoderate force of his desire suggests "troppo ... vigore" (*Purg.* 17.96). Procne, too, demonstrates "troppo ... vigore" in her over-passionate loyalty to her sister, and her excessive enthusiasm for vengeance at the devastating cost of her own child speaks to an *amore* that "al mal si torce" (*Purg.* 17.100).[20] As proof of the dire consequences of love gone wrong, the sisters then stand as apposite signposts along the pilgrim's path through purgatory. They alert the reader to the issues at stake in the *cantica*, and serve to substantiate Virgil's exposition on *amore*'s fundamental position at the origin of sinfulness. Dante's deft employment of this tragic tale of misused love thus drives home the lessons at the very core of *Purgatorio*: before the soul can ascend to paradise, it must be purged and corrected of its "mal amor" (twisted love [*Purg.* 10.2]).[21]

As if in accordance with the classical tradition of periphrastic allusion to the sisters, however, neither Philomela nor Procne is actually named in the *Commedia*. The only indications of their presence in *Purgatorio* are the swallow's "tristi lai," which mark the hour of the pilgrim's dream of the eagle, and the "empiezza" of the woman "che mutò forma," who exemplarily appears as a vision of wrath on the third terrace.[22] Early commentators assumed that Dante was following the Latin versions of the tale, in which the swallow represented Procne, and the nightingale stood for Philomela.[23] Not until the late eighteenth century did a dissenting commentary appear, arguing for an identification of the swallow of *Purgatorio* 9 with Philomela and the nightingale of *Purgatorio* 17 with Procne.[24] Eventually the idea gained momentum to the extent that current commentaries of the *Commedia* will almost invariably identify the *rondinella* with Philomela and the "uccel ch'a cantar più si diletta" with Procne.[25] The logic of this identification is unassailable, despite the early commentators' reversal of it: as many readers have noted, the contexts of *Purgatorio* 9 and *Purgatorio* 17 support the association of the swallow with Philomela and the nightingale with Procne. For example, because a suggestion of rape permeates the first third of *Purgatorio* 9—the verb "rapire" is used twice in seven lines[26]—Dante's reference to the swallow's "primi guai" reasonably refers to rape as well, that is, to Tereus's assault on Philomela. Thus, the *rondinella's* identification with Philomela becomes inevitable. Likewise, the setting of *Purgatorio* 17, the terrace of wrath, confirms that the bird whose *empiezza* qualifies her to be the first of the pilgrim's three visions of anger stands for the sister whom Ovid decisively associates both with anger and impiety, Procne. In the *Ex Ponto* she is named "inpia Procne" (impious Procne [3.1.119]); her vengeance is called "non . . . pie" (not pious) in *Heroides* 15.153; and her *ira* explicitly motivates her violent behavior in the *Metamorphoses'* version of the tale: "iram / non capit ipsa suam" ([Procne] does not contain her own wrath [*Met.* 6.609–10]); "tacitaque exaestuat ira" (she boils up with silent wrath [*Met.* 6.623]). Her primary position as a paragon of wrath on the third terrace thus accords with Ovid's emphatic representation of her ire, just as the repeated references to rape in *Purgatorio* 9 suggest a link with Philomela's experience in the *Metamorphoses*. Dante's allusions to the swallow's "primi guai" and to the "empiezza" of the bird who most delights to sing thus situate the sisters in their respective positions in *Purgatorio*, while his repeated references to their story help highlight the centrality of love to the sins of the penitent souls.

As birds who narrate their *primi guai* through song for eternity, Procne and Philomela stand as fitting figures for just such penitent souls, reflecting on their past experiences in an effort to undergo this process of purgation and correction. The swallow, in fact, explicitly represents the repentant soul in several allegorical readings of birds in the Middle Ages. Hrabanus Maurus, for example, associates the swallow with the penitent spirit in *De universo*, "hirundo autem paenitentium pro peccatis suis typum tenet" (for the swallow stands as a type for one repenting for its sins) as does Pseudo Hugh of St. Victor, who, titling his chapter on the swallow in *De bestiis et aliis rebus* "De hirundinis natura, moraliter animae paenitenti addicta" (On the nature of the swallow, morally judged to be of a penitent spirit), writes "Si nosti clamorem hirundinis, nisi fallor, questum designat animae paenitentis. Clamor enim hirundinis est dolor paenitentis" (If you know the chatter of the swallow, unless I err, this designates the penitent spirit. For the chatter of the swallow is the sorrow of the penitent).[27] Moreover, Pseudo Hugh goes on to read the swallow's movements and songs as an elaborate allegory of contrition, confession, faith, and ascent. The swallow's allegorical identity thus makes it an ideal usher for the soul's entry to purgatory. Situated at the beginning of the pilgrim's climb up the mountain, the swallow sets the stage for Dante's own passage through the stages of repentance.

Even without the swallow's allegorical link to the penitent soul, the presence of Philomela at the beginning of *Purgatorio* 9 would resonate with the pilgrim's painful progress through the terraces of purgatory. After all, Philomela's story speaks to the triumph of resolve over captivity. Even when Tereus deprives her of her capacity to cry out, she devises a means to effect her deliverance. Overcoming a physical inability to escape from the hut, hidden deep in the Thracian woods, "silvis obscura vetustis" (*Met.* 6.521), Philomela stands as a model for the pilgrim, who very nearly fails to free himself from his own dark wood, "selva oscura" (*Inf.* 1.2). As he makes his way through the purgatorial realm, striving to efface the signs of the seven sins inscribed on his brow, Dante recalls Philomela, bearing the *notae* of her trials and transgressions on her breast. The swallow's presence in *Purgatorio* 9, as the pilgrim prepares to enter the terrace of pride and confront his most troubling sin, suggests the relevance of the struggle of Philomela's will to Dante's own arduous pilgrimage.[28] Dante even links the hour when the swallow commences her song to pilgrimage: it is the moment when "la mente nostra, peregrina / più da la carne e men da' pensier presa, / a le sue visïon quasi è divina" (our mind, more pilgrim / from the flesh and less caught up in thoughts, / is more prophetic in its visions [*Purg.* 9.16–18]). Indeed, Philomela, who refuses to allow her corporeal deficiencies, the restrictions of her flesh, to hinder her escape from prison, can easily be read as just such a *mente peregrina*, appearing right before the pilgrim passes through the gate to purgatory to proclaim her kinship with his endeavor. Her song, then, stands as a marker for the crucial passage from an existence limited by the shortcomings of the *carne* to one governed by the aspirations of the *pellegrino*.

The pilgrim's connection to Philomela's experience is further supported by his dream of the eagle. Dante imagines that he is seized by "un'aguglia . . . con penne d'oro" (an eagle / with golden feathers [*Purg.* 9.20]), just as Philomela is raped by a man metaphorically associated with an eagle grasping its prey, "non aliter quam cum pedibus praedator obuncis / deposuit nido leporem Iovis ales in alto" (*Met.* 6.516–17). Both the pilgrim and Philomela are figuratively placed at the mercy of the powerful bird. As Dante learns from Virgil, however, the eagle in his dream actually stands for St. Lucy, whom the Virgin Mary had originally summoned to help Dante. The *Commedia*, then, restages Ovid's tale of violation. The predatory eagle eying Philomela is recast as a benevolent savior aiding the pilgrim; the godless, disordered setting of Ovid's Thrace is replaced by a universe carefully regulated by divine rule; and Philomela's rape is refigured as Dante's Pauline rapture.

Like Paul, Dante is whisked mysteriously toward the divine vision. The Pauline implications of the pilgrim's rapture further suggest a correction of the violent Ovidian scene of rape and indicate the significant distinction between the pilgrim's and Philomela's experiences. At the same time, however, one feature of Paul's encounter with the divine, his inability to express what he sees, is shared by both Philomela and Dante.[29] Throughout the poem, Dante struggles with the challenge of expressing the inexpressible, particularly as he gets closer to the divine vision. Approaching the sphere of the sun in paradise, for example, he attests, "Perch'io lo 'ngegno e l'arte e l'uso chiami, / sì nol direi che mai s'imaginasse" (Though I should call on genius, art and practice, I could not tell it so that it could be imagined [*Par.* 10.43–44]) and, attempting to narrate his vision in the Empyrean, he exclaims, "Oh quanto è corto il dire e come fioco / al mio concetto!" (O how scant is speech, and how feeble to my conception! [*Par.* 33.121–22]). The marvels of the otherworld are evidently so impossible to verbalize that the poet gestures toward abandoning the effort altogether, "chi non s'impenna sì che là sù voli, / dal muto aspetti quindi le novelle" (let him who does not wing himself so that he may fly up thither await tidings thence from the dumb [*Par.* 10.74–75]). According to Dante's assessment of his skill, the deficiency of his account gives it the same descriptive force as silence; he might as well be mute.[30] Dante's *muto* recalls Philomela's *os mutum* (6.574), just as his *s'impenna* brings to mind her subsequent winged escape ("pendebant pennis" [6.668]),[31] but neither the poet of the *Commedia* nor the creator of the damning tapestry need stay silent for long. They are thwarted but not vanquished by their narrative limits.

Philomela and Dante must both contrive new ways to communicate what they have seen. The tongueless girl relates her story through weaving; she places a web on her loom and fashions the text of her tale through the placement of purple marks on a white background. The *notae* thus narrate her story of anguish and speak to her defiant resistance to defeat. For Dante, too, sign-making is indispensable to the revelation of the events of his voyage.[32] The poem operates under the assumption that readers need the indescribable made comprehensible through metaphor and example. As the poet declares at the beginning of his journey through paradise, "Trasumanar significar *per verba* / non si poria; però l'essemplo basti / a cui esperïenza grazia serba" (the passing beyond humanity may not be set in words: therefore let the example suffice any for whom grace reserves that experience [*Par.* 1.70–72). Rhetorical figures can translate the events of the otherworld for the earth-bound. Or as Beatrice explains in what amounts to an articulation of the poetics of the *Commedia*, the saved souls are placed in individual spheres in paradise " . . . per far segno / de la celestïal c'ha men salita" (to afford sign of the celestial grade that is least exalted [*Par.* 4.38–39]). But the *essempli* and *segni* need to be probed for meaning: as Philomela relies on Procne to interpret her *notae* correctly, Dante, too, urges the reader to uncover hidden meaning beneath his narrative, "mirate la dottrina che s'asconde / sotto 'l velame de li versi strani" (consider the teaching that is hidden / behind the veil of these strange verses [*Inf.* 9.62–63]). It is the reader's task to uncover the sense behind the letter, the *dottrina* behind the *segno*.

Procne's accurate understanding of Philomela's tapestry leads to Philomela's freedom, her rescue from the "*miseris . . . rebus*"

(*Met.* 6.575) of her confinement. Similarly, Dante intends a reading of his poem to "removere viventes in hac vita de statu *miserie* et perducere ad statum felicitatis" (remove those living in this life from a state of misery and to lead them to a state of happiness [*Epistola* 13.39]).[33] For both Dante and Philomela, a successful interpretation of the significance of their texts is meant to result in salvation. Moreover, within the fiction of the *Commedia*, the poem brings about Dante's own salvation as well: he is delivered from the *selva oscura* of his soul's error to the splendor of the heavens and the guarantee of his own eternal inclusion in the celestial company.[34]

In Philomela's triumph over her physical handicaps, Dante can find a paradigm for the transcendence of his own bodily restraints; her disability literalizes the limitations imposed by Dante's carnal impulses, the "falso . . . piacer" (false delights [*Purg.* 31.35]) that led him into the dark wood to begin with. Overcoming these restrictions allows Dante to achieve both his spiritual and his artistic aspirations. Unencumbered by the weaknesses of the flesh, the pilgrim ascends to celestial glory;[35] no longer distracted by bodily temptations, the poet rises to a higher theme and devotes himself to a depiction of God's kingdom. The salvific power of Dante's text allows him to free himself from sin, just as Philomela's innovative composition permits her to defy her corporeal impediments and achieve her own liberation.

Despite the applicability of his identification with Philomela, however, Dante does not lose sight of the brutal consequences of Philomela's deliverance. His allusion to Procne's *empiezza*, several cantos after his reference to Philomela, demonstrates Dante's awareness of the tragic consequences of Philomela's artistry. In the story of Procne and Philomela, artistic innovation gives rise to a young boy's death. The poet's recollection of Procne's ruthlessness thus problematizes the victory of Philomela's inventive escape and suggests a wary appreciation for the perils inhering in ingenuity. At the same time, the poet's allusion to Procne's cruelty reminds us of the repercussions of a godless universe and gestures toward the fundamental difference between Pandion's daughters and the pilgrim of the *Commedia*. For Dante, penitence is a reality; contrition and confession purge the repentant soul of sin and prepare him for paradise. For Procne and Philomela, on the other hand, lament and regret effect no change in their circumstances, efface none of the red *notae* marking their breasts. For them, mourning functions merely as emotional release.[36]

Despite the apparent futility of their sorrowful songs, however, Dante seems to make a deliberate choice to highlight the sisters' identities as songbirds in the two passages in the *Purgatorio* that allude to them. Philomela is the *rondinella*, warbling her *tristi lai* in the early hours of the morning and Procne is memorialized as the "uccel ch'a cantar più si diletta." They are constitutionally devoted to self-expression through song, and the *Commedia*'s allusions to them draw particular attention to their perpetual interest in artistic production. They are thus music makers above all. The political conflicts and alliances that form the backdrop for their story may recede; the specifics of their tale may grow blurry and easily confused; their very names may vary as the account of their history is passed from generation to generation and from culture to culture, yet they remain eternal artists, like Dante, forever narrating their pasts and proclaiming their identities through song.

## NOTES

1. I am pleased to have the opportunity to express my tremendous admiration for Robert Hollander. I am grateful for his wisdom, his generosity, and his great good humor. He has been an inspiration to me, and to so many others, as an exceptional scholar, eloquent translator, and dedicated, passionate teacher. I feel thankful to have been his student and lucky to call him my friend.

2. I am using Petrocchi's Italian text of the *Commedia* and Robert and Jean Hollander's translations of *Inferno* and *Purgatorio*. Because the Hollander *Paradiso* is not yet available, I am using Charles Singleton's translation of the final *cantica*. Dante Alighieri, *'La Commedia' secondo l'antica vulgata*, ed. Giorgio Petrocchi, 4 vols. (Milan: Mondadori, 1966–67); trans. Robert Hollander and Jean Hollander, *Inferno*, ed. Robert Hollander (NY: Doubleday, 2000); trans. Jean Hollander and Robert Hollander, *Purgatorio*, ed. Robert Hollander (NY: Doubleday, 2003); trans., Charles S. Singleton, *Paradiso*, (Princeton: Princeton University Press, 1975).

3. Hom, *Od.* 19.515 ff; Hes. *Op.* 568–69; Arist. *Rh.* 3.3.4; Apollod. *Bibl.* 3.14.8; Aesch. *Ag.* 1140–49; and Thuc. 2.29. A lost play of Sophocles', *Tereus*, was devoted entirely to the story. For surveys of the transmission of the Philomela story in the Greco-Roman tradition, see Ignazio Cazzaniga, *La saga di Itis nella tradizione letteraria e mitografica greco-romana*, 2 vols. (Varese-Milan: Cisalpino, 1950–51) and Nicolas Zaganiaris, "Le mythe de Térée dans la littérature grecque et latine," *Platon* 25 (1973): 208–32. See also D'Arcy W.

Thompson, *A Glossary of Greek Birds* (Oxford: Oxford University Press, 1936), 16–22 and 314–25.

4. Not all Latin poets definitively transpose the Greek identification of Procne with the nightingale and Philomela with the swallow. See Cazzaniga, vol.1, 84. The Romans' indeterminacy and their alteration of the tale, however, are an inevitable outcome of the confusing similarities between Procne and Philomela (daughters of Pandion; lovers of Tereus), on the one hand, and the nightingale and the swallow (harbingers of spring; birds with mournful cries; birds reputed to lack tongues), on the other, within the Greek tradition itself. See Zaganiaris, 211, 222–23, and Thompson, 315. Virgil's substitution of "philomela" for the traditional Latin term for nightingale, "luscinia," in *Georgics* 4.511, marks an early example of the name's transferred meaning. In late antique and early medieval Latin, "philomela" comes to function as a synonym for nightingale, and "procne" as a synonym for swallow.

5. Cazzaniga, vol. 1, 81–84, 92. See, for example, Catull. 65.12–14; Hor. *Carm.*, 4.12.5–8; Verg. *Ecl.* 6.74–81; *G.* 4.15; 4.511–15.

6. The commentary tradition unanimously agrees that Dante's references to Philomela and Procne rely on Ovid's detailed version of the story in *Metamorphoses* 6.401–674. Bypassing the Hellenistic poets' allusions to the story, Ovid appears to find his source material in a graver, more extensive version of the tale, perhaps Sophocles' *Tereus*. See Cazzaniga, vol. 1, 81 and Brooks Otis, *Ovid as an Epic Poet*, 2d ed. (Cambridge: Cambridge University Press, 1970), 211.

7. For a reading of Tereus's desire as an outcome of political ambition, see Patricia Klindienst Joplin, "The Voice of the Shuttle is Ours," *Stanford Literature Review* 1 (1984): 24–53.

8. For the Latin texts of Ovid's works I am using those established by the Loeb Classical Library. Ovid, *Metamorphoses,* trans. Frank Justus Miller, 3d ed., rev. G. P. Goold, 2 vols. (Cambridge: Harvard University Press, 1984); *Tristia* and *Ex Ponto,* trans. Arthur Leslie Wheeler, 2d ed., rev. G. P. Goold (Cambridge: Harvard University Press, 1988); *Heroides,* trans. Grant Showerman, 2d ed., rev. G. P. Goold (Cambridge: Harvard University Press, 1986). All translations from Latin texts are my own.

9. For a reading of the murmuring tongue that pays attention to the intersection of sexuality, violence, and the strengths and weaknesses of language in the poem, see Lynn Enterline, *The Rhetoric of the Body from Ovid to Shakespeare* (Cambridge: Cambridge University Press, 2000), 3–5; 88–90.

10. The transmutation of anguish to *ingenium* is a common aphorism in Latin literature. See *Ovid's 'Metamorphoses' Books 6–10*, ed. and comm. William S. Anderson (Norman: University of Oklahoma Press, 1972) 226.

11. Cazzaniga and Franz Bömer both assume the *notae* are letters. Cazzaniga, vol. 2, 43; Franz Bömer, *P. Ovidius Naso, 'Metamorphosen': Kommentar, Buch VI–VII* (Heidelberg: Universitätsverlag, 1976), 157. While it is possible, even likely, that Philomela weaves words into her tapestry, Ovid's text leaves the question open. *Nota* can indeed mean "letter," but it can also retain the vagueness of "sign" or "token."

12. See Charles Segal, "Philomela's Web and the Pleasures of the Text: Ovid's Myth of Tereus in the *Metamorphoses*," in *The Two Worlds of the Poet: New Perspectives on Vergil*, ed. Robert M. Wilhelm and Howard Jones (Detroit: Wayne State University Press, 1992), 283.

13. Ibid.

14. Philomela speaks of her *crimen* (6.541) and cannot look her sister in the eye for fear that she has become Procne's *paelex* (6.606; see also 6.537). This type of behavior is typical in the world of the *Metamorphoses*, where rape victims are considered responsible for their rapes. See the story of Callisto, 2.401–530, esp. 2.447–50. See also Leo Curran, "Rape and Rape Victims in the *Metamorphoses*," *Arethusa* 11 (1978): 213–41 and Amy Richlin, "Reading Ovid's Rapes," in *Pornography and Representation in Greece and Rome*, ed. Amy Richlin (Oxford: Oxford University Press, 1992), 158–79.

15. Anderson, *Ovid's 'Metamorphoses'* 667.

16. 6.596. See Segal, 286.

17. See Otis, 214; Segal, 287; and Leonard Barkan, *The Gods Made Flesh: Metamorphosis and the Pursuit of Paganism* (New Haven: Yale University Press, 1986), 66.

18. See Otis, 214 and Curran, 277.

19. Ovid's interest in the tragic story spills over into texts other than the *Metamorphoses*. See *Am.* 3.12.32; *Her.* 15.153–54; *Ars* 2.383–84; *Fast.* 2.853–55, 4.481–82; *Tr.* 2.389–90, 5.1.59–60; *Pont.* 1.3.39–40.

20. Giovanni del Virgilio's verse allegorization of the Philomela story places misuse of love at the fore: "Naso per historiam incestum condemnat amorem / Et notat obscenus quam male finit amor." *Allegorie Librorum Ovidii Metamorphoseos*, in Fausto Ghisalberti, "Giovanni del Virgilio: Espositore delle *Metamorfosi*," *Giornale dantesco* 34 (1931): 74. John of Garland's treatment of the story also appears to emphasize the relevance of love to the narrative: "Commentatur aves doctrina poetica quippe / Devia poscit avis, / devia poscit amor." Giovanni di Garlandia, *Integumenta Ovidii: Poemetto inedito del secolo XIII*, ed. Fausto Ghisalberti (Messina-Milan: Principato, 1933), 59.

21. Georg Rabuse's work draws a similar conclusion. See "Schwalbe und Nachtigall in der *Göttlichen Komödie*," *Deutsches Dante Jahrbuch* 38 (1960): 172, 186. See also Mark Musa, "The Sensual Pilgrim: Dream 1 of *Purgatory*," *Rivista di studi italiani* 1 (1983): 5 and passim.

22. As readers of the *Commedia* have noted, the "mutò forma" of *Purg.* 17.19 recalls the "mutatas . . . formas" of the proem of the *Metamorphoses* (1.1). See William S. Anderson, "Multiple Change in the *Metamorphoses*," *Transactions of the American Philological Association* 94 (1963): 1–2 for the argument that in the *Metamorphoses*, Ovid's "mutatas formas" stands as a synonym for the Greek word *metamorphosis*.

23. Arnulf of Orléans, whose widespread allegorization of Ovid's *Metamorphoses* would easily have been known to Dante's early commentators, maintains that Philomela's sylvan sojourn destines her to metamorphose into a nightingale while Procne, who lived in a house, necessarily transforms into a swallow. *Allegoriae super Ovidii Metamorphosin*, in Fausto Ghisalberti, "Ar-

nolfo D'Orléans: Un cultore di Ovidio nel secolo XII," *Memorie del reale istituto lombardo di scienze e lettere: Classe di lettere, scienze morali e storiche* 24/2 (1932): 218. Early commentators all appear to conform to Arnulf's belief, identifying the *rondinella* in *Purgatorio* 9 with Procne.

24. Lombardi's commentary of 1791–92 seems to introduce the shift in opinion.

25. Rabuse takes the rare position among twentieth-century readers of maintaining the earlier identification of Philomela with the nightingale. The notes to Robert Durling's translation of *Purgatorio* also tentatively propose the earlier identification. Trans. Robert M. Durling, *Purgatorio*, ed. Ronald L. Martinez and Robert M. Durling (Oxford: Oxford University Press, 2003).

26. "Ed esser mi parea là dove fuoro / abbandonati i suoi da Ganimede, / quando fu *ratto* all sommo consistoro" (*Purg.* 9.22–24); "Poi mi parea che, poi rotata un poco, / terribil come folgor discendesse, / e me *rapisse* suso infino al foco" (*Purg.* 9.28–30; my emphasis).

27. Hrabanus Maurus, *De universo*, PL 3: 252. Pseudo Hugh of St. Victor, *De bestiis et aliis rebus*, PL 177: 42. Isaiah 38:14 provides a possible source for the allegorical association of the swallow with penitence: a moaning suppliant soul is equated with a clamoring swallow, "sicut pullus hirundinis sic clamabo meditabor." For an examination of the swallow's allegorical significance in antiquity, see Zaganiaris, 216–21. Other medieval interpretations of the swallow include Isidore, *Etymologiae* 12.7.70; Vincent of Beauvais, *Speculum naturale*, 16.97; and Brunetto Latini, *Tresor*, 1.165.

28. On Dante's use of Ovid to underscore central issues of the *Commedia*, see in this volume Simone Marchesi, "Distilling Ovid: Dante's Exile and Some Metamorphic Nomenclature in Hell." Marchesi's analysis of the Ovidian subtext of *Inferno* 21–23 looks both at the way Ovid's poetry allows Dante to express autobiographical concerns, and at the way Ovid's poetic framing of his own autobiography provides a model for using intertexts to express these concerns.

29. 2 Cor.12:4. Thomas Aquinas, in the *quaestio* "De raptu," maintains that Pauline rapture itself implies a certain violence. See Thomas Aquinas, *Summa Theologiae*, 2a2ae 175.2. Robert Hollander, *Allegory in Dante's 'Commedia'* (Princeton: Princeton University Press, 1969) 147.

30. Teodolinda Barolini points out that the text of *Paradiso* bears witness to Dante's identification with those unable to speak: the pilgrim is, in fact, mute from *Par.* 9.81 to *Par.* 14.96. *The Undivine 'Comedy': Detheologizing Dante* (Princeton: Princeton University Press, 1992) 197.

31. Much has been written on flight imagery in the *Commedia* generally, and on Dante's use of the word "penne" specifically. See, for example, Hugh Shankland, "Dante *Aliger*," *Modern Language Review* 70 (1975), 765–86; Mark Musa, "Le ali di Dante (e il Dolce Stil Novo): *Purg.* XXIV," *Convivium* 34 (1966), 361–67; R. A. Shoaf, "Dante's *Columbi* and the Figuralism of Hope in the *Divine Comedy*," *Dante Studies* 93 (1975): 27–59; and Lino Pertile, "Il nodo di Bonagiunta, le penne di Dante e il Dolce Stil Novo," *Lettere italiane* 46 (1944): 44–75.

32. See Barolini 186–87.

33. My emphasis. Dante Alighieri, *Epistole*, eds. Arsenio Frugoni and Giorgio Brugnoli, *Opere minori*, vol. 3, tomo 2 (Milan: Ricciardi, 1996). My assumption here is that Dante is the author of the letter to Cangrande. See Robert Hollander, *Dante's Epistle to Cangrande* (Ann Arbor: University of Michigan Press, 1993). Within the *Commedia*, Dante also points to his poem's salvific purpose. See *Par.* 1.34–36 and *Par.* 17.136–42.

34. For Dante's eventual placement among the blessed, see *Inf.* 3.90–93; *Purg.* 2.91–92; *Purg.* 8.58–60; *Purg.* 26.58; *Purg.* 26.73–75; and *Par.* 15.28–30.

35. See *Par.* 1.73–75. I address the ambiguity marking this passage in "The Re-formation of Marsyas in *Paradiso* 1," in *Dante for the New Millennium*, ed. Teodolinda Barolini and H. Wayne Storey (N.Y.: Fordham University Press, 2003), 415. On the distinction between the body and the flesh, see Robert M. Durling, "The Body and the Flesh in *Purgatorio*," in *Dante for the New Millennium*, 183–91.

36. For more on the trecento's complicated response to classical sources, see in this volume Suzanne Hagedorn, "Boccaccio's Manto: Pagan Vision and Poetic Revisions," esp. 62. Both Dante and Boccaccio pick and choose among classical and contemporary influences. Hagedorn points out that Boccaccio ultimately privileges Dante's version of Manto's story over Virgil's. In fact, in making use of some elements of Virgil's story and not others, Boccaccio is further emulating Dante; he allows his work to express artistic approval of his classical source at the same time as he expresses moral disapproval of that source. Likewise, for Dante, Philomela's initial response to Tereus's crime provides a model for an innovative artist, but Procne's presence in the visions of the wrathful registers Dante's discomfort with endorsing the entirety of that response.

# Boccaccio's Manto:
# Pagan Vision and
# Poetic Revisions

## Suzanne Hagedorn

Like Petrarch, who expected to win undying fame from his Latin works rather than his scattered Italian rhymes, Giovanni Boccaccio has earned an enduring literary reputation from his Italian fictions rather than his erudite Latin compilations—*De casibus virorum illustrium, Genealogia deorum gentilium,* and *De mulieribus claris.* With the advent of feminist literary studies, however, the latter work has received renewed attention from scholars, who have discussed its ambiguous portrayal of women and its influence on the medieval debate on women, especially as reflected in the works of Christine de Pizan, who drew heavily upon Boccaccio's brief biographies in writing a defense of her own sex.[1]

Nevertheless, when Boccaccio (or for that matter, any male writer) of the Middle Ages set out to discuss women in history or literature, in a sense, what he was really doing was to discuss their representation by earlier male poets and writers. Women's lives, though they are ostensibly the subject of the text, thus become a pretext for engagement with and contestation of accounts by the male writer's poetic father figures, to invoke Harold Bloom's model of poetic influence.[2] Boccaccio's interest in negotiating these earlier poetic and historic accounts in *De mulieribus claris* manifests itself more clearly in some lives than others—perhaps most notably in his chapter on Dido, which, as Anna Cerbo suggests, stages various ideological conflicts: conflicts between history and poetry, between Petrarch and his predecessors Dante and Virgil.[3] In this

58

essay, I examine another instance in which Boccaccio's presentation of conflicting stories about a heroine reflects underlying poetic tensions: namely, his two successive versions of a chapter on the Theban prophetess Manto in *De mulieribus claris.*[4]

As with his entry on Dido, Boccaccio's portrayals of Manto are motivated by a literary agenda that runs beneath the surface of his narrative: his placement of himself with respect to two powerful poetic father figures, Dante and Virgil. Simone Marchesi has argued earlier in this volume that Dante moves between Brunetto Latini and Ovid as he seeks an appropriate model for the poet-in-exile; so too, Boccaccio's successive drafts of his chapter on Manto document a similar process of reading and shifting between his classical and vernacular poetic forbears, though in this case, I shall argue that the pull of the vernacular poet is more powerful than the classical.[5] Moreover, in view of Jessica Levenstein's analysis of Dante's repeated invocation of the violent Ovidian myth of Philomela and Procne in the *Purgatorio* as a way of marking the difference between the redemptive song of the penitent pilgrim and the mournful, limited songs of his classical forbears, I find it interesting to note that the locus of Boccacio's poetic negotiation between Dante's Christian and Virgil's pagan worldview also takes place over the (dead) body of a mythical woman.[6]

Since Boccaccio's entries on Manto seem to draw particular attention to the conflicts between Dante's and Virgil's accounts of the Theban prophetess that Robert Hollander and other critics have considered in their treatment of this canto, before turning to Boccaccio's chapter, or rather, chapters on Manto, it is necessary to review in some detail the portraits of this character in these earlier writers.[7] In Book X of the *Aeneid,* Virgil treats Manto briefly in the course of describing the forces that followed Aeneas from Etruscan shores, joining the Trojan in his fight against the Rutilians. Here, Virgil catalogues the war chief Ocnus and his forces:

> Ille etiam patriis agmen ciet Ocnus ab oris
> fatidicae Mantus et Tusci filius amnis
> qui muros matrisque dedit tibi, Mantua, nomen,
> (*Aeneid* X, 198–203)[8]

[Another who called up a company from his native shores was Ocnus, son of fate-telling Manto and the Etruscan river, who gave to Mantua its walls and his mother's name.]

Virgil's digression on his native city as he mentions Ocnus makes clear its direct genealogical link to pagan prophecy. Marie Desport's study of this passage discusses its portrayal of "fatidicae Mantus" (prophetic Manto), noting that among all the ancestors with which Mantua was richly endowed, Virgil has chosen to highlight this one, who permits him to consider Mantuans, in a sense, as "diviners." She also stresses the connection between the name Manto and the Greek words "mantis" and "manto" which correspond to the Latin term "vates"—poet-seer, a term favored by Virgil.[9]

Yet Virgil's foundation myth was not the only one available, even to early commentators. Besides recounting Virgil's version, Servius's commentary on this passage gives alternate accounts of Mantua's origins: "Alii . . . referunt" (Others say . . . .) that Ocnus was the son or the brother of Aulestes, the founder of Perugia, and he left the city to found Mantua to avoid a fight with his brother. Another story in Servius's commentary says that Mantua was founded by Tarconus, the son of Tirreneus, and was named Mantua because Tarconus dedicated the city to the father of the Gods, called Mantus in the Etruscan language.[10] Apparently, Virgil's myth of origins, if not his own fictional creation, was one of several competing versions of the foundation of Mantua—and his is the only one that links his hometown genealogically to pagan prophecy.

Other Latin poets' accounts of Manto make no mention of what becomes of the Theban prophetess after the fall of her home city. Seneca's drama *Oedipus* depicts Manto aiding her father in making the sacrifices necessary to consult the oracle of Apollo for King Oedipus. In one scene, Manto describes for her blind parent the horrible omens revealed in the sacrifices. She does not interpret them herself but rather asks her father to unfold their significance.[11] Likewise, Book IV of Statius's *Thebaid* represents Manto as a virgin dedicated to Phoebus, and shows her aiding her father in his divination. Yet, in contrast to Seneca's portrait, Statius depicts Manto as having prophetic powers of her own, weaving a charm that summons and disperses the souls of the dead whom she and her father wish to consult. Statius here acknowledges her powers, but quickly dissociates them from the crimes of female sorcery: He says that her actions are "qualis, si crimina demas, / Colchis et Aeaeo simulatrix litore Circe" [like, (but without their crimes) the Colchian witch or Circe on her Aeaen shore.][12]

Besides these poetic accounts of Manto, Boccaccio had access
to a more "historical" account contained in Pomponius Mela's
survey of world geography, *De Chorographia.*[13] In his discussion of
the regions of Ionia, Pomponius mentions "Lebedos and the sanc-
tuary of Clarian Apollo, founded by Manto daughter of Tiresias
after she fled the Epigones, conquerors of Thebes, and Colophon,
founded by Mopsus, the son of this same Manto."[14] Here, we see
both Manto and her son as the founders of cities, although not of
Virgil's city, Mantua.

Nevertheless, for modern-day readers and for Boccaccio, perhaps the most curious treatment of Manto is that of Dante's *Commedia.* In *Inferno* 20, Dante condemns Manto to the circle of the
diviners, and the description of her by Dante's guide Virgil contains one of the most fascinating moments of textual revisionism
in the *Commedia.* Here, Dante's Virgil makes a speech retracting
the *Aeneid*'s version of the foundation of Mantua, substituting an
account that makes Manto's association with the city casual and
fortuitous rather than causal. This aspect of the canto has been of
perennial interest to commentators, and since it is vital to understanding Boccaccio's chapters, let us turn now to this passage,
which begins as Virgil points out Manto to Dante:

> E quella che ricuopre le mammelle,
>     che tu non vedi, con le trecce sciolte,
>     e ha di là ogne pilosa pelle,
> Manto fu, che cercò per terre molte
>     poscia si puose là dove nacqu'io;
>     onde un poco mi piace che m'ascolte
> Poscia che 'l padre suo di vita uscìo
>     e venne serva la città di Bacco
>     questa gran tempo per lo mondo gìo.
>                     (*Inferno* 20.52–60)[15]

> [And that female whose backward-flowing tresses
> fall upon her breasts so that they are hidden
> and has her hairy parts on that same side,
> was Manto, who searched through many lands
> before she settled in the place where I was born—
> for just a moment hear me out on this.
> After her father had parted from this life
> and the city of Bacchus was enslaved,
> she wandered for a time about the world.]

Virgil's speech then continues with a lengthy digression on the geography of Northern Italian lakes and rivers, and the marshy land on the plain below Lake Benacus (now known as Lake Garda) before he returns to Manto seven tercets later:

> Quindi passando la vergine cruda
> vide terra, nel mezzo del pantano,
> sanza coltura e d'abitanti nuda.
> Lì per fuggire ogne consorzio umano
> ristette con suoi servi a far sue arti,
> e visse, e vi lasciò suo corpo vano.
> Li uomini poi che'ntorno erano sparti
> s'accolsero a quel loco, ch'era forte
> per lo pantan ch'avea da tutte parti
> Fer la città sovra quell'ossa morte;
> e per colei che 'l loco prima elesse
> Mantüa l'appelar sanz'altra sorte.

> ෩ ෩ ෩

> Però t'assenno che, se tu mai odi
> originar la mia terra altrimenti,
> La verità nulla menzogna frodi.
> (*Inferno* 20.82–93; 97–99)

[When she passed that way, the cruel virgin
    saw dry land in the middle of marsh
    where no one lived and no one tilled the soil
There, to avoid all company, she stopped,
with only servants, to ply her magic arts.
There she lived and left her empty body.
Later on, the people scattered round about
    collected there because it was protected
    by the marsh on every side.
They built the city over those dead bones
    and, after her who first had claimed the spot,
    named it Mantua, with no spells or incantations

෩ ෩ ෩

I charge you, therefore, should you ever hear
    my city's origins described another way,
    allow no lie to falsify the truth.]

Virgil's narrative makes it clear that Manto has no son, and that the city named for her is founded literally over her dead body, by strangers rather than a direct descendant. Moreover, in the closing lines of the passage, Dante makes his Virgil condemn any other account of his city's foundation as a fraud, thus making him retract the story of Mantua's foundation in the *Aeneid*. As Francesco D'Ovidio argued early in the twentieth century, Dante's portrayal of Virgil in this scene shows the Latin poet dissociating himself from the diviners that he sees; by giving an alternate myth of origins that eliminates the direct genealogical link between the prophetess Manto and his hometown, Dante's Virgil avoids any taint of the magical practices with which he was associated in various medieval legends.[16]

Though this passage is interesting enough in itself, the figure of Manto is connected with another problem in Dante's text: namely the fact that she alone, of all of the characters in the *Commedia*, is placed twice—once in Malebolge with the augurers in the passage cited above, and once in Limbo, as Virgil tells Statius in Purgatorio 22.113 that "la figlia di Tiresia" (the daughter of Tiresias) along with several other of Statius's heroines resides with him in Limbo. This famous crux has occasioned much discussion among Dante critics. Robert Hollander has commented at length upon it, relating the two Mantos in the *Commedia* to the larger problem of Dante's salvation of Statius and condemnation of Virgil; while Virgil's textual construct is condemned to suffer in hell, Statius's character, though not saved like Statius himself, is allowed to dwell in a better place.[17]

Boccaccio clearly knew Dante's source texts, and perhaps had also noticed the bilocation problem in the *Commedia*. In the first stage of his Manto chapter, Boccaccio conflates elements from various sources, but nevertheless, this version seems to have a more Virgilian cast than his later one. Boccaccio associates Manto with Theban history, placing her biography directly after a chapter dealing with Jocasta, Queen of Thebes. He begins his discussion of the prophetess in this chapter with the words "Mantho fatidica," echoing the Virgilian phrase "fatidicae Mantus" (prophetic Manto).[18] In this sentence, he celebrates the fame of the prophetess using metaphors of brightness (fama prefulgens) and sparks (fulgoris favillula), conventional figures that are nonetheless reminiscent of Boccaccio's preface to *De Claris Mulieribus* itself, which praises the book's potential dedicatee, Queen Joan of Jerusalem and Sicily, speaking of "ingens regius fulgor" (her . . . dazzling

royal luster) and denigrates his own work as "opusculi tenuis et
fere semisopita favillula" (the flickering flame of my little book so
small and weak).[19] In the introduction, it is Queen Joan's bright
fame that threatens the "favillula" of Boccaccio's work; in the
opening sentence of his first chapter on Manto, Boccaccio says
that "small sparks of the brightness of Manto's fame still survive
into our age"—presumably, his own work is one of these poetic
sparks. This sentence is thus indirectly Virgilian by way of Dante's
Virgil, for the association with sparks and poetic fame is one that
Dante's Statius makes in *Purgatorio* 21 when he says of Virgil:

> Al mio ardor fuor seme le faville
>     che mi scaldar de la divina fiamma
>     onde sono allumati più di mille;
> de l'Eneïde dico . . .
>
> (Purgatorio 21.94–97)[20]

> [The sparks that kindled the fire in me
>     came from the holy flame
>     from which more than a thousand have been lit—
> I mean the Aeneid . . .]

The second sentence of Boccaccio's original chapter further
picks up on this association of sparks and fame by linking Manto's
reputation with the art of reading sparks (pyromancy), learned from
her father as well as other divinatory arts, including augury. Here,
perhaps, Boccaccio remembers the accounts of the various sorts of
divination used by Tiresias and Manto in the *Thebaid* or Seneca's
*Oedipus*. Boccaccio is quick to denounce such arts as "against our
religion" but nonetheless considers Manto's skills something special. His description of Manto's wanderings—"longum in exilia
acta per orbis tractus varios" (she been driven into exile for a long
time in various parts of the earth)—echoes the sense of Dante's
line, "Manto fu che cercò per terre molte." Boccaccio then turns to
Pomponius Mela's version of Manto's wanderings, denouncing
with Christian contempt the oracle that she founded.

In its list of various itineraries for the Theban prophetess, Boccaccio's rhetoric in this version of the chapter echoes that of
Servius's Virgil commentary as it enumerates the legends surrounding the foundation of Mantua. "Alii . . . . confirmant" (others
say)—namely, Dante and Virgil, that either as a virgin or having

given birth to Citheonus (which is Boccaccio's mysterious misreading of the Virgilian phrase "ciet Ocnus") Manto chose to settle
on the marshes. Here, Boccaccio prefers the poetic as opposed to
the "historical" readings of the foundation of Mantua offered by
Servius; he follows Virgil and Dante in making the etymology of
the city's name descend from Greek Manto rather than an Etruscan god. Nevertheless, despite its Virgilian beginning, at the end
of this chapter, Boccaccio's account is closer to Dante's version in
its assertion that an unnamed "they" rather than Manto's son
founded a city on her grave. The chapter ends by stressing the double signification of the word Mantua, which memorializes both
the city and its legendary first settler. In this treatment of Manto,
Boccaccio clearly struggles to sort out the conflicting accounts of
Dante and Virgil, and to reconcile them with the story Pomponius
tells. If this Manto does not come off as a shining example whom
Boccaccio urges his female readers to imitate, neither is she an infernal sorceress.

   In his later revision of this chapter, Boccaccio greatly strengthens his attack on Manto's divinatory arts. From the start, she is
identified with her father, the seer Tiresias. Boccaccio omits the
meditation on the sparks of Manto's fame with which he had earlier begun, and now seems far more interested in Manto's ability
to read sparks than in the sparks of her fame, condemning her pyromancy as occurring through "dyabolico opere" (diabolical agency). In cataloging the various types of divination Manto practiced,
Boccaccio includes a powerful one that he omitted from his previous treatment of her: namely, that Manto "suis artibus spiritus
immundos et inferorum manes coegit in voces et responsa dare
quarentibus" [she summoned up by means of her arts unclean
spirits, and she compelled the shades of the dead to speak and to
answer those who questioned them]. Boccaccio's ascription of
necromancy to Manto may come from a reading of Statius's *Thebaid*, in which, as mentioned above, Manto's arts help her father
speak with the ghost of Oedipus's father; alternately, it may come
from Boccaccio's development of a hint in Dante's portrait of
Manto. As Hollander points out, Benvenuto da Imola's commentary on *Inferno* 20 notes that Manto's disordered tresses and the
epithet "cruda" seem to come from the description of the loath-
some witch Erictho in Lucan's *Pharsalia*.[21] In a particularly gruesome scene, one of Pompey's sons has this horrifying hag call up

the ghost of a man newly dead in order to answer questions. By including necromancy among Manto's skills, Boccaccio's account
thus seems to be following Dante more closely in assimilating the
evil Erictho's characteristics to his Manto.

After this disturbing touch of the Dantesque underworld, Boccaccio again turns to Pomponius Mela's account of Manto's Asian
journey before relating Virgil's version of her settlement. However, even though Boccaccio follows Virgil in giving Manto a son,
his rhetoric here closely echoes Dante's. Boccaccio imitates Inferno 20's long topographical excursus on rivers and the situation
of Mantua with his own mapping of Manto's wandering from
Cisalpine Gaul to Lake Garda and finally to the site of Mantua.

Likewise, Boccaccio again follows Dante in his harsher account
of Manto's site-selection procedure, suggesting that one of the reasons that Manto chooses the unhealthy place is "ut suis cantationibus posset vacare liberius" [to be able to practice her spells
with greater freedom]. This claim resembles that of Inferno 20.85-
86 : "Lì per fuggire ogne consorzio umano, / ristette con suoi servi
a far sue arti" (There, to avoid all company, she stopped, with only
servants, to ply her magic arts). After this homage to Dante, Boccaccio shifts abruptly back to the Virgilian foundation myth, saying that Citheonus (that is, Ocnus) founded the city and named it
for his mother. Though this particular observation seems more
Virgilian than Dantesque, Boccaccio gives Inferno 20, or rather,
Dante's Virgil the last word on Manto's fate, noting that some say
that Manto preserved her virginity unto death. Boccaccio's text,
however, does not end there. Lest the reader interpret her chastity
as a sign of purity or goodness (for in De mulieribus claris, Boccaccio repeatedly praises this womanly virtue in his other biographies), Boccaccio makes sure his reader realizes that even Manto's
virginity cannot mitigate her "nephastis...artibus," (wicked arts),
ending this version of the chapter with a strong denunciation of
Manto's divinatory arts worthy of the Commedia itself.

Like the earlier version of the chapter, this retelling of Manto's
story (or rather, of the stories told by male poets and historians
about her) privileges the poetic, Virgilian-Dantesque account of
the foundation of Mantua rather than the more historical accounts compiled by either Servius or Pomponius Mela. But this
time, Boccaccio ends by declaring in no uncertain terms his alle-
giance to Dante's Christian vision through his concluding state-

ment that Manto died a virgin followed by his vehement peroration on Manto's evil practices. Boccaccio's moralizing revision of this chapter is in keeping with changes that he made to other biographies in *De mulieribus claris*, which show that for Boccaccio, as a Christian humanist, pagan texts were deeply attractive, but at the same time presented profound moral difficulties.

The second of Boccaccio's two Mantos, then, seems to be the one that Dante puts in Hell; perhaps the other would have ended up with Virgil in Limbo, since her exploits and her fame seems to be described in more benign terms. In any event, Boccaccio's redrafting of the chapter suggests his ambivalence about both her character and his classical source texts. While he does not eliminate the Virgilian version of Manto's life entirely, Boccaccio recasts his own work in such a way that he takes greater account of Dante's clear articulation of the tragic limitations of pagan—and more specifically, of Virgilian—vision. Boccaccio's harsher attitude toward divination in the second and final version shows his decision to value Dante's Christian moral vision over that of his classical sources.

### APPENDIX: BOCCACCIO'S TWO CHAPTERS ON MANTO

Boccaccio's first draft of his chapter on Manto from Vatican Library Codex Urbinate lat. 45, as printed in Giovanni Boccaccio, *De Mulieribus Claris* ed. Vittorio Zaccaria, in *Tutte le Opere di Giovanni Boccaccio*, Vol 10 (Milan: Mondadori, 1967), 506:

> Mantho fatidica mulier et thebana adeo fama prefulgens fuit ut in nostrum usque evum perseveret eius fulgoris favillula. Hec Tyresie thebani preclari vatis filia sub eruditissimo patre talium pyromantiam egregie didicit sic et ad vaticinia exquirenda fibras atque precordia seu exta cesarum pecudum intueri, nec non garritus volucrum atque volatus meditari. Que etsi veritate, et plurimum, careant, et nostre sint adverse religioni, non tamen muliebre intrasse ingenium mirabile minus. His tamen florens et magna facta nominis, post fedata infanda cede Thebanorum fratrum iniqua odia et sue civitatis a Creonte occupatum imperium, longum in exilium acta per orbis tractus varios—ut non nulli volunt—devenit in Cariam ibique Mopsum eisdem suis artibus postea insignem virum, quo tamen ex patre nescio, peperit et demum

Clarii Apollinis templum condidit, non inter antiquorum detes-
tanda facinora minimum, quin imo inter alia celeberrimum re-
sponsorum oraculum. Alii vero omisso numquid ex Caria an
potius ex occupata patria sumpta fuga, eam in Ytaliam devenisse
confirmant et tandem seu virgo seu ex Tybri iam Cithone enixo
inter paludes, ex Benaco nondum Venetorum lacu effusas, sibi
sedem et cineribus suis elegisse perpetuam quibus desuper cum
condidissent civitatem posteri eam de suo nomine dixere Manthuam. Quo nomine et nos insignem civitatem cognoscimus et
Manthonis invicem memoriam reservamus.

Translation:

Manto, a Theban prophetess, was of such bright fame that small
sparks of its brightness persist in our age. This daughter of Tiresias (the most famed of Theban seers) learned pyromancy, advised
by her father, most erudite in such matters, and learned to ob-
serve the entrails, stomachs, and significant organs of slaugh-
tered animals in order to inquire into prophetic matters, as well
as learning to meditate on the sounds and flights of birds. Although these [skills] are lacking in truth and are against our religion, they are not the less impressive for a woman to have attained. Nevertheless, although she was excellent in them and
had acquired a great reputation, after the iniquitous feuding of
the Theban brothers had been befouled by unspeakable slaughter
and the control of her city had been usurped by Creon, and she
had been driven into exile for a long time in various parts of the
earth—as some say—she came to Caria and in that place gave
birth to Mopsus (later a famous man by means of those same arts)
though I do not know who was his father—and finally she founded the temple of the Clarian Apollo, a deed not least among the
detestable acts of the ancients, for indeed among them it was the
oracle most celebrated for its advice. Without saying whether her
flight took place from Caria or her occupied country, others say
that she came to Italy and finally (either a virgin or already having
given birth to Cithonus, who was fathered by Tiberus) she chose
a perpetual seat for herself and her ashes among the marshes not
yet poured out from Lake Benacus of the Veneto, where, when
later people came to found a city they called it Mantua from her
name. And by this name we know the famous city and preserve
the memory of Manto.

Boccaccio's later version of the Manto chapter as given in Giovanni Boccaccio, *De Mulieribus Claris* ed. Vittorio Zaccaria, in

*Tutte le Opere di Giovanni Boccaccio,* Vol 10 (Milan: Mondadori, 1967), 126–28:

Mantho, Thyresie, maximi Thebanorum vatis, filia, tempore Edipi Regis filiorumque fuit insignis. Hec quidem sub patre magistro tam pronpti atque capacis fuit ingenii, ut pyromantiam, vetustissimum Caldeorum, seu—ut volunt alii—Nembroth inventum, adeo egregie disceret, ut evo suo nemo melius flammarum motus colores et murmura, quibus, nescio quo dyabolico opere, futurorum dicunt demonstrationes inesse, cognosceret. Preterea fibras pecudum et taurorum iecinora et quorumcunque animalium exta perspicaci cognovit intuitu; traxitque sepissime—ut creditum est—suis artibus spiritus immundos et inferorum manes coegit in voces et responsa dare querentibus. Sane cum iam bello cecidissent argivi reges qui Thebas obsederant, occupassetque Creon civitatis imperium, hec—ut placet aliquibus—regem novum fugiens, secessit in Asyam ibique Clarii Apollonis fanum, postea celeberrimum divinatione, instituit et Mopsum, inclitum sui seculi vatem, esto ex quo conceptum non prodat antiquitas, peperit. Alii vero aliter sentiunt dicuntque eam cum complicibus quibusdam suis, post thebanum bellum, errasse diu et tandem in Ytalium devenisse ibique Tyberino iuncta cuidam, concepisse ex eo et peperisse filium, quem Cithconum dixere, a quibusdam Byanorem etiam vocitatum; et inde cum prole in Cisalpinam Galliam transiecisse, ubi com palustria loca, Benaco contermina lacui, comperisset sua natura munita, seu ut suis cantationibus posset vacare liberius, seu vite residuum securius ducere, media in palude, in supereminente aquis solo, posuisse sedem et ibidem post tempus mortuam atque sepultam. Circa cuius tumulum aiunt Cithconum civitatem suis constituisse eamque de matris nomine Manthuam vocitasse. Quidam vero arbitrati sunt eam in mortem usque constanti proposito virginitatem servasse: floridum quippe atque sanctissimum opus et laudabile plurimum, ni illud nephastis suis labefactasset artibus Deoque vero, cui dicanda est, virginitatem servasset.

Translation by Virginia Brown, ed. and trans., *Famous Women: Giovanni Boccaccio* (Cambridge, Mass.: Harvard University Press, 2001), 120–21:

Manto, daughter of Tiresias, the greatest soothsayer of Thebes, was renowned in the time of King Oedipus and his sons. Her father's pupil, she had such a quick and capable mind that she became expert in the ancient art of pyromancy discovered by the

Chaldeans or, as some authorities would have it, by Nimrod. In her age no one understood better the movements of flames, their colors and murmuring, wherein are said to be contained, as through some diabolical agency, indications of the future. Moreover, Manto also knew well how to interpret the entrails of sheep, the livers of oxen, and the vital organs of any other animal. Often, so people believed, she summoned up by means of her arts unclean spirits, and she compelled the shades of the dead to speak and to answer those who questioned them.

When the Argive kings besieging Thebes fell in battle and Creon had taken control of the city, Manto (according to some sources) fled the new king and went to Asia. There she built the temple of Apollo Clarius, later famed for its oracle, and she gave birth to Mopsus, a distinguished soothsayer in his time, although the ancients do not tell us the name of his father.

A different version recounts that Manto wandered for a long time after the Theban war with some of her companions and finally reached Italy. Here she married a certain Tiberinus, conceived, and gave birth to a son called Citheonus by some and Bianor by others. Manto then went with her child to Cisalpine Gaul. Finding naturally fortified swampy areas near Lake Garda, she settled on some higher ground in the middle of the marsh, either to be able to practice her spells with greater freedom or so as to spend the rest of her life in safer surroundings. There she eventually died and was buried. Citheonus is said to have built a city for his followers near her grave and to have named it Mantua after his mother.

Other authorities, however, believe that Manto resolutely preserved her virginity until her death. This would have been a splendid, holy, and praiseworthy thing to do, had she not stained such an action with her wicked arts and had she preserved her virginity for the true God, to whom it should be consecrated.

## NOTES

1. See, for example, Constance Jordan, "Boccaccio's In-Famous Women: Gender and Civic Virtue in *De Mulieribus Claris*" in Carole Levin and Jeanie Watson, eds., *Ambiguous Realities: Women in the Middle Ages and the Renaissance* (Detroit: Wayne State University Press, 1987), 25–47 and Patricia Phillippy, "Establishing Authority: Boccaccio's *De Claris Mulieribus* and Christine de Pisan" *Romanic Review* 77 (1989): 167–94.

2. Harold Bloom, *The Anxiety of Influence* (New York: Oxford, 1975).

3. Anna Cerbo, "Didone in Boccaccio," in *Annali Istituto Universitario Orientale, Napoli, Sezione Romanza* 21 (1979): 177–219.

4. Citations of the text are from Giovanni Boccaccio, *De Mulieribus Claris,* ed. Vittorio Zaccaria, in *Tutte le Opere di Giovanni Boccaccio,* Vol 10 (Milan: Mondadori, 1967). English translations are cited from Virginia Brown, ed. and trans., *Famous Women: Giovanni Boccaccio* (Cambridge, Mass.: Harvard University Press, 2001).

5. See Simone Marchesi, "Distilling Ovid: Dante's Exile and Some Metamorphic Nomenclature in Hell" earlier in this volume for a discussion of Dante's shifts from Brunetto to Ovid in the *Inferno.*

6. See Jessica Levenstein, "Philomela, Procne, and the Song of the Penitent in Dante's *Purgatorio,*" contained in this volume.

7. Clearly, my interpretation of Boccaccio's Manto is deeply indebted to Robert Hollander's discussions of this character in Dante's *Commedia,* especially the essays "The Tragedy of Divination in Inferno XX" in his *Studies in Dante* (Ravenna: Longo, 1980), 131–218 and "Dante's Misreadings of the Aeneid in Inferno 20" in Rachael Jacoff and Jeffrey T. Schnapp, The Poetry *of Allusion: Virgil and Ovid in Dante's Commedia* (Stanford: Stanford University Press, 1991), 76–93.

8. For Virgil's text, see R. D. Williams, ed., *The Aeneid of Virgil,* Vol. 2 (New York: St. Martin's Press, 1987); for the English translation, see W. D. Jackson Knight, trans., Virgil, *The Aeneid* (Harmondsworth: Penguin, 1956).

9. Marie Desport, *L'Incantation Virgilienne: Virgile et Orphée* (Bordeaux: Imprimeries Delmas, 1952), 446–48.

10. See G. Thilo and H. Hagen, eds., *Servii grammatici qui feruntur in Vergilii carmina comentarii* (Leipzig, 1884), 412–13.

11. See Seneca's *Oedipus,* lines 303–83 in Frank Justus Miller, ed. and trans., *Tragedies: Seneca* (Cambridge, Harvard University Press, 1998), I.452–61.

12. Statius, *Thebaid* IV 550–51. For the Latin text, see J. H. Mozley, trans, *Statius* Vol. 1 (Cambridge: Harvard University Press, 1967); for the translation, see Statius, *Thebaid,* trans. A. D. Melville (Oxford: Clarendon Press, 1992).

13. See Pomponius Mela, *Chorographie,* ed. and trans. A. Silberman (Paris: Les Belles Lettres, 1988).

14. *De Chorographia* I, 17, 89: "Lebedos Clariique Apollinis fanum, quod Manto, Tiresiae filia, fugiens victores Thebanorum Epigonos, et Colophon, quam Mopsus eiusdem Mantus filius statuit."

15. The text of Dante's *Commedia* cited here was established by Giorgio Petrocchi and reproduced in Robert and Jean Hollander, trans., *The Inferno* (New York: Random House, 2000), from which I quote the translation.

16. See Francisco D'Ovidio, "Dante e la magìa," and "Ancora su Dante e la magìa" in his *Studii sulla Divina Commedia* (Milan-Palermo: Sandron, 1901), 76–112; 113–49.

17. See Hollander, "Tragedy of Divination," 205–18. Among the other more recent treatments of this problem is Richard Kay, "Dante's Double Damnation of Manto," in *Res Publica Litterarum* (1978): 113–49. Kay concludes that Dante saves the pious fictional heroine of Statius' *Thebaid* while condemning the actual historical personage of Manto.

18. The text of this version, found in Zaccaria, ed., 506 is reprinted in the appendix to this essay.

19. See Virginia Brown, ed. and trans., *Famous Women: Giovanni Boccaccio* (Cambridge: Harvard University Press, 2001), 3.

20. The text of the *Purgatorio* is that edited by Giorgio Petrocchi; the translation is that of Robert and Jean Hollander, *Purgatorio* (New York: Random House, 2003).

21. See Hollander, "Tragedy of Divination," 190.

# *Nolite iudicare*: Dante and the Dilemma of Judgment

LAUREN SCANCARELLI SEEM

I BEGIN THIS ESSAY WITH AN EXERCISE. ROBERT DURLING, IN *THE Figure of the Poet in Renaissance Epic*, fruitfully examines four Renaissance texts by taking as his point of departure moments of authorial self-representation. He focuses on episodes in each epic where the author offers a portrait of himself as poet.[1] The exercise here is to borrow Durling's term in order to try to locate a "figure of the poet" in Dante's *Commedia*. As one has come to expect in Dante studies, I am not the first to attempt this exercise. In 1373, Benvenuto Da Imola produced a promising candidate of his own—the Sibyl of *Paradiso* 33. Durling's phrase was, of course, unknown to Benvenuto, yet the *trecento* commentator clearly saw the Sibyl as a representation of the figure of Dante the poet. Benvenuto's gloss on the Sibyl compares her role in reproducing Apollo's oracle to Dante's role in reproducing the visionary experience necessary to write the *Commedia*.[2]

Benvenuto, in recognizing the parallels between the Sibyl's function as oracle and Dante's as writer, identified a convincing figure of the poet in the *Commedia*. My own candidate for a portrait of Dante as author within his own text, however, shows Dante in one of the less attractive aspects of that role: that of judge. There are some disturbing correspondences between Dante's posture as author and Minos's as judge in *Inferno* 5. There, Minos is described as the sinners come before him,

> essamina le colpe ne l'intrata;
> guidica e manda secondo ch'avvinghia.
> Dico che quando l'anima mal nata

li vien dinanzi, tutta si confessa;
e quel conoscitor de le peccata
vede qual loco d'inferno è da essa;
cignesi con la coda tante volte
quantunque gradi vuol che giù sia messa.
                                    (*Inferno* 5.5–12)[3]

[He examines each offender at the entrance,
judges and dispatches as he encoils himself.
I mean that when the ill-begotten soul
stands there before him it confesses all,
and that accomplished judge of sins
decides what place in Hell is fit for it,
then coils his tail around himself to count
how many circles down the soul must go.]

Minos, snarling as he wraps his tail around himself, is undeniably
an absurd figure, yet it would be a mistake to allow his grotesque
appearance to mask the importance of his function in the poem.
Minos not only dispatches each sinner to an appropriate circle, he
pronounces judgment by deciding just what circle that should be.
Minos has the distinction of being the sole judge of all who enter
Hell. In performing his task, Minos parodies both judicial procedure and Christ's promised role as judge in the Last Judgment. The
same, however, could be said of Dante in writing the *Commedia*.
Whatever his potential disclaimers are, Dante establishes himself
as the single and final judge of the souls who populate his text.
Moreover, while Minos's considerable jurisdiction is limited to
placing those already condemned to Hell, it is Dante, as author of
the poem, who has passed the sentence. Dante's parody of judgment in the figure of Minos is ultimately a self-parody.

A reading of Minos as a representation of Dante himself points
to a paradox that lies at the very heart of the *Commedia*'s poetics.
Unless we accept the poem as a divinely authorized text, it is
Dante, on his own authority, who passes judgment on hundreds of
souls as he assigns each soul a place in heaven or hell. Dante
usurps for himself the eschatological privilege that Christian theology reserves for God alone.

"Nolite iudicare," Christ preached in his Sermon on the Mount,
"Do not judge and you will not be judged." Although perhaps the
best known, this is but one of the scriptural dictates against stand-

ing in judgment over one's fellow man. Paul calls several times for
restraint in judgment, including I Corinthians 4:5: "There must be
no passing of premature judgment. Leave that until the Lord
comes."[4] Yet, paradoxically, at the same time that he is acting in
the face of clear biblical injunctions against the passing of judgment, Dante admonishes his readers not to presume to know who
is saved and who is damned. Dante even produces his own version
of Paul's warning when he has the Eagle of Jupiter intone,

> E voi, mortali, tenetevi stretti
> a giudicar: ché noi, che Dio vedemo,
> non conosciamo ancor tutti li eletti;
> *(Paradiso* 20.133–35)

[And you, mortals, keep yourselves restrained in judging; for we,
who see God, know not yet all the elect.]

Even the blessed do not know who is saved, who is damned, yet
the integrity of the *Commedia* depends on Dante's claim to have
access to this privileged knowledge. The eagle's warning against
presumption in judging threatens to dismantle the moral and narrative strategies of the very poem in which it is found. Divine
judgment invalidates the *Commedia* for attempting to portray divine judgment.

The *Commedia*'s judgments are, of course, most damning for
those it consigns to hell, but it is in the *Paradiso* that Dante offers
an extended consideration of his own paradoxical stance. In his
third *cantica* Dante retrospectively questions the enterprise that
he has been engaged in since the *Inferno*—writing his own account of divine judgment. Dante offers us an opportunity to examine the poem just where the poem seems to be examining itself
and its own claims. At the literal center of the *Paradiso*, in Mars,
in what is arguably one of the poem's most significant encounters,
Dante meets his ancestor Cacciaguida. Dante expresses to Cacciaguida well-merited, if ultimately self-serving hesitation at the
prospect of presenting an uncensored version of the knowledge he
has supposedly acquired concerning the fate of certain souls. Cacciaguida's response, "tutta tua vision fa manifesta" [make manifest all that you have seen] *(Par.* 17.128), gives, in effect, a commission to Dante to write the *Commedia* and in doing so gives
also a validation of the judgments he passes.

Dante carefully surrounds this central episode authorizing his poem, and the judgments that it makes, with the *Commedia*'s two explicit injunctions against the passing of judgment. The encounter with Cacciaguida is framed on one side by the warning Dante places in the mouth of St. Thomas of Aquinas in the Heaven of the Sun:

> Non sien le genti, ancor, troppo sicure
> a guidicar, sì come quei che stima
> le biade in campo pria che sien mature;
> ch'i'ho veduto tutto 'l verno prima
> lo prun mostrarsi rigido e feroce,
> poscia portar la rosa in su la cima;
> e legno vidi già dritto e veloce
> correr lo mar per tutto suo cammino,
> perire al fine a l'intrar de la foce.
> Non creda donna Berta e ser Martino,
> per vedere un furare, altro offerere,
> vederli dentro al consiglio divino;
> ché quel può surgere, e quel può cadere.
>                         (*Par.* 13.130–42)

[Moreover, let folk not be too secure in judgment, like one who should count the ears in the field before they are ripe; for I have seen first, all winter through, the thorn display itself hard and stiff, and then upon its summit bear the rose. And I have seen ere now a ship fare straight and swift over the sea through all her course, and perish at the last as she entered the harbor. Let not dame Berta and squire Martin, if they see one steal and one make offering, believe to see them within the Divine Counsel; for the one may rise and the other may fall.]

The eagle's Pauline warning in the sphere of Jupiter in *Par.* 20.133–35 against passing judgment cited above ("E voi mortali, tenetevi stretti . . ."), completes the frame. These twin injunctions against the passing of judgment are both thematic and structural companion pieces. Read in tandem, the two strongly worded admonitions deny the possibility of human access to divine judgment and have broad implications for the text in which they are found, a poem that presumes to judge all. The warnings, however, are also specifically linked to two surprise witnesses to God's judgment. The first injunction has, as one of its several subtexts, the presence of

Solomon among the lights in the Sun, while Ripheus's appearance in Jupiter more directly occasions the second admonition.

Solomon and Ripheus have a good deal more in common than an acquaintance with them outside of Dante's text would suggest. Both appear in the *Commedia* as "fifth lights." Solomon is *"la quinta luce"* (*Par.* 10.109) of the twelve that make up the first circle of saved souls in the Sun; Ripheus is *"la quinta delle luci"* (*Par.* 20.69) that together comprise the eye of the eagle in Jupiter. Even more important than this parallel numerical position, both are meant to surprise Dante's readership: Solomon because of the intense debate as to whether he was saved or damned, and Ripheus because he is a pagan without any patristic history of redemption who appears in the pages of the *Commedia* in the most Christian of places.

The admonitions that follow their appearances are directed toward any reader who expresses surprise at finding Solomon and Ripheus among the saved, for to be surprised by who appears in Heaven is to reveal a presumption that one could have possibly known what any human's fate would be. But more specifically, the warnings are directed at the two men who would probably be the most surprised to find Solomon and Ripheus among Dante's blessed: St. Augustine and Virgil. St. Augustine would most likely be quite astonished to find in Heaven the man whom he believed had lost his early promise and wisdom to carnal love. Similarly, Virgil would probably be quite surprised to find in Paradise Ripheus, a minor character from his *Aeneid* whom Virgil had quickly dispatched to the shades in combat.

In the heaven of the Sun, Thomas Aquinas identifies the blessed lights for Dante: first himself, then Albertus Magnus, Gratian, Peter Lombard, and then,

> La quinta luce, che'è tra noi più bella,
> spira di tale amor, che tutto 'l mondo
> là giù ne gola di saper novella:
> entro v'è l'alta mente u' sì profondo
> saver fu messo, che, se 'l vero è vero,
> a veder tanto non surse il secondo.
> (*Par.* 10. 109–14)

[The fifth light, which is the most beautiful among us, breathes with such love that all the world there below thirst to know tid-

ings of it. Within it is the lofty mind to which was given wisdom
so deep that, if the truth be the true, there never rose a second of
such full vision.]

Dionysius the Areopagite, Orosius, Boethius, Isidore of Seville,
Bede, Richard of St. Victor, and Siger complete the first circle. The
fifth of the circle's lights has always been identified as Solomon.

While Aquinas is accorded the honor of speaking for the first
circle, as Bonaventure is the spokesman of the second circle, Solomon has a certain distinction of his own among the twenty-four
souls named in the Sun. First, of course, is the honor conveyed in
the periphrastic description of Solomon as being the most beautiful of the distinguished souls who grace the circle. Then, Aquinas
returns to his description of Solomon some three *canti* later (*Par.*
13.35–42) to offer a lengthy explication of what it was that he
meant when he said of Solomon, "a veder tanto non surse il secondo." In addition, apart from each circle's "representative"—
Aquinas and Bonaventure—Solomon is the only other member of
either circle to be accorded a speaking role. In *Paradiso* 14.37–60
Aquinas falls silent, and it is Solomon who promulgates the doc-
trine of the resurrection of the body to the pilgrim.

In addition to having an expanded role among the wise lights of
the Sun, Solomon was probably meant to be the fourth heaven's
biggest surprise and this in a heaven that includes the surprising
appearances of Siger and Joachim. A reading of the early commentators on the *Commedia*, probably the closest we can come to
having any sort of access to the reaction of the poem's original audience, shows that these earliest readers seem to register more
surprise at Solomon's inclusion than at the presence of either the
heretical Siger or Joachim. The remarks of the *antiqui commenta-
tori* refer to the debate among theologians in the Middle Ages as to
whether Solomon was saved or damned. Solomon's idolatry and
concupiscence in old age is recorded in I Kings 11.1–4: "King
Solomon loved many foreign women. . . . He had seven hundred
wives of royal rank and three hundred concubines. When Solomon
grew old his wives swayed his heart to other gods." The Bible is
silent on Solomon's fate, leaving his ultimate destiny, or at least
his reputation, in the hands of the various exegetes who wish to
speculate on the matter.[5] The commonly accepted interpretation
of Aquinas's comment that "tutto 'l mondo / là giù ne gola di saper
novella" (*Par.* 10.110–11) is that the world hungers for news of the

condition of Solomon's soul, to find out whether he is saved or not. The contention over his fate becomes his identifying feature when Solomon makes his appearance in the *Commedia*.

The twenty-four souls named in the Sun are involved in a complicated web of commentary and countercommentary. Perhaps the theologian whose life and works are most intertwined with that of the other eleven souls who share the first circle with him is Aquinas. Aquinas studied under Albertus Magnus, wrote commentaries on Peter Lombard, Boethius, and the Pseudo-Dionysus, and attacked the teachings of Siger. Aquinas provides the most extreme example, but involvement with the works of one's fellow theologians is the rule, not the exception of the fourth heaven. Isidore of Seville, the ninth theologian in the first circle, was among those who judged Solomon in his own writings and found him wanting. In his "*De ortu et obitu partum,*" Isidore holds that Solomon's immorality excluded the king from ultimate salvation.[6] Presumably like Gregory, who Dante tells us in *Paradiso* 28.133–35 argued for an "incorrect" hierarchical ordering of the angelic circle and upon his death realized his "mistake" when he saw the Angelic circles and smiled at his error, Isidore must have "*di sè medesmo rise*" when he saw that Solomon was one of his companions in the Heaven of the Sun.

Yet Isidore of Seville was hardly alone in his presumptive judgment of Solomon, and in Augustine of Hippo Solomon found his harshest judge of all. Augustine finds numerous opportunities to make his position on Solomon clear. In the *De civitate Dei* Augustine gives an extended gloss on Nathan's prophesy of 2 Samuel 7.5–16, a prophecy that promises God's extended favor to David and his offspring:

> I will preserve the offspring of your body after you and make his sovereignty secure. It is he who shall build a house for my name, and I will make his royal throne secure for ever. I will be a father to him and he a son to me; if he does evil, I will punish him with the rod such as men use, with strokes such as mankind gives, Yet I will not withdraw my favor from him, as I withdrew it from your predecessor. Your House and your sovereignty will always stand secure before me and your throne be established for ever.

This prophecy, quite reasonably, is assumed to refer to Solomon. Augustine roundly refutes this interpretation:

Hanc tam grandem promissionem qui putat in Salomone fuisse completam, multum errat. Adtendit enim quod dictum est: *Hic aedificabit mihi domum*, quoniam Salomon templum illud nobilissimum struxit, et non adtendit: *Fidelis erit domus eius et regnum eius usque in aeternum coram me*. Adtendat ergo et aspiciat Salomonis domum plenam mulieribus alienigenis colentibus deos falsos et ipsum ab eis regem aliquando sapientem in eandem idolatriam seductum atque deiectum; et non audeat existimare Deum vel hoc promisisse mendaciter vel talem Salomonen domumque eius futuram non potuisse praescire.

[Anyone who supposes that this magnificent promise was fulfilled in Solomon is greatly mistaken. For he notes only the words: "He shall build me a house," inasmuch as Solomon erected that most noble temple, and ignores these words: "His house shall be faithful to me and his reign shall endure for ever in my sight." Let him then take note and consider Solomon's house, full of alien women who worshipped false gods, and the king himself, who, though a wise man once, was seduced and degraded to the same idolatry. And let him not dare think that God made this promise deceitfully, nor that he was unable to foresee that Solomon and his house would be like this.][7]

Augustine is able to find redemption for David after his lapse into sinfulness with Bathsheba; but in his *De doctrina christiana* (3.21.31), Augustine explicitly excludes David's son from the same possibility for grace. David's passion is forgiven since it passed on like a "guest." According to Augustine there is no such forgiveness for the unfortunate Solomon since his carnal love took possession of him. Augustine's harshest words of all for Solomon are found is his *Contra Faustum Manichaeum*. There Augustine writes of Solomon, "Nec mihi prorsus occurrit, quid saltem in allegoria boni significet" [nor does anything at all about him occur to me that even allegorically indicates anything good].[8]

Just as Augustine's disapproval of Solomon has a strong presence in the body of Augustine's work, Augustine himself has a strong presence in the fourth heaven, but it is a presence that takes the form of conspicuous absence.[9] The name Augustine appears twice within the Heaven of the Sun, once in the first circle, once in the second. In the first circle the seventh light is introduced by periphrasis as,

Ne l'altra piccioletta luce ride
quello avvocato de' tempi cristiani
del cui latino Augustin si provide.
(*Par.* 10.118–20)

[In the next little light smiles that defender of the Christian times,
of whose discourse Augustine made use.]

The soul being introduced is that of Orosius, who is described as
providing the intellectual fodder that Augustine would later use.
On first reading, this identification fits well into the pattern of in-
terconnection between the writings of the various theologians
who make up the circle. Augustine did make great use of Orosius's
writings. However Augustine is not one of the twelve lights who
make up the lesser circle.

In *Paradiso* 12 we are introduced to twelve more theologians
who together comprise the second garland of light. Again the
reader comes upon the name *Augustin.* Bonaventure first introduces himself and then identifies the second and third souls, "Illuminato e Augustin son quici," (*Par.* 12.130). For one brief line it
would be reasonable for the reader to believe that Augustine of
Hippo is here in the sun's second circle, but this premature conclusion is scuttled immediately by the identification that follows,

Illuminato e Augustin son quici,
che fuor de' primi scalzi poverelli
che nel capestro a Dio si fero amici.
(*Par.* 12.130–32)

[Illuminato and Augustine are here, who were of the first unshod
poor brethren that with the cord made themselves God's friends.]

Here we have not Augustine of Hippo, but a quite different Augustine, an early follower of St. Francis. Although the name Augustine appears twice within the fourth sphere, Augustine himself
is not to be found in the Heaven of the Sun. The reader is kept in
suspense concerning Augustine's place in Dante's scheme of the
afterlife until *Paradiso* 32.35. There St. Bernard points out to the
pilgrim some of the saints seated in the Rose. Bernard indicates to
Dante, "Francesco, Benedetto e Augustino / e altri." Augustine is
assuredly in the most exalted of places and in the most exalted of

company, yet by just one word he misses being one of the *"altri,"* an unnamed member of the chorus, so to speak, although a member of the chorus of the blessed to be sure.

Dante leaves no doubt that Augustine, Isidore, and the other theologians who have made errors of judgment concerning Solomon's salvation are among the saved, but they are still among those targeted by the final speech that Dante gives to Thomas Aquinas. At various points in their writings, they too have been *"troppo secure / a guidicar"* (*Par.* 13.130–31). Like *donna Berta* and *ser Martin*, they had behaved as though they had seen within *consiglio divino*. But divine counsel is inaccessible to humans, and that is the message driven home in *Paradiso* 20, which serves as both complement and corollary to *Paradiso* 13 and its warning against precipitous judgment.

The companion piece to *Paradiso* 13's injunction is found in the heaven of Jupiter with its just rulers. There the souls show themselves in a curious form of divine sky writing as they spell out the phrase *"Diligite iustitiam qui iudicatis terram."* (*Par.* 18.91–93). The line is, of course, the opening verse of *The Book of Wisdom*, a work ascribed to Solomon. Solomon and the honorific description accorded him by Aquinas in the Heaven of the Sun as being without equal in kingly wisdom immediately become the background against which the sixth sphere and its just rulers should be read.

It is in the sixth heaven that Dante addresses an issue that has been smoldering since *Inferno 4* when Dante saw the virtuous heathens relegated to Limbo—the ultimate fairness of divine justice. In the sixth heaven, the pilgrim silently challenges the rightness of divine judgment when he asks the unvoiced question of wherein lies the justice that condemns a virtuous heathen who has no access to Christianity. The Eagle delivers a chastising reply,

> Or tu chi se', che vuo' sedere a scranna,
> per giudicar di lungi mille miglia
> con la veduta corta d'una spanna?
> (*Par.* 19.79–81)

[Now who are you who would sit upon the seat to judge a thousand miles away with the short sight that carries but a span?]

The fate of the virtuous heathens, and in particular the fate of Virgil, the heathen in whom Dante has the greatest personal investment, has weighed heavily on the pilgrim. The Eagle's response is not an attempt to justify what seems to the pilgrim to be patently unfair, but an outburst against man's pride and presumption in questioning God's judgment in the first place. In *Paradiso* 19 the Eagle comments not once but three times within the span of a single canto on the limited perspective available to man from which to contemplate divine judgment. Even before the Eagle gives voice to Dante's concern, only to lambaste him for having the temerity to formulate it in the first place, it asserts:

> Però ne la giustizia sempiterna
> la vista che receve il vostro mondo,
> com'occhio per lo mare, entro s'interna;
> che, ben che da la proda veggia il fondo,
> in pelago nol vede; e nondimeno
> èli, ma cela lui l'esser profondo.
> (*Par.* 19.58–63]

[Therefore the sight that is granted to your world penetrates within the Eternal Justice as the eye into the sea; which, though from the shore it can see the bottom, in the open seas it sees it not, and none the less it is there, but the depth conceals it.]

The Eagle drives home the same point home yet a third time when it pronounces:

> . . .Quali
> son le mie note a te, che non le 'ntendi,
> tal è il guidicio etterno a voi mortali.
> (*Par.* 19.97–99)

[As are my notes to you who understands them not, such is the Eternal Judgment to you mortals.]

In *Paradiso* 19 Dante, through the collective voice of the just rulers who comprise the Eagle, places a triple insistence on the inability of man to comprehend the judgments that God has passed. Yet if the Eagle's admonitions launch a preemptive strike against anyone who might dare to question God's judgment, in the very next canto it also offers a surprise witness to this inscrutable eternal judgment—Ripheus. The fifth soul to make up the eyebrow of the Eagle is introduced,

> Chi crederebbe giù nel mondo errante
> che Rifeo Troaino in questo tondo
> fosse la quinta de le luci sante?
> (*Par.* 20.67–69)

[Who would believe, down in the erring world, that Ripheus the Trojan was the fifth of the holy lights in this circle?]

As Teodolinda Barolini points out, this is a "nonrhetorical rhetorical question." Ripheus's appearance is meant to shock, to be beyond belief.[10] As the Eagle comments, "La prima vita del ciglio e la quinta/ ti fa maravigliar" [The first soul of the eyebrow and the fifth make you marvel] (*Par.* 20.100–101). But while there is at least a tradition bolstering the salvation of the first light, Trajan, there is no such tradition to turn to in order to find justification for Ripheus's appearance in heaven. The only history Ripheus brings to Dante's text is that provided by Virgil in the pages of the *Aeneid*. There Ripheus is mentioned three times. The first two mentions, though seemingly casual, build to a climax in the Trojan's death. Ripehus is first seen among a group of Trojan warriors with Aeneas (*Aen.*II.339). Then some sixty lines later (*Aen.*II.394) Ripheus rushes into battle. His third and final mention is at his death (*Aen.*II.426–28) when he is accorded his epitaph:

> cadit et Rhipeus, iustissimus unus
> qui fuit in Teucria, et servantissimus aequi
> (dis aliter visum);

[Ripheus, too, falls. He was first among the Teucrians for justice and for doing right (the gods saw it differently).][11]

Virgil in his stance as recorder of history testifies that Ripheus was the most righteous of the Trojans, but remarks that his gods reached a different conclusion.

Ripheus's salvation within the pages of the *Commedia* has deep implications for Virgil as Dante plays a sophisticated literary game with Virgil's text. Virgil's ultimate judgment of Ripheus is contrasted with Dante's, while the judgment of Virgil's "dèi falsi e bugiardi" [false and lying gods] (*Inf.* 1.72) is set against the kinder judgment of Dante's Christian God. A minor character manages to receive achieve salvation while his celebrated author is denied the same fate. As Robert Hollander has pointed out, the encounter with Ripheus underscores Virgil's fate and brings into sharp relief the pathos of the saved character versus his damned author. At the same time Dante allows Virgil's text to function as a form of scripture, one that can guarantee the salvation of a soul on its own authority, although this honor is blunted by Virgil's inability to save himself. Yet underneath all of these various levels of meaning there lies the strong possibility that Dante might very well be doing to Virgil what Augustine did to Solomon.[12]

The appearance of Ripheus occasions the Eagle's final outburst against presumptive judgment cited above, "E voi, mortali, tenetevi stretti a giudicar" (*Par.* 20.133–34). The Ripheus episode, and indeed all of *Paradiso* 19 and 20, raises the question of whether there is justice in God's judgment along with its complement of whether men have any access to this judgment. These are the questions, now voiced explicitly in Jupiter, which were implicit in the heaven of the Sun in both Solomon's fate and Aquinas's warning in *Paradiso* 13 that we must not presume to know anyone's fate. Just because we see one stealing and another making pious offering, Aquinas warns, God may yet save the former and damn the latter. The Eagle's injunction against making judgments is stronger than Aquinas's. Even the blessed who see God are granted only limited knowledge and do not know all the elect. If this intelligence is denied even to those who now occupy heaven, the Eagle asks, how can mere mortals presume to have access to this knowledge?

A corollary to the prohibition against passing judgment is that the standard of judgment you apply to others will be in turn applied to you. In Romans 2:2 we find, "In judging others you condemn yourself since you behave no differently from those you judge," and Christ's command of "*nolite iudicare*" continues, "as you measure out, so it will be measured out to you." The principle is put into play in the *Commedia*. Dante's treatment of Virgil and Augustine is retrospectively conditioned by their treatment of Ripheus and Solomon. Ripheus's presence in Heaven underscores Virgil's fate in Hell, and the extended treatment accorded Solomon in the Sun may possibly be meant to counter Augustine's scant mention in Heaven.

Yet as much as the invectives against the passing of judgment
can be read as being directed toward Virgil and Augustine, the
*Commedia* takes its sharpest aim at itself. Cornelius a Lapide in
his commentary on Matthew relates a cautionary tale that comes
from St. Dorotheus's *Doctrina*:

> An angel once brought the soul of an adulterer to a certain old
> man who had condemned him. "Here is the dead man whom you
> have judged," the angel says to the old man, "where should I take
> his soul, to Heaven or to Hell? Since you have appointed yourself
> judge of the dead in the place of Christ, then judge this soul." At
> the angel's words the old man was overcome with compunction.
> He begged for pardon and did penance for the rest of his life.[13]

The warnings against judgment that Dante has Thomas Aquinas
and the Eagle deliver intimate that Dante is quite cognizant of the
fact that by writing the *Commedia* he runs the risk of being like
Dorotheus's old man. Dante uses the twin injunctions to question
not only the validity of the particular judgments he has made in
writing his poem and assigning each soul a place, but also to question whether any judgment at all is possible. Underlying these
concerns about the possibility of judgment is the potential that if
the principle of "as you measure out, so it will be measured out to
you" holds true, then Dante himself could be held accountable at
his own final reckoning for the judgments of damnation that he
has passed as an author. In other words, it is Dante himself who
teasingly suggests the possibility that there is always the chance
that he is doing to Virgil and Augustine what Virgil and Augustine
did to Ripheus and Solomon.

I began this essay by considering the possible aptness of Minos
as a figure of the poet in Dante's text. I would like to conclude by
further speculating that the *Commedia* also contains a figure of
the anti-poet. In *Paradiso* 18.130 Dante reproachfully addresses
Pope John XXII as "tu che sol per cancellare scrivi" (you who write
only to cancel). In John XXII Dante presents a figure of unjust writing. Lest this sounds too fanciful, consider the context in which
the line appears. The Heaven of Jupiter opens with writing, the
writing of the just souls that spells out a message for the pilgrim.
The message is one about justice, "*diligite iustitiam qui iudicatis
terram.*" John serves as a cautionary figure for Dante. John's writing represents an abuse of authority and presents a figure of the

*Commedia* at its darkest—as writing that runs the risk of condemning unjustly. Dante is well aware that the charge that the *Commedia* makes against John XXII is one that could in turn be leveled against Dante himself.

## NOTES

1. Robert Durling, *The Figure of the Poet in Renaissance Epic* (Cambridge: Harvard University Press, 1965).

2. In *Paradiso* 33 Dante describes his memory of his vision of the empyrean,

> Così la neve al sol si disigilla;
> così al vento ne le foglie levi
> si perdea la sentenza di Sibilla.
> (*Par.* 33.64–66)

Benvenuto (*Comentum super Dantis Aldigherij Comoediam*, vol. 5, 517) glosses these lines, "Sicut enim responsum Apollinis, qui erat Deus sapientiae, traditum sapienti Sybillae scribebatur in folio et asportabatur a vento; ita visio Dei, qui est vera et summa sapientia, ostensa Danti sapienti, scripta fuit in mente mobili quae evolvitur tamquam folium ad ventum, Sybilla enim arrepta spiritu Apollinis perdebat memoriam eorum quae viderat dum esset arrepta: ita autor post raptum suum reversus ad se perdidit memoriam eorum quae viderat tempore raptus."

3. I am using the text of the *Commedia* established by Giorgio Petrocchi as found in the English translation of Robert and Jean Hollander for *Inferno* (New York: Doubleday, 2000). Because the Hollander *Paradiso* is not yet available, I am using Charles Singleton's translation for *Paradiso* (Princeton: Princeton University Press, 1975).

4. "Do not judge and you will not be judged" is found in Matthew 7:1 and in Luke 6:37. "There must be no passing of premature judgment" is found in I Corinthians 4:5. Other examples of biblical injunctions against the passing of judgment include "no matter who you are, if you pass judgment you have no excuse. In judging others you condemn yourself, since you behave no differently from those you judge" (Romans 2:1.2), and "You shall never pass judgment on a brother or treat him with contempt" (Romans 14:10). These and all English translations from the Bible are from *The Jerusalem Bible*, ed. Alexander Jones (New York: Doubleday & Co., 1968).

5. For a discussion of how Solomon was viewed in the Middle Ages, and in particular by the church fathers, see M. Bose, "From Exegesis to Appropriation: The Medieval Solomon," in *Medium Aevum*, 65.2 (1996): 187–210. See also Michele Scherillo, *Alcuni capitoli della biografia di Dante* (Torino: Ermanno Loescher, 1896), 299–311 and Gian Roberto Sarolli, *Prolegomena alla "Divina Commedia"* (Firenze: Leo. S. Olschki Editore, 1971), 210–15.

6. Isidore of Seville condemns Solomon in his *"De ortu et obitu patrum,"* which can be found in the *Patrologiae Cursus Completus: Series Latina*, ed. J. P. Migne (Paris: Garnier Freres, 1844–1864), vol. 42, 459. The *Series Latina* will hereafter be abbreviated as Migne, *PL*.

7. Augustine, *De civitate Dei contra paganos*, XVII.viii; the Latin text and English translation are from the Loeb classical library edition, trans. by Eva M. Sanford and W. M. Green (Cambridge: Harvard University Press, 1965), 5:280–82.

8. Augustine, *Contra Faustum Manichaeum*, cap. LXXXVIII. Latin text from Migne, *PL*, vol. 42, 459; the translation from the Latin is my own. Augustine in *De doctrina christiana* (3.21.31) compares David's sinfulness to that of his son and says, "On the other hand, in his son Solomon, this lust did not pass on like a guest. It took possession of his kingdom. Holy Scriptures does not keep silent about it, but condemns him as a lover of women. The beginning of his reign shone with his desire for wisdom. But that which he had obtained through spiritual love, he lost through carnal love" (translation my own).

9. Olga Grlic, in a very interesting essay, also notes St. Augustine's absence from the pages of the *Commedia*. She finds parallels between Augustine's conversionary experience in his *Confesssions* and the conversionary experience given to Statius in the *Commedia*. In her reading, Statius becomes a figure of Augustine while Virgil's writing fulfils the function of scripture. See Olga Grlic, "Dante's Statius and Augustine: Intertexuality in Conversionary Narrative" in *Medievalia et Humanistica*, XXI (1995): 73–84.

10. See Teodolinda Barolini, *Dante's Poets* (Princeton: Princeton University Press, 1984), 254–56.

11. The Latin text is from *The Aeneid of Virgil*, edited and with introduction and notes by R. D. Williams (New York: St. Martin's Press, 1987). The English translation is my own.

12. For much of my thinking about Dante's encounter with Ripheus I am greatly indebted to Robert Hollander's *Il Virgilio dantesco: tragedia nella "Commedia"* (Firenze: Olschki, 1983).

13. Cornelius a Lapide, *Commentaria in Scripturam Sacram* (Paris: Ludovicus Vivèr, 1868), 206.

# Chaucer as *Vates*?:
# Reading Ovid through
# Dante in the *House of Fame*,
# Book 3

JAMIE C. FUMO

Poca favilla gran fiamma seconda:
   forse di retro a me con miglior voci
   si pregherà perché Cirra risponda.

[A great flame follows a little spark: perhaps, after me, prayer
shall be offered with better voices, that Cyrrha may respond.]
               —Dante, *Paradiso* 1.34—36

IN HIS ELEGANT AND INFLUENTIAL *ALLEGORY IN DANTE'S COMMEDIA*,
Robert Hollander, insisting upon Dante's fundamental difference
in outlook from that of Ovid's medieval allegorizers, remarks that
Dante was "a great scholar for whom literature was a form of life
and not merely a pretext for simple-minded interpretation."[1] Indeed, Dante so deeply and idiosyncratically internalized his Virgil,
Ovid, Statius, and so on that it became impossible for poets writing in the shadow of Dante's genius, such as Chaucer and Boccaccio, to ignore the compelling—even transformative—mediation of
Dante's reading of the classical poets. It is to the fascinating Chaucerian afterlife of what is perhaps Dante's most audacious act of
Ovidian revisionism, the invocation to Apollo in *Paradiso* 1, to
which this essay turns, with the aim of tracing Chaucer's own
"living out" of one important segment of Dante's poetic journey.

As many critics have observed, Chaucer's rewriting of Dante's
invocation at the beginning of the third book of his most adven-
turously Dantean poem, the mock-visionary *House of Fame*, con-

tributes importantly to the poem's deflation of Dante's *Comme-dia* as a merely human burlesque that trivializes the mission of the *viator*, the authority of his guides, and, at least in the fragmen-tary form in which the poem survives, the possibility of enlight-enment itself.[2] If Chaucer's subversion of Dante's *Commedia* in the *House of Fame* is incontrovertibly systematic, however, the level of skill with which the English poet reworked Dante's ex-travagantly allusive Italian in his own invocation to Apollo has proven more difficult to characterize.[3] I intend to argue in this essay that Chaucer's engagement with *Paradiso* 1 at the beginning of the third book of the *House of Fame* is both more serious and more subtle than most critics have allowed, and, further, that the Ovidian background of Dante's invocation—which Robert Hol-lander established beyond doubt in his 1969 study—forms the key to appreciating Chaucer's transformation of it. Chaucer's invoca-tion of Apollo is usually understood to punctuate the English poet's characteristically self-abnegating rejection of the classical tradition of the poet as a vessel of prophetic truth, as daringly Christianized by Dante (who conflates Apolline inspiration with Pauline spiritual transport).[4] I contend instead that Chaucer *shares* with Dante a fundamental interest in defining the poet's role as *vates*. Indeed, Chaucer's treatment of Apollo here, as elsewhere in his poetry, is shaped by a sense of ambivalence and irony that does not so much underscore Chaucer's hesitation about claiming a vatic prerogative as his attunement to the true complexity of the classical definition of vatic poetics, as "authorized" by Apollo, god of poetry and prophecy. This poetics, marked especially by Ovid's influence, is one that proves unable to separate the transcendent experience of inspiration from the reality of failure, breakdown, and loss. To Dante, this phenomenon constitutes the "tragedy" of the *Commedia*,[5] to be corrected and metamorphosed into Chris-tian "comedy" in passages like the invocation of *Paradiso* 1. Chaucer, on the other hand, seems more interested in the problem than the solution.

Few critics would claim that the *House of Fame*, which dates from early in Chaucer's career (c.1379–80),[6] is one of Chaucer's best works, but it is unquestionably one of his most lively, witty, and provocative; it showcases the active and inquisitive poetic mind that would later produce two of the greatest medieval poems, *Troilus and Criseyde* and the *Canterbury Tales*. This unfinished dream vision marks several "firsts" in English literature: most importantly for our purposes, it is the first poem written in English to show the influence of Dante and the first to invoke the Muses (unless we take Chaucer's *Anelida and Arcite* to be earlier); one could add that it is also the first to feature an eagle (borrowed from *Purgatorio* 9) who has read Plato, a summary of all twelve books of the *Aeneid*, and, it would seem, a scholastic proof of the physics of flatulence. Though its subject matter is the stuff of fantasy literature and allegory, it is especially interesting for being semiautobiographical: it takes as its subject Chaucer's own angst-filled attempt to understand the nature of his vocation as poet in the context of the myriad works of genius that constitute his literary influences.

After having invoked Morpheus early in the first book, and Venus and the Muses in the second, Chaucer calls upon Apollo's aid upon beginning the last, most important book of the poem, in which "Geffrey" reaches his destination in the Houses of Fame and Rumor:

> O God of science and of lyght,
> Appollo, thurgh thy grete myght,
> This lytel laste bok thou gye!
> Nat that I wilne, for maistrye,
> Here art poetical be shewed,
> But for the rym ys lyght and lewed,
> Yit make hyt sumwhat agreable,
> Though som vers fayle in a sillable;
> And that I do no diligence
> To shewe craft, but o sentence.
> And yif, devyne vertu, thow
> Wilt helpe me to shewe now
> That in myn hed ymarked ys—
> Loo, that is for to menen this,
> The Hous of Fame for to descryve—
> Thou shalt se me go as blyve
> Unto the nexte laure y see,
> And kysse yt, for hyt is thy tree.
> Now entre in my brest anoon!
> (1091–1109)[7]

This, of course, is modeled upon Dante's strikingly different invocation of Apollo near the beginning of the first canto of the *Par-*

*adiso*, the inauguration of his transit from the highest point of earth to the celestial beyond. Chaucer consciously echoes the structural position of this Dantean passage by placing it at the beginning of the third book of his own visionary poem, just before reaching his comic "heaven"—a destination quite different from the rarefied realm of spirit into which Dante's eagle delivers him. While earlier generations of critics found in the invocation of Apollo proof that Chaucer was "the first Englishman to share Dante's sense of the worth of poetry and of the act of poetic creation" (interestingly, Chaucer's invocation was included as the first excerpt in Ernest Rhys's 1894 collection of "The English Poets in Defence and Praise of their Own Art"),[8] more recent critics have understood Chaucer to emphasize instead his self-enforced distance from claims of poetic superiority and the poet's elevated mission—this in contrast with Dante, whose matching invocation makes precisely those claims:

> O buono Appollo, a l'ultimo lavoro
>   fammi del tuo valor sì fatto vaso,
>   come dimandi a dar l'amato alloro. . . .
> Entra nel petto mio, e spira tue
>   sì come quando Marsïa traesti
>   de la vagina de le membra sue.
> O divina virtù, se mi ti presti
>   tanto che l'ombra del beato regno
>   segnata nel mio capo io manifesti,
> vedra'mi al piè del tuo diletto legno
>   venire, e coronarmi de le foglie
>   che la materia e tu mi farai degno.
>                    (*Paradiso* 1.13–15, 19–27)

[O good Apollo, for this last labor make me such a vessel of your worth as you require for granting your beloved laurel. . . . Enter into my breast and breathe there as when you drew Marsyas from the sheath of his limbs. O divine Power, if you do so lend yourself to me that I may show forth the image of the blessed realm which is imprinted in my mind, you shall see me come to your beloved tree and crown me with those leaves of which the matter and you shall make me worthy.]

Both Dante's and Chaucer's invocations concern the poet's wish for Apollo to help them articulate memories imprinted in their minds. Nonetheless, whereas Chaucer's invocation dwells centrally upon why he *does not* want to be crowned with Apollo's laurel—he only wants to kiss the laurel in deference—the whole point of Dante's invocation is his desire to be crowned with the laurel. To Dante's open invitation to future genius, with which this essay began, Chaucer seems, in effect, to reply (with his Wife of Bath), "lordynges, by youre leve, that am nat I."[9] This would appear to amount to a straightforward repudiation of Dante's celebration of the poet's role as *vates*, a vessel of inspired truth; indeed, it has become a critical commonplace to characterize Chaucer's poetics as essentially nominalist (or, to some, "postmodern") in both attitude and structure, expressed through contingency, skepticism, and fragmentation rather than the sort of theological order achieved by Dante.[10] John Fyler compares Chaucer's and Ovid's similar resistance to the vatic precedents of Dante and Virgil in order to define the playfully skeptical tone of their poetic self-presentations:

> Each [i.e., Chaucer and Ovid] is . . . a *poeta* and only by comic indirection a *vates*. The difference is important: the *vates* can present truths he could not normally discern, because he is speaking for a numinous power that allows him to escape human limitations; the *poeta*, on the other hand, is self-consciously trapped by those limitations. The effect is comic irony[.][11]

Fyler's position is provocative, but it is weakened by its lack of consideration of the complexity added by Dante's own uses of Ovid. I argue, in contrast, that Chaucer was in fact more fascinated by the vatic ideal of inspired, prophetic truth—a model of poetry specifically associated with Apollo, god of the *vates*—than he has been given credit for. A consideration of the Ovidian sources of these invocations reveals that Chaucer, far from having simply repudiated Dante's vatic poetics, has restored this poetics to its proper Ovidian register, reminding us of the essentially deconstructive and precarious nature of vatic triumph. In fact, rather than rejecting an identification with Apollo, Chaucer surprisingly (and ironically) embraces it.

The most striking feature of Dante's invocation is his ingenious reimagination of the Ovidian myth of Apollo's flaying of Marsyas for challenging him, the god of music, to a musical contest, when Dante begs Apollo to inspire him by drawing him out of his limbs, just as he did to Marsyas. Ovid narrates Marsyas's story in *Fasti* 6.697–710 and *Metamorphoses* 6.383–400, the latter passage forming Dante's source:

> satyri reminiscitur alter,
> quem Tritoniaca Latous harundine victum
> adfecit poena. "quid me mihi detrahis?" inquit;
> "a! piget, a! non est" clamabat "tibia tanti."
> clamanti cutis est summos direpta per artus,
> nec quicquam nisi vulnus erat; cruor undique manat,
> detectique patent nervi, trepidaeque sine ulla
> pelle micant venae; salientia viscera possis
> et perlucentes numerare in pectore fibras.
> 
> (*Met.* 6.383–91)[12]

[Another recalled the satyr whom the son of Latona (i.e., Apollo) had conquered in a contest on Pallas's reed, and punished. "Why do you tear me from myself?" he cried. "Oh, I repent! Oh, a flute is not worth such price!" As he screams, his skin is stripped off the surface of his body, and he is all one wound: blood flows down on every side, the sinews lie bare, his veins throb and quiver with no skin to cover them: you could count the entrails as they palpitate, and the vitals showing clearly in his breast.]

Medieval commentators claim quite reasonably that the point of Ovid's tale of Marsyas is to illustrate the dangers of artistic presumption and pride, Marsyas's obliviousness to his human limitations.[13] It is worth noting, however, that Ovid's portrayal of Apollo in this episode is equally unflattering: his punishment of his challenger seems extremely excessive, veritably cruel and unusual, given that Marsyas's presumption, for which he honestly repents, is only briefly and vaguely described, and that his fate elicits the sympathy of all of nature, whose tears—rather than Marsyas's blood —form a river that bears Marsyas's name.[14]

What for Ovid's Marsyas was the punishment of grotesque physical torture becomes, in Dante's Christian poetics, an image of spiritual rapture: this Apollo acts allegorically in the name of the Christian God to free Dante's soul forcibly from the prison of its sinning flesh. This reinscription of Ovid demonstrates, in Brownlee's adroit formulation, how in the *Paradiso* "Ovid's narratives of transformation operate as extended, yet necessarily inadequate and incomplete, metaphors for Christian transfiguration."[15] Dante here imagines a conversion—a metamorphosis—from a human state to a spiritual state, a renovation of the body to accommodate a perception of Heaven, a process called by Robert Hollander "transhumanization" (from "trasumanar," *Par.* 1.70), that continues throughout the *Paradiso*, until such time as Dante achieves face-to-face vision.[16] By the same token, as other critics have observed, Dante's metaphorical flaying imagines a deliverance from all that Marsyas represents—pride, presumption, irreverence—as Dante takes on the project of describing the secrets of Heaven in the Italian vernacular, a project that runs a real risk of succumbing to these damnable sins.[17] Dante deranges Ovid's myth even further when he, as the transformed Marsyas, then reaches for Apollo's laurel crown—an act, he implies, which is no longer an image of presumption, but an assertion of legitimate entitlement. Paradoxically, Dante's flaying will empower him to produce music worthy of (indeed, superior to) the god, and will unite him with Apollo in an almost erotic union—rather than, as in Ovid's version, establishing the distance between the poet's humanity and Apollo's divinity. Dante will join Apollo, rather than compete with him. And by the end of the *Paradiso*, Dante will leave even this typological Apollo/Christ behind, along with his Muses (compare *Par.* 2.8–9 and 23.55–63), "unable," as Michael Kensak puts it, "to record in Apollonian verse a song which transcends Apollo."[18]

What happens to Marsyas in Chaucer's rewriting of Dante's invocation? It would seem at first that he simply disappears; Chaucer strikingly eliminates Dante's flaying image and emphasizes instead his polite distance from Apollo. Shortly after this invocation in the *House of Fame*, however, we encounter Marsyas among the other famous musicians who entertain Fame in her royal court ("And Marcia that loste her skyn, / Bothe in face, body, and chyn, / For that she wolde envien, loo, / To pipen bet than Appolloo" [*HF* 1229–32]); it would seem that Chaucer has deliberately excised Marsyas from his invocation and transferred him to this spot in his narrative. There is no doubt, however, that Chaucer understood and was impressed by Dante's flaying image, for he echoes it in a scene in *Troilus and Criseyde* in which Criseyde plans on committing suicide, but is too squeamish to handle a sword and so plans to starve herself to death instead, "Til I my soule out of my breste unshethe" (*Tr* 4.776). Here Chaucer causes Criseyde to repeat Dante's image of Apollo unsheathing Marsyas from the scab-

bard of his limbs, and with some literary sophistication: she re-
places the feared literal sword with a metaphorical one.[19] But even
as Chaucer's invocation of Apollo eliminates the Marsyas myth
from the surface of the text, it restores it to its original Ovidian
register. For the Chaucer who nervously invokes Apollo is *wary* of
presumption and insolence ("Nat that I wilne, for maistrye, / Here
art poetical be shewed" [*HF* 1094–95]); he remembers the fate of
Marsyas and takes pains to make Apollo aware that he is *not* like
Marsyas—this in contrast with Dante, who needed to be *like*
Marsyas, to experience his flaying, in order to free himself from
the satyr's sins.

In Chaucer's invocation, we can see two different dynamics at
work. First, in restoring to the Marsyas myth its Ovidian function
as a warning against presumption, Chaucer foregrounds the general theme of his own relation to Dante as poet—for Dante, in a
sense, is the Apollo figure by whom Chaucer is here inspired, and
to whom Chaucer does not want to appear presumptuous; we
should recall Chaucer's insistence later in the poem that he himself does not seek fame.[20] Second, in rewriting Dante's wish to attain the laurel crown as the more humble promise simply to kiss
the next laurel tree he sees, Chaucer has again pressed back
through Dante's text to an Ovidian scene that stands behind it: the
origins of the laurel in the myth of Daphne's transformation. At
the moment that the desperate Apollo catches the virgin Daphne
after a long pursuit, Daphne prays to be transformed into an ever-
green laurel tree. Apollo grasps her in her changed form, can even
feel her heart beating beneath the bark, and tries to kiss her, but
the bark shrinks from his kisses ("refugit tamen oscula lignum"
[*Met.* 1.556]). Nonetheless, Apollo wins in the end: he fashions her
leaves into a crown and appropriates it as an emblem of poetic and
martial victory. As Robert Hollander has demonstrated, Dante
himself wove together the scene of Apollo's pursuit of Daphne in
*Metamorphoses* 1 and the episode of Marsyas's flaying in *Metamorphoses* 6: the Ovidian Apollo's desire for Daphne explains Dante's "amato alloro" (1.15) and "diletto legno" (1.25); his "per triun-
fare o cesare o poeta" (1.29) reflects Ovid's connection of the laurel
with Roman military triumph; and, perhaps most interestingly, the
Ovidian Apollo's celebration of the powers of his deity may have
suggested Apollo's potential as a (figurally) Christian inspirer, as
we see in *Paradiso* 1.[21] However, whereas Dante takes up the last

image of Ovid's Daphne episode—the laurel crown— Chaucer fastens upon the penultimate: like Ovid's Apollo, he merely attempts to kiss the laurel tree, the tree that shrinks from kisses.[22] As with his Ovidian rewriting of the Marsyas subtext, Chaucer here undermines Apollo even in praising him, by reminding us that it was the pathetic failure of Apollo that engendered the symbol of the laurel as a mark of poetic triumph in the first place.

Indeed, I suggest that Chaucer's separate treatment of Marsyas just over one hundred lines later in the *House of Fame* may well point back to the Daphne intertext yet again. Chaucer's presentation of Marsyas as *female*—"Marcia that loste her skyn" (*HF* 1229) —has provoked many elaborate theories: Alfred David, for example, explains Chaucer's error by means of a variant reading of an interpolation in the *Roman de la Rose*, in which "Marse" is described as a female satyr, while Jane Chance and David Wallace take psychological approaches to what they believe is an intentional alteration on Chaucer's part, signaling Chaucer's experimentation with a feminized authorial position.[23] I offer another theory, equally speculative. The feminine Marcia is intended as a counterpart to the feminine Daphne, who tragically discovered not that she was unable to "pipen bet" than Apollo, but that she could not outrun him. Chaucer's addition of gratuitous detail here—Marcia lost her skin "Bothe in face, body, and chyn" (*HF* 1230)—may simply be filler, but it has no precedent in the episode of Marsyas's flaying as narrated in the *Metamorphoses*, the *Fasti*, the *Paradiso*, or the interpolation in the *Roman de la Rose*. This sort of anatomical catalogue of soon-to-be-lost body parts is, however, very common in Ovid's vivid descriptions of the moment of metamorphosis, of which Daphne's is an excellent example:

> vix prece finita torpor gravis occupat *artus*,
> mollia cinguntur tenui *praecordia* libro,
> in frondem *crines*, in ramos *bracchia* crescunt,
> *pes* modo tam velox pigris radicibus haeret,
> *ora* cacumen habet: remanet nitor unus in illa.
> (*Met.* 1. 548–52; emphases added)

[Scarce had she thus prayed when a down-dragging numbness seized her *limbs*, and her soft *sides* were begirt with thin bark. Her *hair* was changed to leaves, her *arms* to branches. Her *feet*, but now so swift, grew fast in sluggish roots, and her *head* was now but a tree's top. Her gleaming beauty alone remained.]

Chaucer's curiously appealing formulation "loste her skyn" also lends his Marcia a rather different character than the male Marsyas of his sources. In contrast with Ovid's grotesque paradox ("quid me mihi detrahis?" [*Met.* 6.385]) and Dante's echo of the language of martyrdom ("sì come quando Marsïa traesti / de la vagina de le membra sue" [*Par.* 1.20–21]), Chaucer's portrayal of Marcia's trauma sounds at once more trivial—as if Marcia had merely lost her jacket—and more appropriate to *other* forms of Ovidian metamorphosis: namely, the loss of identity that corresponds with enforced change.[24] The loss of skin—as it is transformed into something else, especially bark—often marks such loss of identity in the *Metamorphoses*, as in Myrrha's transformation: "duratur cortice pellis" [her skin (changed) to hard bark] (*Met.* 10.494). Whatever the precise relationship of Chaucer's Marcia to Ovid's Daphne in this passage, it is at least partly through Chaucer's deflation of Apollo from Christlike inspirer to failed lover in his Book 3 invocation that the English poet, rejecting Dante's precedent, makes room for the *unreformed* Marsyas in his comic Heaven.

Indeed, it could be said that if Dante is essentially concerned with transhumanization in his treatment of the Marsyas myth, Chaucer is interested instead in *humanization*—of Apollo and, in turn, the poet inspired by him.[25] He reminds us of Apollo's "human" side by stepping clear of his imagined wrath in the Book 3 invocation, and also recalling, in the flippant reference to "Marcia that loste her skyn," Ovid's insinuation of Apollo's insecurities, his readiness to abuse his powers of deity in order to prove that they exist. But even as Chaucer rejects both the Ovidian and Dantean subject positions of Marsyas here in making his request, he subtly couches his praise of Apollo in an irony that may have been "inspired" by Dante's "amato alloro," but that immediately takes on a life of its own: the unflattering erotic etiology of Apollo's claim to the laurel, a symbol that is at the very heart of the vatic project as Dante imagines it.

Chaucer's ironic jab at Apollo, as I see it, has two important implications for Chaucer's "art poetical." First, the Ovidian connection between poetic vocation and erotic failure, crystallized in Apollo's experience and dramatized by Chaucer's promised "kysse," establishes a mythological context for Chaucer's pose throughout his early works as a poet who is a failed lover—for so,

too, is Ovid's Apollo. As is often noted, Chaucer relishes presenting himself as a non-lover or a failed lover, who nonetheless serves
the servants of Love through his poetry, even when this constitutes a major change to his sources (e.g., Dante in the *House of
Fame* and Boccaccio in the *Troilus*). From disavowals of active
love service Chaucer nearly always turns to affirmations or manifestations of his bookishness (e.g., *BD* 30–61; *HF* 613–28; *PF* 8–14;
*Tr* 1.15–49), and even in the *House of Fame*, in which Geffrey's free
pass to the House of Fame is presented as divine "recompensa-
cion" for those literary labors which are love's surrogate, his vision of the inner workings of Fame and the unmediated passions
of "Loves folk" proves, of course, to be every bit as bookish as the
walls of his hermitical London study (*HF* 665, 675). In other
words, Apolline poetics—in the deconstructive, ironic mode in
which Ovid presents it—seems fundamentally relevant to one of
Chaucer's most characteristic literary games.[26]

Second, for all the differences in his emphasis and for all his
protestations of humility, Chaucer one-ups Dante in his transformation of the Apollo invocation. Quite mischievously, Chaucer
flirts with Dante's forthright claim of the vatic prerogative even
while appearing to reject it by rewriting Dante's sublime paradox
of Ovidio-Christian inspiration in his own ironic terms. While
avoiding presumption, Chaucer equates himself—a second, more
discreet Marsyas—with Apollo after all: by promising only to kiss
the laurel, not to claim it, he reenacts the very action of Apollo
himself in *Metamorphoses* 1. In so doing, Chaucer maps himself
onto Apollo in a way that is complementary to, yet wholly distinct from, the spiritually purged Dantean Marsyas's (legitimized)
assumption of the laurel crown. Unlike Dante, however, Chaucer
uses the invocation to critique Apollo in the very act of identifying himself with him (whereas Dante reserves his critique for *Paradiso* 23). Chaucer achieves this delicate balance by exploiting the
allusive potential of his own self-deprecation: in reenacting Apollo's kiss, he allows himself to be the butt of the humor while tac-
itly showing the project of poetic triumph that Apollo symbolizes
to be at best a precarious illusion and, at worst, a sham.

The extent of Apollo's ambivalences as a rhetorical and narrative presence, as well as his particular relevance to medieval nego-
tiations with classical antiquity, is wide-ranging, and well beyond
the scope of the present study.[27] For Ovid at least, Apollo's "hu-

manity" compromises his divinity especially in treatments of his love for human beings and his humanlike powerlessness in the realm of love. With Hyacinthus in Book 10 of the *Metamorphoses* as with Daphne, the origins of poetry for Ovid emerge from scenes of failed Apolline healing: failed art is transformed into artistic triumph. Though Apollo's divine powers fail to secure the elusive Daphne (much less cure himself of love for her) and are too weak to heal the dying Hyacinthus, Apollo finally recoups victory from tragedy by appropriating the laurel as the crown of poets, and by inscribing words of mourning on the petals of the flower into which the dead Hyacinthus has been transformed. Loss, contingency, and irony—the ingredients of a poetics that scholars such as Fyler has *opposed* to the vatic model—in fact inform vatic poetics and Apolline rhetoric in two essential ways. On the one hand, vatic poetics can enact a kind of art that is transformative and consolatory: the triumph of poetry that renders loss beautiful (the loss of Daphne, the loss of control over the self) and grants the illusion of eternal possession. On the other hand, however, such art is merely a kind of illusion, an attractive exterior that conceals, and potentially is compromised by, a core of failure, imperfection, and loss. Chaucer's invocation of Apollo in the *House of Fame*, in other words, shows the models of vatic, Dantean poetry, and an Ovidian poetics of contingency to exist in a relationship that is symbiotic, not antithetical.

I conclude by considering two rather surprising responses to Dante's and Chaucer's invocations of Apollo, one visual and the other literary. The first is the Sienese artist Giovanni di Paolo's lavish illustration of *Paradiso* 1 in the famous Yates-Thompson codex of the *Commedia*, produced around 1445 for Alfonso V of Aragon, King of Naples, and now held by the British Library. Illustrations of Dante's invocation of Apollo were very rare, and no one before Giovanni di Paolo had attempted to represent visually its sublime paradox.[28] In di Paolo's illustration, Apollo, dressed in golden armor and standing in front of a laurel tree and the twin peaks of Parnassus, holds two laurel crowns in his hands, gesturing toward Dante, who stands on his right, as the Muses look down at him approvingly from the sky. On Apollo's left side is a grove of laurels and the dead Marsyas, body slashed, reaching up toward Apollo as if rising from the dead. To Marsyas's left stands a naked orange figure playing a flute, who, according to Pope-

Invocation of Apollo, *Paradiso* 1. Illustrated by Giovanni di Paolo (c. 1445) B. L. Yates-Thompson 36, fol. 129r. By permission of the British Library.

Hennessy, could either be Pan (whose competition with Apollo was sometimes conflated with that of Marsyas) or a second Marsyas. If the latter, it is unclear whether this second Marsyas, who structurally corresponds with Dante in the layout of the illustration, is intended to represent the living Marsyas who competed with Apollo or the flayed Marsyas whose spiritual resurrection is an image of Apollo's inspiration.[29] What is most interesting for our purposes are two details pictured by di Paolo but not implied in Dante's text. First, Apollo is portrayed as *handing* the laurel crown to Dante. Second, Dante, who is kneeling, does not reach out for the crown, but holds his hands back, as if to show his modesty. Taken together, these alterations suggest that di Paolo was uncomfortable with the daring implications of Dante's claim, the thoroughness of his subversion of the Marsyas narrative. As a result, di Paolo emphasizes Dante's humility: rather than portraying the poet in the act of seizing the laurel himself, on the authority of his transformative inspiration by the Christianized Apollo, the artist instead presents Apollo as firmly in charge, physically handing the laurel to Dante who, much like Chaucer in the *House of Fame*, seems concerned to maintain his distance.

The second response I wish to consider, this one to Chaucer's invocation, is from Book Four of Spenser's *Faerie Queene*, in which Chaucer's unfinished *Squire's Tale* is continued at length. Before embarking upon his continuation, Spenser invokes Chaucer's pardon and aid:

> Then pardon, O most sacred happie spirit,
>     That I thy labours lost may thus reuiue,
>     And steale from thee the meede of thy due merit,
>     That none durst euer whilest thou wast aliue,
>     And being dead in vaine yet many striue:
>     Ne dare I like, but through infusion sweete
>     Of thine owne spirit, which doth in me surviue,
>     I follow here the footing of thy feete,
> That with thy meaning so I may the rather meete.
>                                        (*FQ* 4.2.34)[30]

Though some have thought that Spenser is imagining a process of Pythagorean metempsychosis in this invocation,[31] I would suggest that Spenser has instead (or, perhaps, in addition) modeled this passage on Chaucer's invocation of Apollo in the *House of*

*Fame*, here presenting Chaucer as the Apollo figure. Spenser certainly knew the *House of Fame*: he drew upon it in the depiction of the court of Philotime in *FQ* 2.7,[32] and he may allude to it here in *FQ* 4.2 in the declaration, two stanzas earlier, that Chaucer is "On Fames eternall beadroll worthie to be fyled" (4.2.32) as well as in the attention to the instability of texts in stanza 33 (recall that Fame's palace is built on a mountain of melting ice).[33]

Like Chaucer's invocation of Apollo in the *House of Fame*, Spenser's invocation of Chaucer is presented in a guarded fashion, as if it were a potential usurpation. Spenser claims that he would not "dare" steal from Chaucer his due merit (cf. "Nat that I wilne, for maistrye, / Here art poetical be shewed" [*HF* 1094–95]). Rather, anything of worth that Spenser produces will be due to Chaucer's agency, the "infusion sweete / Of thine owne spirit" (cf. "Appollo, thurgh thy grete myght, / This lytel laste bok thou gye! . . . / Now entre in my brest anoon!" [*HF* 1092–93, 1109]). Like Chaucer, Spenser specifically calls on his inspirer's aid in prosody—"I follow here the footing of thy feete"[34] (cf. "But for the rym ys lyght and lewed, / Yit make hyt sumwhat agreable, / Though som vers fayle in a sillable /. . . helpe me to shewe now / That in myn hed ymarked ys" [*HF* 1096–98, 1102–3])—and, in connection with this, emphasizes *meaning* over the importance of precise details: "That with thy meaning so I may the rather meete" (cf. "And that I do no diligence / To shewe craft, but o sentence" [*HF* 1099–1100]). But perhaps most importantly, Spenser has followed Chaucer in using this invocation, with all of its subtextual Apolline layers, to negotiate and mythologize his artistic identity in relation to a great poet who has come before him. In a sequence of transformations that is the stuff of Ovidian fantasy, Marsyas has become Dante, Dante has become Chaucer, and finally, Chaucer has become Apollo.

Though Chaucer's early readers, including Spenser, could be accused of misreading Chaucer by heralding him as an Apollo figure, a lofty, vatic poet, missing the cynical and self-deprecating tone for which Chaucer is better known today, a more careful understanding of how Apollo and the poet's vatic role were actually imagined by Ovid, Dante, and Chaucer should compel us to temper our criticism. Chaucer's invocation of Apollo in the *House of Fame*, which, as I have argued, is directly implicated in his larger "ars poetical," is, for all its gothic juxtaposition of tentativeness and ambition, in a real sense *more* faithful to the spirit of classical precedent than was Dante's. Considering that Geffrey twists Apollo's arm so impishly in the invocation of Book 3, it is perhaps appropriate that, if the poem's collapse at the feet of a "man of gret auctorite" bears any weight, Apollo appears not to have granted Geffrey's prayer.

## NOTES

All quotations and translations from the *Paradiso* are from Dante Alighieri, *The Divine Comedy: Paradiso*, ed. and trans. Charles S. Singleton (1977; Princeton: Princeton University Press, 1982).

1. Robert Hollander, *Allegory in Dante's* Commedia (Princeton: Princeton University Press, 1969), 206.

2. Important accounts of the *House of Fame*'s systematic irony include Robert B. Burlin, *Chaucerian Fiction* (Princeton: Princeton University Press, 1977), 45–58; John M. Fyler, *Chaucer and Ovid* (New Haven: Yale University Press, 1979), 23–64; Piero Boitani, "What Dante Meant to Chaucer," *Chaucer and the Italian Trecento*, ed. Boitani (Cambridge: Cambridge University Press, 1983), 117–25.

3. For example, A. C. Spearing, *Medieval to Renaissance in English Poetry* (Cambridge: Cambridge University Press, 1985), 28–29, attributes Chaucer's alterations of Dante to misconstrual. Howard H. Schless, *Chaucer and Dante: A Revaluation* (Norman, Okla: Pilgrim Books, 1984), represents a generally "conservative" approach to Dante's influence on Chaucer which is outweighed, at least in bulk, by the steady stream of recent books that have attempted to establish (some more convincingly than others) the breadth and subtlety of Chaucer's use of Dante: e.g., Karla Taylor, *Chaucer Reads 'The Divine Comedy'* (Stanford: Stanford University Press, 1989); Richard Neuse, *Chaucer's Dante: Allegory and Epic Theater in* The Canterbury Tales (Berkeley: University of California Press, 1991); Ann W. Astell, *Chaucer and the Universe of Learning* (Ithaca: Cornell University Press, 1996); Warren Ginsberg, *Chaucer's Italian Tradition* (Ann Arbor: University of Michigan Press, 2002).

4. See Kevin Brownlee's excellent discussion of this paradox in "Pauline Vision and Ovidian Speech in *Paradiso* 1," *The Poetry of Allusion: Virgil and Ovid in Dante's* Commedia, eds. Rachel Jacoff and Jeffrey T. Schnapp (Stanford: Stanford University Press, 1991), 202–13.

5. Cf. Robert Hollander, "Tragedy in Dante's *Comedy*," *Sewanee Review* 91 (1983): 240–60.

6. For an overview of the problem of dating the *House of Fame*, see A. J. Minnis with V. J. Scattergood and J. J. Smith, *Oxford Guides to Chaucer: The Shorter Poems* (Oxford: Clarendon Press, 1995), 167–72. Schless, 41, favors an earlier date.

7. All citations of Chaucer are from *The Riverside Chaucer*, ed. Larry D. Benson, 3d ed. (Boston: Houghton Mifflin Co., 1987). Abbreviations of Chaucer's works follow the example of this edition.

8. J. A. W. Bennett, *Chaucer's* Book of Fame (Oxford: Clarendon Press, 1968), 101; Ernest Rhys, ed., *The Prelude to Poetry: The English Poets in Defence and Praise of their Own Art* (1894; London and Toronto: J. M. Dent; New York: E. P. Dutton, 1927), 1–2. Chaucer's company in the volume includes Sidney, Milton, Dryden, and Shelley.

9. *Canterbury Tales* III.112. This essay's epigraph should be compared with the imagistic conjunction of sparks, fame, and prophecy in Dante and Boccaccio as analyzed by Suzanne Hagedorn in her contribution to the present volume.

10. See, most pertinently, Sheila Delany, *Chaucer's House of Fame: The Poetics of Skeptical Fideism* (Chicago: The University of Chicago Press, 1972); Robert M. Jordan, *Chaucer's Poetics and the Modern Reader* (Berkeley: University of California Press, 1987); Holly Wallace Boucher, "Nominalism: The Difference for Chaucer and Boccaccio," *Chaucer Review* 20:3 (1986): 213–20; and the references catalogued in William H. Watts and Richard J. Utz, "Nominalist Perspectives on Chaucer's Poetry: A Bibliographical Essay," *Medievalia et Humanistica* n.s. 20 (1993): 147–73. Often, this characterization of Chaucer's poetics is also used to differentiate Chaucer's "medieval" qualities from changing ideas of poetry in the fifteenth century and the English Renaissance (much of which poetry, of course, was directly influenced by Chaucer): see, e.g., Lois A. Ebin, *Illuminator, Makar, Vates: Visions of Poetry in the Fifteenth Century* (Lincoln: University of Nebraska Press, 1988), 1–18, and Carol A. N. Martin, "Authority and the Defense of Fiction: Renaissance Poetics and Chaucer's *House of Fame*," *Refiguring Chaucer in the Renaissance*, ed. Theresa M. Krier (Gainesville: University Press of Florida, 1998), 40–65.

11. Fyler, *Chaucer and Ovid*, 22.

12. All *Metamorphoses* citations and translations are from Ovid, *Metamorphoses*, ed. and trans. Frank Justus Miller, rev. G. P. Goold, 3d ed., The Loeb Classical Library (1916; Cambridge: Harvard University Press; London: William Heinemann, 1984), 2 vols.

13. See the references listed in B. G. Koonce, *Chaucer and the Tradition of Fame: Symbolism and* The House of Fame (Princeton: Princeton University Press, 1966), 200, n. 51.

14. Eleanor Winsor Leach, "Ekphrasis and the Theme of Artistic Failure in Ovid's Metamorphoses," *Ramus* 3:2 (1974), 102–42, and H. le Bonniec, "Apollon dans les *Métamorphoses* d'Ovide," *Journées Ovidiennes de Parménie: Actes du Colloque sur Ovide (24–26 juin 1983)*, ed. Jean Marc Frécaut and Danielle Porte, Collection Latomus 189 (Brussels: Revue d'Études Latines, 1985), 145–74, miss Ovid's point here by focusing, respectively, on Marsyas's misdeed and on Ovid's clinical, distancing tone in the passage (Leach, 127; le Bonniec, 154–56). Rather, this episode must be understood as one example among many in the *Metamorphoses* of Apollo appearing too defensive about his own divinity, too intent upon proving those powers that have not received the proper recognition (because of his inauspicious beginnings, as the son of the

persecuted Latona, on the then-obscure island of Delos). As we will see, Chaucer's rendering of Dante's invocation to Apollo underscores the god's indecorous tendencies. I pursue this reading of Ovid's Apollo at greater length in a book in development, *The Legacy of Apollo: Antiquity, Authority, and Chaucerian Poetics.*

15. Brownlee, "Pauline Vision," 204. On Dante's revisions of Ovidian metamorphosis more generally, see Kevin Brownlee, "Dante and the Classical Poets," *The Cambridge Companion to Dante,* ed. Rachel Jacoff (Cambridge: Cambridge University Press, 1993), 111–18, and Warren Ginsberg, "Dante, Ovid, and the Transformation of Metamorphosis," *Traditio* 46 (1992), 205–33. The present discussion should be compared with Jessica Levenstein's illumination of Dante's allusions to Procne and Philomela in the *Purgatorio,* which comparably sublimate an Ovidian scene of grotesque violation.

16. Hollander, *Allegory,* 201–4; cf. Brownlee, "Pauline Vision," 213. As Robert Hollander points out in "The Invocations of the *Commedia,*" *Studies in Dante* (Ravenna: Longo Editore, 1980), 33, it is fitting that five out of nine of the *Commedia*'s invocations occur in the *Paradiso,* wherein Dante's need for heavenly aid is most pronounced (and, of course, is an important theme in itself). On Dante's revision of Ovid's Marsyas, see the insightful recent article by Jessica Levenstein, "The Re-Formation of Marsyas in *Paradiso* 1," *Dante for the New Millenium,* ed. Teodolinda Barolini and H. Wayne Storey (New York: Fordham University Press, 2003), 408–21.

17. See Peter S. Hawkins, "The Metamorphosis of Ovid," *Dante and Ovid: Essays in Intertextuality,* ed. Madison U. Sowell (Binghamton, NY: Medieval & Renaissance Texts & Studies, 1991), 31–34, and Brownlee, "Pauline Vision," 202–13, esp. 207. From the perspective of Christian humanism, the topos of the invocation itself demands that the poet negotiate a potentially dangerous balance between, on the one hand, the spiritual perils of presumption involved in "commanding" the Muse and, on the other, the humility appropriate to prayer. In *Paradise Lost,* Milton goes one step beyond Dante to make the epic's invocations into "sustained explorations of the poet's subjectivity" (Walter Schindler, *Voice and Crisis: Invocation in Milton's Poetry* [Hamden, CT: Archon Books, 1984, 12]). Dante's Marsyas, in fact, functions rather like Milton's Satan as regards the invocatory ethic: just as Milton, throughout his invocations, confronts the Satanic potential in his epic project ("if all be mine, / Not Hers who brings it nightly to my ear" [*PL* 9.46–47]), and just as the incapacitation of the Satanic impulse within himself corresponds with the actual diminution of Satan as a potent, attractive force in *Paradise Lost,* so does Marsyas represent the Ovidian skin that Dante must, quite literally, shed. Cf. Hawkins, 21–34; Schindler, 88–92; and, on the invocation topos more generally, Ernst Robert Curtius, *European Literature and the Latin Middle Ages,* trans. Willard R. Trask (1953; New York: Harper & Row, 1963), 228–46.

18. Michael Kensak, "Apollo *exterminans*: The God of Poetry in Chaucer's *Manciple's Tale,*" *Studies in Philology* 98:2 (2001), 154 (more broadly, 151–55). The ultimate rejection of Apollo and the Muses is something of a convention of Christian epic; the topos appears, as Kensak shows, in Alain de Lille's *Anticlaudianus* and Chaucer's *Canterbury Tales* as well as Dante's *Paradiso*; A. J.

Minnis adds Joseph of Exeter's *De bello Trojano* to the list (*Oxford Guides*, 174, 179). See also Jeffrey T. Schnapp's argument, in *The Transfiguration of History at the Center of Dante's* Paradise (Princeton: Princeton University Press, 1986), 139, that "Christ's hermeneutic and epistemological ascendancy over Apollo" forms the thematic heart of the *Paradiso*'s Christian rewriting of the *Aeneid*.

19. B. A. Windeatt, ed., *Troilus & Criseyde* (1984; London: Longman, 1990), 4.776 n., notes the resemblance between Criseyde's expression and Dante's image.

20. The use of invocations to place oneself strategically in the stream of literary tradition is, of course, an important feature of the convention, for example in Virgil's backward look at Homer in "arma virumque cano," as he proposes to condense (and reinvent) the Greek bard's Iliadic arms and Odyssean man in a single epic.

21. Hollander, *Allegory*, 204–9.

22. Nicholas R. Havely, in his edition of *The House of Fame* (Durham: Durham Medieval Texts, 1994), notes that Chaucer's tree-kissing finds its source in Ovid's *Metamorphoses* 1, and remarks that "this may therefore be a case in which Ch[aucer] is being more Ovidian than Dante (in *Par.* 1) is" (lines 1106–8 n.). Minnis repeats Havely's observation and comments upon Chaucer's diminution of Apollo in this invocation from "God of science and of light" to hapless lover (*Oxford Guides*, 177–78), a phenomenon that I explore more fully above. Cf. Piero Boitani, *Chaucer and the Imaginary World of Fame* (Cambridge: D. S. Brewer, 1984), 163.

23. Alfred David, "How Marcia Lost Her Skin: A Note on Chaucer's Mythology," *The Learned and the Lewed: Studies in Chaucer and Medieval Literature*, ed. Larry D. Benson (Cambridge: Harvard University Press, 1974), 19–29 (followed by Schless, 70–71); Jane Chance, *The Mythographic Chaucer* (Minneapolis: University of Minnesota Press, 1995), 45–82; David Wallace, *Chaucerian Polity: Absolutist Lineages and Associational Forms in England and Italy* (Stanford: Stanford University Press, 1997), 249–51.

24. Of course, Ovid often highlights the more profound continuity of identity beneath what superficially appears as loss or arbitrary change. For a cogent account of this feature of Ovidian metamorphosis, see Joseph B. Solodow, *The World of Ovid's* Metamorphoses (Chapel Hill: University of North Carolina Press, 1988), 174–92.

25. Cf. Boitani, "What Dante Meant," 120: "Geoffrey is denied the 'transumanar', the passing beyond humanity that Dante undergoes in *Paradiso*, I."

26. Petrarch, in the *Canzoniere* (which Chaucer knew at least in part), appropriates a similar mythic complex—an Apolline persona, failed love, and poetic success—in a very different spirit.

27. I am currently devoting a book to the full dimensions of this issue.

28. John Pope-Hennessy, *Paradiso: The Illuminations to Dante's Divine Comedy by Giovanni di Paolo* (London: Thames and Hudson, 1993), 35, pl. 32, reproduces an early example of the invocation's depiction in a late-fourteenth-century manuscript held by the Biblioteca Marciana in Venice.

29. If the flute-playing figure does indeed represent the flayed, "risen" Marsyas—and I tend to believe it does—then the imagery of the *Purgatorio*'s com-

plementary invocation to the Muses (in condemnation of the Pierides, Marsyas's counterparts in artistic presumption) may implicitly be at work here: "Ma qui la morta poesì resurga, / o sante Muse, poi che vostro sono" (Here from the dead let poetry rise up, / O sacred Muses, since I am yours). Text and translation from Dante Alighieri, *Purgatorio*, trans. Jean and Robert Hollander (New York: Doubleday, 2003), 1.7–8. My reading of the illustration differs from that of Edith Wyss, *The Myth of Apollo and Marsyas in the Art of the Italian Renaissance* (Newark: University of Delaware Press, 1996), who believes that di Paolo simply opposes Apollo with the presumptuous (living) Marsyas, thus reinforcing the simplistic medieval allegorizations of Marsyas that Dante supersedes: "Dante's metaphorical introduction of the myth into his invocation has been turned into a bodily presence. The illuminator is unable to distinguish between an allegorical allusion and the main body of thought in Dante's poem" (34–35). The illustration in question, with commentary, is reproduced in Pope-Hennessy, 70–71.

30. Edmund Spenser, *The Faerie Queene*, ed. Thomas P. Roche, Jr. with C. Patrick O'Donnell Jr. (1978; London: Penguin Books, 1987).

31. See *The Works of Edmund Spenser: A Variorum Edition*, ed. Edwin Greenlaw et al., vol. 4 (Baltimore: Johns Hopkins University Press, 1935), 4.2.34 n.

32. See John A. Burrow's entry, "Chaucer, Geoffrey," in *The Spenser Encyclopedia*, ed. A. C. Hamilton et al. (Toronto: University of Toronto Press, 1990), 147.

33. Cf. Bennett, 110.

34. Could there be a further allusion here to Dante's following in Virgil's footsteps (in which Chaucer becomes the Virgil figure)? Cf. *Inf.* 1.136 and *Purg.* 5.62 and see also Statius, *Thebaid*, 12.816–17.

# O'erpressed Spirits
# in Shakespeare's *Pericles*

### William Robins

I$_{\text{N}}$ MORE WAYS THAN ONE, THIS ESSAY ON SHAKESPEARE'S *PERICLES* IS about the return to the past. First, there is this essay's own history, for it had its start as the epilogue to a dissertation written under the tutelage of Robert Hollander, John V. Fleming, and Peter Brown on the reception of the ancient romance of Apollonius of Tyre.[1] For over a decade it has been variously abandoned, revived with interest, and then given up for lost among the shipwrecks on my desk. Now, with an opportunity to show my respect for Robert Hollander, I have felt driven by some irresistible imperative to rescue the piece, resuscitate it, and reunite it with the context of its own origin. It is not about Dante, and only mentions Boccaccio in passing, yet Robert Hollander as a teacher always encouraged intellectual explorations that moved well beyond the confines of Italian literature; he has always been an admirer of Shakespeare, a keen interpreter of romance plots, and an exemplary practitioner of comparative approaches to literary texts, and this essay is offered in thanks for that. So if this essay's own history of separation and reunion, of loss and recovery, recapitulates the basic pattern of romance narrative, so much the better, for it is this pattern of loss and recovery that animates *Pericles* just as it animates other retellings of the Apollonius story. Shakespeare very deliberately recasts the tale's main characters in order to explore how experiences of loss and recovery strike at something very deep in the human psyche, and it is the burden of this essay to tease out that dimension of the play.

Shakespeare's *Pericles* gives prominence to several episodes where characters enter and exit unconscious states. These episodes are crucial for establishing the play's relationship to the genre of romance, for creating its general atmosphere of "wonder," and for setting its grounds for characterological self-identity. As a consequence, these scenes have held, and still hold, a central place in interpretations of the play as a whole.[2] In this essay, I want to focus especially on the last of these three issues—the nature of characterological identity—re-examining these scenes in order to grasp the conditions of human subjectivity at stake in Shakespeare's dramaturgy.[3]

The approach offered here is a comparative one. *Pericles* recasts the tale of Apollonius of Tyre, an ancient Latin romance that engendered numerous medieval and early modern adaptations. Shakespeare's version has often been compared to the two versions of the tale that served as direct sources for the play—John Gower's *Confessio Amantis* and Lawrence Twyne's *Patterne of Painefull Adventures*—but only rarely with the ancient Latin *Historia Apollonii Regis Tyri* or its other progeny. By contrasting *Pericles* with several of these versions (and to some other ancient romances as well), I hope to draw attention to the real novelty of Shakespeare's play, which represents, I will argue, notably different parameters of human agency and selfhood.

The first episode to look at comes near the middle of the play, and in it the loss of consciousness is diagnosed as a condition of "o'erpressed spirits." Thaisa, the wife of King Pericles, has been buried at sea and her coffin has washed ashore near Ephesus where the doctor Cerimon revives her:

> Cerimon
>                          ... This chanced tonight.
> 2 Gentleman
>      Most likely, sir.
> Cerimon
>                      Nay, certainly tonight,
> For look how fresh she looks. They were too rough
> That threw her in the sea. Make a fire within;
> Fetch hither all my boxes in my closet.
> Death may usurp on nature many hours,
> And yet the fire of life kindle again
> The o'erpressed spirits. I heard of an Egyptian
> That had nine hours lain dead, who was
> By good appliance recovered.

> *Enter one with napkins, and fire.*
> Well said, well said; the fire and cloths.
> The rough and woeful music that we have,
> Cause it to sound, beseech you.
> The viol once more. How thou stirr'st, thou block!
> The music there! I pray you, give her air.
> Gentlemen, this queen will live. Nature awakes;
> A warmth breathes out of her! She hath not been
> Entranced above five hours. See, how she 'gins
> To blow into life's flower again.
> *1 Gentleman*                The heavens,
> Through you, increase our wonder, and set up
> your fame forever.
> *Cerimon*                She is alive!
>
> > (3.2.76–96)[4]

In most versions of the tale, this moment of the queen's revival from a "false-death" occurs very differently. In the late antique *Historia Apollonii Regis Tyri*, the episode is presented as a somewhat comic moment: the doctor is greedy and inadequate, and it is not he but rather one of his young students who decides to warm and massage the corpse.

> When he saw the corpse of the beautiful young girl being placed on the pyre, he looked at his teacher and said: "What is the cause of this recent unexplained death?" The teacher said: "Your arrival is timely; the situation requires your presence. Take a jar of unguent and pour it over the body of the girl to satisfy the last rites." The young man took a jar of unguent, went to the girl's bier, pulled aside the clothing from the upper part of her body, poured out the unguent, ran his suspicious hands over all her limbs, and detected quiescent warmth in her chest cavity. The young man was astounded to realize that the girl was only apparently dead. He touched her veins to check for signs of movement and closely examined her nostrils for signs of breathing; he put his lips to her lips, and, detecting signs of life in the form of slight breathing that, as it were, was struggling against false death, he said, "Apply heat at four points." When he had had this done, he began to massage her lightly, and the blood that had coagulated began to flow because of the anointing." When the young man saw this, he ran to his teacher and said: "Doctor, the girl you think is dead is alive."[5]

The erotic suggestions implied by rubbing a dead princess's body with oil are elaborated upon by some reworkings of the tale, as in Twyne's *Patterne of Painefull Adventures*, one of Shakespeare's main sources for *Pericles*, and even more explicitly in Boccaccio's *Filocolo*, where this episode from the *Historia Apollonii* is adapted into a scene of what Hollander speaks of as "necrophiliac thrills":[6]

> he . . . tooke hir in his armes, and not satisfied therwith, he began to feele her here and there, and to put his hand into hir frosen breast among the cold dugs. But afterwards (being become more bolde than was meete) to seeke out under the riche attire whiche she had on, the secrete parts of the body, going and feeling with a fearful hande hither and thither till at the last he spread the same upon hir stomacke, where as with a feeble motion he felt the weake pulses somewhat to move. He then became very fearful, but yet love made him bolde, and therfore trying further with a more assured hede, he knew that she was not dead. . . . He caused great fires to be made, to the end to comfort the colde membres, wherunto the lost forces did not therby returne in due sort: by occasion wherof, as one peradventure discrete in such a case, willed a solemne hote house to be prepared, wherein he caused first to be strowed many vertuous herbes, and after placed the Gentlewoman therin, causing hir as it was mete for one in that plight to be tenderly looked unto. In the which hotehouse, after she had for a time made her abode there, the bloud coagulate about the heart, began thorow the receyved heate to disperse by the colde vaines, and the spirites half dead began to return to their places.[7]

In contrast with these comic and erotic renderings, Gower's retelling of the story in his *Confessio Amantis* omits the role of the student, ascribes the requisite zeal and knowledge to the "gret Phisicien" Cerymon, and downplays the anointing of the body.[8] Shakespeare opts to follow Gower here, so that in *Pericles* there is likewise no rivalrous disciple, no implication of greed or necrophilia, but the activity of a learned doctor seeking for signs of life in a queen.

Shakespeare adds to this episode a remarkable suggestion: Thaisa may in fact have died. At least, Cerimon's statement that "Death may usurp on nature many hours" encourages us to entertain the possibility that death could, during its initial stage, be reversed. According to Cerimon, Thaisa is in a state of being "entranced," perhaps with that word's etymological sense of being "in transit" between life and death. The play does not insist that Thaisa has actually died, but it does open up the possibility, with the concomitant implication that Thaisa's revival is either a wondrous resurrection or else a natural event worth thinking of in unnatural, marvelous terms. It is not a miracle of Christian faith (despite the inevitable parallel with the resurrection of Christ), but a miracle, or near miracle of summoning natural forces, effected by the powers of the magus, Cerimon. In all other versions of the story, the queen is treated with therapies that place the body in a position where it will recover naturally from its weakness. Indeed, in a medieval Italian rendition, the *Cantari di Apollonio di Tiro* by Boccaccio's friend Antonio Pucci, not only is the quickening of the pulse through the application of an unguent accounted for physiologically, but also the power of the doctor is explicitly demystified: "For many women have passed out from cold during childbirth, as is well recorded."[9] But in *Pericles*, Cerimon has control not only over therapies for the body but perhaps to some degree even over the life-forces themselves. As one of Cerimon's admirers affirms: "hundreds call themselves / Your creatures, who by you have been restored" (3.2.40–41).

As Greek and Latin fictional narratives were published and translated during the sixteenth century, the ancient genre to which the story of Apollonius of Tyre once belonged was again brought to light.[10] Accordingly, Shakespeare knew a literary context for the story that was significantly different from the one known by, say, Boccaccio, Pucci, or Gower. *Pericles*, in fact, bears traces of this new contextualization. In the scene of Thaisa's revival, Cerimon's lines: "I heard of an Egyptian / That had nine hours lain dead, who was / By good appliance recovered" (3.2.83–85), suggest that Shakespeare read the story of Apollonius in light of ancient fiction, for they seem to allude to Apuleius's *Golden Ass*, or Heliodorus's *Aethiopica*, or both. It has been suggested recently that the doctor's words might refer to a scene in the *Golden Ass* where an Egyptian prophet, Zachlas, animates a corpse, causing the spirit of a man to return to testify how he was murdered.[11] So far unnoticed, I believe, is an even closer resonance with a similar episode of Egyptian necromancy in Heliodorus's novel, in a scene where the heroine Charicleia watches a sorceress revive a son who has recently died:

for the old woman thinking that she had now gotten a time
wherein she should neither be seene, nor troubled of any, first
digged a pitte, then made she a fire on both sides thereof, and in
the middes she layd her sonnes body, and taking an earthen potte
from a three footed stoole which stoode thereby, poured honey
into the pytte: out of another shee poured milke, and so did shee
out of the thirde, as though shee had done some sacrifice . . . and
doing many monstrous and strange thinges beside these, at
length bowing her selfe downe to the dead body of her sonne, and
saying somewhat to him in his eare, awaked him, and by force of
her Witchcrafts made him stand up soudainely.

This manipulation of the dead belongs to illicit sorcery, and the
maguslike Egyptian high priest Kalisiris explains to Charicleia
that true sages do not attempt such unnatural rites:

for it becometh not the priestes, either to take delight, or bee present where such thinges are dooing. But they ought by sacrifices,
and lawfull prayers enquire, not by shamefull sorceries, which
are conversant aboute the earth, and dead creatures, of which sort
is the Aegyptians practise, which chaunce at this time, hath
caused us to see.[12]

In Shakespeare's character Cerimon, the therapies of medicine and
the rites of necromancy are merged, giving Shakespeare's scene a
tone very different than that in the relevant passages of the *Historia Apollonii* or Apuleius or Heliodorus. Unnatural resuscitation
appears legitimized, as medicine extends its power beyond the
therapeutic treatment of the body toward a control over the conditions of life. A sampling of critical reactions to *Pericles* would
demonstrate how thoroughly our sympathy for the plight of the
queen has been eclipsed by our awe for the powers of the doctor.

Thaisa enters another state of "o'erpressed spirits" during the
final scene of the play, when she faints upon being reunited with
her husband Pericles. During her lapse of consciousness, Cerimon
again takes charge of the situation:

*Thaisa*                          Voice and favour!
         You are, you are, O royal Pericles!
*Pericles*
         What means the nun? She dies. Help, gentlemen!
*Cerimon*
         Noble sir,

> If you have told Diana's altar true,
>   This is your wife.
> *Pericles*                    Reverend appearer, no,
>   I threw her overboard with these very arms.
> *Cerimon*
>                    Upon this coast, I warrant you.
> *Pericles*                    'Tis most certain.
> *Cerimon*
>   Look to the lady. O, she's but overjoyed.
>   Early one blustering morn this lady was
>   Thrown upon this shore. I oped the coffin,
>   Found there rich jewels; recovered her, and placed her
>   Here in Diana's temple.
> *Pericles*                    May we see them?
> *Cerimon*
>   Great sir, they shall be brought you to my house,
>   Whither I invite you. Look, Thaisa is
>   Recovered.
> *Thaisa*                    O, let me look!
>   If he be none of mine, my sanctity
>   Will to my sense bend no licentious ear,
>   But curb it, spite of seeing. O my lord,
>   Are you not Pericles? Like him you spake,
>   Like him you are. Did you not name a tempest,
>   A birth and death?
> *Pericles*                    The voice of dead Thaisa!
> *Thaisa*
>   That Thaisa am I, supposed dead
>   And drowned.
> *Pericles*
>                    Immortal Dian!
> *Thaisa*                    Now I know you better.
>   When we with tears parted Pentapolis,
>   The king my father gave you such a ring.
>                                        (5.3.13–39)

In all other versions of the tale of Apollonius of Tyre, the reunited King and Queen face each other without mediation by some third party. They command full possession of their own stories, so that it is always the queen herself who recounts the history of her resuscitation and of her subsequent admittance to Diana's temple at Ephesus. In *Pericles*, by contrast, the doctor who restored life to Thaisa wields such knowledge and power that he becomes the keeper of her tale, the guardian of its tokens and the one who can speak it forth. Thaisa participates in the further disclosure of her identity only after Cerimon has explained her situation to her husband.

The collapse of Thaisa here is not merely an effect arising from a dramatic moment of recognition, or *anagnorisis*, for even after reviving she still requires some confirmation that this man is indeed her husband. Fainting is in part a retreat into an interior "sanctity" that is contrasted to conscious "sense." Pericles, in the subsequent lines, speaks about his excess of personal emotion in related terms:

> *Pericles*
> This, this! No more, you gods. Your present kindness
> Makes my past miseries sports. You shall do well,
> That on the touching of her lips I may
> Melt and no more be seen. O come, be buried
> A second time within these arms.
>
> (5.3.40–44)

The reunion of Pericles and Thaisa is an occasion for deep joy, one for which a vocabulary of excess—sanctity, dissolution, burial—is employed. Personal interiorities of joy are moments of excess, "overjoyed" moments severable from the possibility of conscious explanation. The power of explanation has been ceded to a third party, the omnicompetent, maguslike Cerimon.

The reunion of Pericles and Thaisa occurs only after the reunion of Pericles with his daughter Marina in an equally climactic recognition scene. The reunion of father and daughter, which provides the last episode of "o'erpressed spirits" that I will examine, shows yet again that omnicompetent third-parties have a crucial function in this play. In the hold of Pericles' ship, Marina and Pericles finally stand before each other, unaware of the other's identity; when Marina names her father, Pericles turns to his counselor Helicanus for help in understanding this unexpected turn of events.

> *Marina*                    . . . Why do you weep? It may be
> You think me an impostor. No, good faith.
> I am the daughter to King Pericles,
> If good King Pericles be.

*Pericles*                    Ho, Helicanus?
*Helicanus*
    Calls my lord?
*Pericles*
    Thou art a grave and noble counsellor,
    Most wise in general. Tell me if thou canst
    What this maid is, or what is like to be,
    That thus hath made me weep?
*Helicanus*                    I know not,
    But here's the regent, sir, of Mytilene,
    Speaks nobly of her.
*Lysimachus*                    She never would tell
    Her parentage. Being demanded that,
    She would sit still and weep.
*Pericles*
    O Helicanus, strike me honoured sir,
    Give me a gash, put me to present pain,
    Lest this great sea of joys rushing upon me
    O'erbear the shores of my mortality
    And drown me with their sweetness. O, come hither,
    Thou that beget'st him that did thee beget,
    Thou that wast born at sea, buried at Tarsus,
    And found at sea again! — O Helicanus,
    Down on thy knees, thank the holy gods as loud
    As thunder threatens us, this is Marina!
    —What was thy mother's name? Tell me but that,
    For truth can never be confirmed enough,
    Though doubts did ever sleep.
*Marina*
    First sir, I pray, what is your title?
*Pericles*
    I am Pericles of Tyre.

                                   (5.1.167–94)

Let me comment upon this part of the scene by drawing attention to the play's most striking divergence from the way earlier versions of the story handle this episode: Pericles' reliance upon his counselor. At the moment of recognition, when Marina utters Pericles' name, Pericles shouts repeatedly for his counselor Helicanus, who comes to his side and, with Lysimachus, answers questions about the girl. Pericles' questions and his raptures are addressed only occasionally, and only secondarily, to Marina herself; his immediate response is to turn instead to these other men of authority.

In the *Historia Apollonii*, when Apollonius grasps that he is speaking with his lost daughter, he calls for his friends and family, and only in their presence does he tell his daughter who he is, so that the reunion between king and princess occurs in the view of public witnesses as Apollonius recovers his twin roles of father and of ruler:

> Apollonius, hearing these signs, exclaimed tearfully in a loud voice: "Run here servants, Run here friends, and put an end to a father's longing!" All who heard the shout came running, and even Athenagoras, the prince of that city ran, and he found Apollonius on the neck of Tarsia crying and saying: "This is my daughter Tarsia, for whom I have been mourning, which is why I put on renewed tears and renewed grief. For I am Apollonius of Tyre, who commended you to Stranquilione. Tell me, what was your nurse called?" And she said: "Lycoris." Then Apollonius began to cry out even more strongly: "You are my daughter!" And she said: "If it is Tarsia you seek, I am she." Then he rose up, embraced her, kissed her, and wept.[13]

In contrast to the public world at stake in this version, in Gower and in Twyne the reunion is a private one between two individuals, occurring in the sight of God alone: "For god, which wot here hol entente / Here hertes bothe anon descloseth."[14] In all of these pre-Shakespearean versions, Apollonius and his daughter speak to each other directly, and the recognition involves restoring a proper reciprocity to their relationship. Shakespeare's introduction of Helicanus and Lysimachus does not return the scene to an ancient, public setting, for it is in front of only these two men that the reunion occurs. Moreover, the counselors do not simply witness, rather they mediate the recognition. Pericles turns to them for assurance, as if their knowledge of events is more to be trusted than his own. Pericles' deeply personal joy is accompanied by doubts about whether he really understands his own experience. Pericles' understanding is no longer guaranteed by the restoration of a hierarchy of social roles, as was the case in the *Historia Apollonii*; Pericles' understanding is guaranteed instead by the presence of advisors who make the king's acts of recognition and self-recognition possible.

The intensely personal individuality of Pericles' reaction is movingly staged here and in the subsequent lines of the scene. Brought out of his excess of despair, the king does not immediately recover a stable, socially responsible position, but instead bounds into an excess of joy:

*Pericles*                          I embrace you, sir.
        —Give me my robes.
                            I am wild in my beholding.
        O heavens bless my girl!
                            But hark, what music?
        Tell Helicanus, my Marina, tell him
        O'er point by point, for yet he seems to doubt,
        How sure you are my daughter. But what music?
*Helicanus*
        My lord, I hear none.
*Pericles*                    None?
        The music of the spheres! List, my Marina.
*Lysimachus*
        It is not good to cross him. Give him way.
*Pericles*
        Rarest sounds! Do ye not hear?
*Lysimachus*
        Music, my Lord? I hear—
*Pericles*                    Most heavenly Music!
        It nips me unto list'ning, and thick slumber
        Hangs upon mine eyes; let me rest.
*Lysimachus*
        A pillow for his head. So, leave him all.
                                    (5.1.210–22)

Instead of a king restored to the exercise of power and concerned with vengeance and weddings, as in earlier accounts, we see a character so stunned by his joy that he hears music no one else hears, and collapses into slumber.

To explain Shakespeare's intervention we can again point to the works of Greek romance, where emphasis on individual desire is in fact much greater than it is in the Latin *Historia Apollonii*, and where excessive personal joy is often as much a feature of reunions as is the restabilization of social rank. Longus's *Daphnis and Chloe* offers the closest parallel in a scene of joy and reunion that combines enigmatic music with the collapse of a hero for

love. The episode in Longus's novel is set, like the reunion of Pericles and Marina, in the outskirts of Mitylene on the island of Les-
bos. As Chloe returns from having been captured by pirates, she is
accompanied by mysterious music from an invisible source.
Chloe's flocks jump to the music, "as if," as Amyot's version has
it, "they wished to let her know they celebrated her deliverance,"
yet the tune has no effect upon the flocks of others. When Daphnis
sees Chloe, "he descended to the plain as fast as he could, crying at
the top of his voice: 'O Nymphs! O Pan!' and running to embrace
Chloe he was seized with such great joy that he fell to the ground
in a swoon." Revived by her kisses, Daphnis sits with Chloe under
their favorite oak tree, and she tells him all about her capture and
escape.[15] This passage from Longus is probably only obliquely related to *Pericles*, yet there are some striking similarities. A pleasant music comes from an invisible, supernatural source; the
music elicits a celebration of deliverance, yet it works its magic
only selectively; the male hero embraces the female heroine and
then swoons for joy. The use of supernatural music to suggest an
intimately emotional moment distinguishes the recognition scene
of *Pericles* from other renditions of the story of Apollonius of Tyre,
and this alteration may, like the detail about Egyptian necromancy, have been suggested to Shakespeare by his reading of
Greek romances. Yet if this is the case, there is an important contrast to be drawn. In *Daphnis and Chloe*, the divine music of Pan
was heard by all onlookers, even if it affected the flocks differently, whereas in *Pericles* it is Pericles alone who experiences a music
no one else can hear. The result is the dramatization of a deeply
personal and interior source of feeling, even more selectively individualized (and even more incommunicable to others) than in the
Greek romance.

    In all three episodes of "o'erpressed spirits," the individual pro-
tagonists Thaisa and Pericles have ceded the interpretation of
their own plights to external, secular bodies of knowledge. If Cerimon represents early modern fantasies about the powers of
medicine, Helicanus represents similar fantasies about statecraft.
And yet, even as they rely upon these omnicompetent advisors,
Thaisa and Pericles also have access to an overwhelming interiority of joy. Indeed, these contemplative depths are now so entirely
personal that they cannot be communicated adequately. The interiority of the self seems severed from the languages through which

it might be conveyed: Thaisa and Pericles have access to the former, but must rely upon third parties who preside over the latter. Thus when Lysimachus cynically comments about the music heard by Pericles, "It's not good to cross him; give him way," we see how wide is the gap between Pericles' interiority and the structures of knowledge that he relies upon to interpret his place in the world. This gap might be presented in performance by *not* playing music during this scene, thus distancing Pericles' interiority from the interpretive jurisdiction of the audience as well.[16]

Shakespeare does give us one way of visualizing Pericles' depths of interiority. When he collapses for joy, Pericles receives a vision of the goddess Diana—the play's sole supernatural event.

*Diana*
> My temple stands in Ephesus. Hie thee thither,
> And do upon mine altar sacrifice.
> There when my maiden priests are met together,
> [      ] before the people all,
> Reveal how thou at sea didst lose thy wife.
> To mourn thy crosses with thy daughter's, call
> And give them repetition to the life.
> Perform my bidding, or thou liv'st in woe;
> Do it, and happy, by my silver bow.
> Awake and tell thy dream.

*Pericles*
> Celestial Dian, goddess argentine,
> I will obey thee. Helicanus!

*Helicanus*                                        Sir?

*Pericles*
> My purpose was for Tarsus, there to strike
> The inhospitable Cleon; but I am
> For other service first. Toward Ephesus
> Turn our blown sails: eftsoons I'll tell thee why.

>                                        (5.1.227–42)

Having received this summons from the supernatural, Pericles emerges from his trauma with a sense of direction and with a will to order Helicanus rather than simply rely on him. The deep interiority of the self, which in crucial ways has been severed from worldly structures of authority, here takes on legitimacy and new purposiveness because of its grounding in an otherworldly source.

In previous versions of the story of Apollonius of Tyre, this vision has nothing to do with the heightened emotions of the scene of recognition. In the *Historia Apollonii*, for example, supernatural guidance comes only after the reunion at Mytilene is complete, after Apollonius has firmly reestablished his roles as father and as king, after the princess has been married to the local prince, and after her tormentor has been punished. For Shakespeare, however, the onset of divine guidance is a crucial feature of the king's emotional swooning. Here, the vision does not come to a character who has already recovered his equilibrium but rather to one who requires just such a summons in order to right himself. Instead of functioning primarily as a sign of providential guidance, Pericles' vision of Diana acts as a grounding for the hero's capacity to claim an agency of his own.

The *Historia Apollonii* recounts that "In a dream [Apollonius] saw someone who looked like an angel."[17] In Gower's version, this angelic messenger is replaced by God himself, "The hihe god, which wolde him kepe."[18] *Pericles* alters the given traditions to make the summons come instead from the goddess Diana. From the perspective of the Greek romances, Diana is entirely appropriate for this role. Diana's importance for the characters and plots of Greek fiction is undeniable, as is evident, to take just one example, in Achilles Tatius's *Leucippe and Clitophon*: "The Goddesse [Diana] appeared in the night privatly to Sostratus, and foretolde him that he shoulde finde a daughter and a sonne in law at Ephesus."[19] Once again it seems likely that Shakespeare has reconsidered the narrative logic of the story of Apollonius in light of ancient Greek fiction.[20] Yet ancient romances are fully polytheistic realms where characters cultivate their personal rapports with various deities, and neither lovers nor family members are expected to share the same divine cult. By contrast, Shakespeare's play establishes a common bond of devotion to Diana: Pericles, Marina, and Thaisa are all devotées of Diana, even before Diana's temple at Ephesus becomes Thaisa's place of refuge. When Pericles vows to keep his hair uncut, he makes the vow to Diana. When he places the infant Marina in the care of others, he entrusts her to Diana. As for Thaisa, her first words upon her resuscitation are "O dear Diana, where am I?" (3.2.104), so that for her, as well as for her husband, Diana is associated with that personal sanctity which lies beyond conscious articulation.

In other words, the guarantee of interior autonomy, for Thaisa as for Pericles, is apprehension of a transcendent force. This act of apprehension is personal and not shared with any onlookers, yet it can lead to a renewed commitment to interpersonal bonds of family love especially because Thaisa, Pericles and Marina all discern the transcendent divine through the figure of Diana. Pericles finally gains self-possession not through reunion with Marina, nor through reoccupying his public role as a king among counselors, although these events set the process going; he achieves his resolve only by opening up to a supernatural force, a realm of otherworldliness, that in a deep way connects him with his daughter and wife who share this inarticulable sanctity. The summons from beyond promotes an intuition of a personal interiority that nevertheless remains essentially divorced from external structures for making sense of it. His personal selfhood is anchored in an otherness, at once transcendent and interpersonal, that social institutions do not mediate.

If we ask how *Pericles* differs from other versions of the story of Apollonius of Tyre, these episodes of "o'erpressed spirits" suggest that Shakespeare's most salient and persistent intervention involves recasting the grounds of characterological identity. On the one hand, Thaisa and Pericles experience a radical interiority; they have access to an interior selfhood that is deeply private, and that also serves as a basis for the most meaningful interpersonal bonds. On the other hand, Thaisa and Pericles are notably divorced from some of the languages that might make sense of who they are; they have crucially ceded the tasks of self-regulation and self-interpretation to the authoritative representatives of important bodies of knowledge, namely medicine and statecraft. Both the depth of interiority and the reliance upon third-parties are new features of Shakespeare's treatment of the tale. Instead of characters who possess full knowledge of their own stories, their own desires, and their own social positions, Thaisa and Pericles exhibit a rupture between the intuition and the interpretation of selfhood.

The play does have a figure for whom self-identity is achieved: Marina, the daughter of Thaisa and Pericles. Marina never faints, just as she never capitulates to others. That Shakespeare makes her one of the main objects of our wonder is uncontestable. On her falls all of the play's nostalgia for a past world, in which individuals are fully present to themselves and deal with other individuals on the basis of unmediated reciprocity. Marina alone of all the characters can say, "I . . . am / No other than I appear" (5.1.95–96). Throughout the play admiration for her more holistic kind of self-identity is mixed with the acceptance of a new order of affairs, a new interrelation of the private self and the institutions surrounding it. Thaisa and Pericles, by contrast, reveal the burden of a different set of concerns. Self-presence is not possible in any strong sense. Rather, an elusive internal selfhood is concomitant with the ceding of powers of regulation and interpretation.

Until recently, criticism of *Pericles* has remained relatively insulated from the poststructuralist transvaluation of subjectivity that, drawing upon the work of Althusser, Lacan, and Foucault, shook the field of Shakespeare studies in the 1980s and 1990s. After all, Shakespeare's late romances seem much less committed to the realistic depiction of characters moving through social space, relying instead on archetypal or aestheticized notions of characterological identity. Perhaps this is why readings of the play abound that treat Pericles' final restoration as a quasi-Christian allegory of providential redemption, or as a kind of liberal-humanist story of how a true selfhood is achieved through love and a hard-won self-awareness. To take just one recent example, de Alvarez argues that *Pericles* stages an allegory of the formation of a unified soul: "As White says, Pericles is the only Shakespearean character who actually hears the music of the spheres. And the one who hears the music of the spheres can only be the one whose soul is in perfect harmony. . . . The harmony of the soul achieved at the end is the coming together of all three parts of the soul—the appetitive, the spirited, and the intellective."[21] My reading of the play is diametrically opposed to this. There is no final harmony of the soul for Pericles or for Thaisa, but rather a striking noncoincidence of individual desire, spiritual guidance, and frameworks of interpretation. Nor are the doctor and counselor to be read as benevolent allegories of personal growth, but they ought rather to be taken for what they are, agents of powerful discourses of knowledge to which Pericles and Thaisa have capitulated.

But while there is room for more suspicious readings of *Pericles*, this does not necessarily mean that a foucauldian vocabulary is entirely appropriate to the situation. In such formulations, the apparent autonomy and interiority of human selfhood is not an essential, universal truth, but is an effect of the disciplinary forces that structure society; subjectivity is the product of impersonal relations of power, and thus the liberal humanist notion of a self-authored and self-present personality independent of social structures is an illusion. In *Pericles*, the role played by the institutions of medicine and statecraft in guiding the identity-formation of the protagonists suggests that Shakespeare's exploration of character might bear some affinity with such antihumanist accounts of subject positions. Yet Pericles and Thaisa, even while they are denied a truly autonomous, self-apprehending self-presence, nevertheless do gain access to a newly discovered depth of selfhood that social institutions do not touch.

The complexity of this dynamic might offer support to the recent work in Shakespeare studies that would complicate poststructuralist formulations of subjectivity by attending to potential ways in which human agency, creativity, and resistance are not always already controlled by institutions of power. Hugh Grady argues that in many plays Shakespeare "implicitly and presciently criticized the theories of power and the subject which dominated the insurgent Shakespeare criticism of the 1980s. For example, it seems to me, he depicts subjectivity as something of a dialectical negation of power, not as a mere effect of its operations; as an orientation to multiple potential selves or identities, not merely the production of a unitary one; as a mental space critically distanced from, and not entirely defined by, the circulating ideologies and discourses of institutions of power."[22] Attention to *Pericles* should benefit from and contribute to this new critical direction. In *Pericles*, the controlling power of institutions occurs concomitantly with a reinvention of the individual self at a deeper level of "sanctity." Far from implying a return to full self-presence, this reinvention is pictured in Shakespeare's *Pericles* as predicated upon the self's noncoincidence with itself. Even at moments of physical and psychological extremity, even when authoritative discourses step in with their own controlling operations, even when subjectivity itself is undergoing its own decomposition, Pericles and Thaisa retain, and to a degree recompose, their subjective integrity at some level.[23] In Shakespeare's play, the omnicompetence of external discourses over one's selfhood and the inexpressibly deep (and not illusory) interior autonomy of the self are presented as perhaps irrevocably tangled up with each other.

In this play structured around loss and recovery, episodes of nonconscious experience provide occasions for imagining the self's noncoincidence with itself, both in its severance from structures of self-understanding and in its interior summons from an apparently transcendent force. The reliance upon statecraft and medicine is answered by an openness to an irreducible otherness that is quasidivine and that is also a fundamental principle of intersubjectivity. The moments of o'erpressed spirits in *Pericles*—near-death, excess joy, vision—establish these new limits of characterological identity in the model world of romance, as an ancient tale is translated to the early modern stage.

## NOTES

1. The earlier version exists in William Randolph Robins, "Epilogue: The Renaissance and Shakespeare's *Pericles*," in "Ancient Romance and Medieval Literary Genres: Apollonius of Tyre," (PhD dissertation, Princeton University, 1995), 201–23.

2. See the introductions and commentaries to the three recent editions of the play: William Shakespeare, *Pericles, Prince of Tyre*, ed. Doreen DelVecchio and Antony Hammond [The New Cambridge Shakespeare] (Cambridge: Cambridge University Press, 1998); William Shakespeare and George Wilkins, *A Reconstructed Text of Pericles, Prince of Tyre*, ed. Roger Warren [The Oxford Shakespeare] (Oxford: Oxford University Press, 2003); and William Shakespeare, *Pericles*, ed. Suzanne Gossett [The Arden Shakespeare, Third Series] (London: Arden Shakespeare, 2004), 1–163. Criticism of *Pericles*, and especially of the play's relationship to traditions of romance, include Northrop Frye, *The Secular Scripture: A Study of the Structure of Romance* (Cambridge: Harvard University Press, 1976); John Arthos, "*Pericles, Prince of Tyre*: A Study of Dramatic Uses of Romantic Narrative," *Shakespeare Quarterly* 4 (1953): 257–70; Derek Traversi, *Shakespeare: The Last Phase* (London: Hollis & Carter, 1954); Northrop Frye, *A Natural Perspective: The Development of Shakespearian Comedy and Romance* (New York: Columbia University Press, 1965); Howard Felperin, *Shakespearean Romance* (Princeton: Princeton University Press, 1972); Andrew Welsh, "Heritage in Pericles," in *Shakespeare's Late Plays: Essays in Honor of Charles Crow*, ed. Richard C. Tobias and Paul G. Zolbrod (Athens: Ohio University Press, 1974), 89–113; Barbara A. Mowat, *The Dramaturgy of Shakespeare's Romances* (Athens: University of Georgia Press, 1976); Robert W. Uphaus, *Beyond Tragedy: Structure & Experience in Shakespeare's Romances* (Lexington: University Press of Kentucky, 1981); Terence Cave, *Recognitions: A Study in Poetics* (Oxford: Oxford University Press, 1988); Elizabeth Archibald, " 'Deep Clerks She Dumbs': The Learned Heroine in Apollonius of Tyre and *Pericles*," *Comparative Drama* 22 (1988–89): 289–303; Robert M.

Adams, *The Four Romances* (New York: Norton, 1989); H. W. Fawkner, *Shakespeare's Miracle Plays: Pericles, Cymbeline, and The Winter's Tale* (Rutherford, N.J.: Fairleigh Dickinson University Press, 1992); Richard Hillman, *Intertextuality and Romance in Renaissance Drama: The Staging of Nostalgia* (New York: St. Martin's Press, 1992); Ruth Nevo, "The Perils of *Pericles*," in *The Undiscover'd Country: New Essays on Psychoanalysis and Shakespeare,* ed. B. J. Sokol (London: Free Association Books, 1993), 150–78; Robert S. Miola, *Shakespeare and Classical Comedy: The Influence of Plautus and Terence* (Oxford: Oxford University Press, 1994); T. G. Bishop, *Shakespeare and the Theatre of Wonder* (Cambridge: Cambridge University Press, 1996); Robert Henke, *Pastoral Transformations: Italian Tragicomedy and Shakespeare's Late Plays* (Newark: University of Delaware Press, 1997); Constance Jordan, *Shakespeare's Monarchies: Ruler and Subject in the Romances* (Ithaca: Cornell University Press, 1997); Stephen J. Lynch, *Shakespearean Intertextuality: Studies in Selected Sources and Plays* (Westport, CT: Greenwood Press, 1998); David Skeele, ed., *Pericles: Critical Essays* (New York: Garland, 2000); Maurice Hunt, "Shakespeare's *Pericles* and the Acts of the Apostles," *Christianity and Literature* 49 (2000): 295–309; F. Elizabeth Hart, "Cerimon's 'Rough' Music in *Pericles* 3.2," *Shakespeare Quarterly* 51 (2000): 313–31; F. Elizabeth Hart, " 'Great is Diana' of Shakespeare's Ephesus," *Studies in English Literature* 43 (2003): 347–74; Barbara Mowat, " 'I tell you what mine Authors saye': *Pericles,* Shakespeare, and *Imitatio*," *Archiv für das Studium der neueren Sprachen und Literatur* 240 (2003): 42–59; Amelia Zurcher, "Unitimely Monuments: Stoicism, History and the Problem of Utility in *The Winter's Tale* and *Pericles*," *ELH* 70 (2003): 903–27.

3. I use the name "Shakespeare" and the word "playwright" to refer to the authorizing agency of the whole of *Pericles,* whether this be the work of William Shakespeare alone or of collaborators. The episodes I discuss are among those for which there is the least doubt about Shakespeare's actual authorship.

4. Citations of *Pericles* are by act, scene, and line from Shakespeare, *Pericles,* ed. Gossett, although I have omitted the editor's suggested—and, for my purpose, too suggestive—stage directions (I have restored the reading of the Quarto for the one direction that does appear), and I have made a few cosmetic changes (here, emending "sets" to "set" in line 3.2.95). The textual problems presented by *Pericles* are particularly thorny. My arguments would not be changed by taking an early printing such as that of the first quarto (1609) as my text; see *Shakespeare's Plays in Quarto: A Facsimile Edition of Copies Primarily from the Henry E. Huntington Library,* ed. Michael J. B. Allen and Kenneth Muir (Berkeley: University of California Press, 1981), 751–86.

5. Gerald N. Sandy, trans., *The Story of Apollonius of Tyre,* in *The Collected Ancient Greek Novels,* ed. B. P. Reardon (Berkeley: University of California Press, 1989), 753–54. For the Latin text, see *Historia Apollonii Regis Tyri,* ed. Gareth Schmeling (Leipzig: Teubner, 1988), Redactio A 26–27, 19–20. For the medieval and renaissance reception of the story of Apollonius of Tyre, see Elimar Klebs, *Die Erzählung von Apollonius aus Tyrus: eine geschichtliche Untersuchung über ihre lateinischen Urform und ihre späteren Bearbeitungen* (Berlin: Reimer, 1889); *Historia Apollonii Regis Tyri,* ed. G. A. A. Kortekaas (Gronin-

gen: Brouma's Boekhuis, 1984); Elizabeth Archibald, *Apollonius of Tyre: Medieval and Renaissance Themes and Variations* (Cambridge: D. S. Brewer, 1991).

6. The phrase is from Robert Hollander, *Boccaccio's Dante and the Shaping Force of Satire* (Ann Arbor: University of Michigan Press, 1997), 141. See Giovanni Boccaccio, *Filocolo*, ed. Antonio Enzo Quaglio, in *Tutte le opere di Giovanni Boccaccio*, ed. Vittore Branca, vol. 1 (Milan: Mondadori, 1967). For Boccaccio's use of the *Historia Apollonii* in the *Filocolo*, and subsequently in *Decameron* X.4, see Francesco Mazzoni, "Una presunta fonte del Boccaccio," *Studi Danteschi* 29 (1950): 192–96, and Pier Massimo Forni, *Adventures in Speech: Rhetoric and Narration in Boccaccio's Decameron* (Philadelphia: University of Pennsylvania Press, 1996), 80. Compare Laurence Twyne, *The Patterne of Painefull Adventures*, in *Narrative and Dramatic Sources of Shakespeare*, 8 vols., ed. Geoffrey Bullough (London: Routledge and Paul, 1957–75), 6:447–50.

7. Giovanni Boccaccio, *A pleasaunt disport of divers Noble Personages* (London: H. Byneman, 1567), ff. 55r–55v [reprinted in facsimile as Giovanni Boccaccio, *Filocopo. London 1567* (Amsterdam: Theatrum Orbis Terrarum, 1970)].

8. John Gower, *Confessio Amantis* 8.1159–226, in *The Complete Works of John Gower*, ed. G. C. Macaulay (Oxford: Clarendon Press, 1899–1902), 3:417–19.

9. "Ché molte donne son già tramortite / Per freddo in parto, e ciò scritto si trova." Antonio Pucci, *Cantari di Apollonio di Tiro*, ed. Renzo Rabboni (Bologna: Commissione per i testi di lingua, 1996), 3.15.3–4, p. 31.

10. On the impact of the Greek romances on renaissance literature, see Samuel Lee Wolff, *The Greek Romances in Elizabethan Prose Fiction* (New York: Columbia University Press, 1912); Carol Gesner, *Shakespeare and the Greek Romance: A Study of Origins* (Lexington: University Press of Kentucky, 1970); Thomas Hägg, *The Novel in Antiquity* (Oxford: Blackwell, 1983); Giles Barber, *Daphnis and Chloe: The Markets and Metamorphoses of an Unknown Bestseller*, Panizzi Lectures 1988 (London: British Library, 1989). The original generic relation of the *Historia Apollonii* to Greek romance is discussed in David Konstan, *Sexual Symmetry: Love in the Ancient Novel and Related Genres* (Princeton: Princeton University Press, 1994); Gareth Schmeling, "Historia Apollonii Regis Tyri," in *The Novel in the Ancient World*, ed. Gareth Schmeling (Leiden: Brill, 1996), 517–51; and William Robins, "Latin Literature's Greek Romance," *Materiali e discussioni per l'analisi dei testi classici* 35 (1996): 207–15.

11. Shakespeare, *Pericles*, ed Suzanne Gossett, 300.

12. Heliodorus, *An Æthiopian History*, trans. Thomas Underdowne, in *The Tudor Translations*, ed. Charles Whibley, vol. 5, (London: D. Nutt, 1895), 169–70. As far as I know, this parallel has not been previously mentioned. Hoeniger suggests a parallel with a passage from Lucian (where, however, the time between death and resuscitation is twenty days, and there is no mention of an Egyptian); William Shakespeare, *Pericles*, ed. F. D. Hoeniger (London: Methuen, 1963), 91. The text preserved in George Wilkins, *The Painefull Adventures of Pericles Prince of Tyre*, ed. Kenneth Muir [English Reprint Series 8] (Liverpool: University Press of Liverpool, 1953), 63–64, may present the original Shakespearean text more accurately than does the Quarto: "I have read of

some Egyptians, who after foure hours death, . . . have raised impoverished bodies, like to this, unto their former health." Many commentators prefer Wilkins's reading, because it seems more appropriate in a case like this to speak of the learned practitioner, rather than the restored person, as an Egyptian. In the *Golden Ass*, as in Wilkins, the reviver is Egyptian, but not the revived. The Heliodoran source, where one Egyptian resuscitates another, would explain both versions. Compare the way Shakespeare alludes to a different episode from Heliodorus's romance in the Duke's words in *Twelfth Night*: "Why should I not, had I the heart to do it, / Like to th' Egyptian thief at point of death, / Kill what I love?" (5.1.115–18); see Hägg, *The Novel in Antiquity*, 195.

13. *Historia Apollonii Regis Tyri*, Redactio B 45, ed. Schmeling, 77; translation mine. One redaction of the *Historia Apollonii* presents Apollonius immediately running toward his daughter: "Apollonius ran to embrace her after she had finished her tearful lamentations. He began to weep for joy and to speak. 'You are my daughter Tarsia, my one and only hope and the light of my eyes'." *Historia Apollonii Regis Tyri*, Redactio A 45, ed. Schmeling, 38; translation Sandy, 767. The text of Redactio A in this passage is probably confused.

14. Gower, *Confessio Amantis* 8.1668–747; compare Twyne, *Patterne of Painefull Adventures*, 467–68.

15. I quote Jacques Amyot's translation from *Histoire des pastorales et bocageres amovrs de Daphnis et de Chloé traduite de Grec en François* (Rouen, 1599). There is an Elizabethan translation of Amyot's text by Angel Day (1587), in which the relevant passage ends slightly differently; *Daphnis and Chloe: The Elizabethan Version*, ed. Joseph Jacobs London: D. Nutt, 1890), 77–78.

16. For this possibility in performance, see Shakespeare and Wilkins, *A Reconstructed Text of Pericles, Prince of Tyre*, ed. Warren, 58.

17. "The Story of Apollonius of Tyre," trans. Sandy, 769; *Historia Apollonii Regis Tyri* Redactio A 48, ed. Schmeling, 40.

18. Gower, *Confessio Amantis* 8. 1788–1803, 434.

19. Achilles Tatius, *The History of Leucippe and Clitophon*, trans. William Burton [Facsimile of London:1597] (Amsterdam: Theatrum Orbis Terrarum, 1977), 132.

20. On Diana in *Pericles*, see Hart, "Cerimon's 'Rough' Music in *Pericles* 3.2"; and Hart, " 'Great is Diana' of Shakespeare's Ephesus," (although I remain unconvinced of the significance of the connection between Diana and Cybele that Hart argues for).

21. Leo Paul S. de Alvarez, "The Soul of the Sojourner: *Pericles, Prince of Tyre*," in *Shakespeare's Last Plays: Essays in Literature and Politics*, ed. Stephen W. Smith and Travis Curtwright (Lanham, Md.: Lexington, 2002), 197–215.

22. Hugh Grady, *Shakespeare, Macchiavelli, and Montaigne: Power and Subjectivity From Richard II to Hamlet* (Oxford: Oxford University Press, 2002), 5–6.

23. See the remarkable rewriting of Foucault's history of madness, and of Foucault's paradigms of subject formation, in Marcel Gauchet and Gladys Swain, *La pratique de l'esprit humain* (Paris: Gallimard, 1980), translated as *Madness and Democracy: The Modern Psychiatric Universe*, trans. Catherine Porter (Princeton: Princeton University Press, 1999).

# II
## Reading the Moderns

# Ernst Robert Curtius
## and Dante as a Reader
## of Medieval Latin Authors

EARL JEFFREY RICHARDS

NO MEDIEVAL WRITER IN THE VERNACULAR PROBABLY EVER READ medieval Latin authors with as much intelligence and sensitivity as Dante, and no modern reader probably ever tried to read Dante with as much intelligence and sensitivity within this context of medieval Latinity before Ernst Robert Curtius. Robert Hollander's scholarship devoted to Dante can be understood within the tradition of Curtius. That Dante himself invites us to situate his work within the context of reading is perhaps most obvious in the final vision of the unity of creation in *Paradiso* 33, 85–90, which in fact alludes to the concrete situation of reading medieval Latin texts:

> Nel suo profondo vidi che s'interna,
>         legato con amore in un volume,
>         ciò che per l'universo si squaderna:
> sustanze e accidenti e lor costume
>         quasi conflati insieme, per tal modo
>         che ciò ch'i' dico è un semplice lume.

[In its depth I saw ingathered, bound by love in one single volume, that which is dispersed in leaves throughout the universe; substances and accidents and their relations, as though fused together in such a way that what I tell is but a simple light.][1]

As intellectually and spiritually moving as the image of the loose pages of creation ultimately being bound in single volume with love (and as appealing as this vision of coherence is to any scholar plagued by chaos), and as well known as this passage is as an example of "The Book As Symbol," signaled by Curtius, it alludes in the first place quite simply and quite directly to the practices current from 1200 to 1450 in the book trade in Italian (and other) universities, the *pecia* system.[2] This overlooked link to the actual practice of reading and copying texts offers perhaps a fruitful approach to the question of Dante's relationship to overlapping medieval Latin *traditions*—to recall Peter Dronke's phrase[3]—from the Church to the University to the law courts to the ducal courts. In this brief tribute to Hollander the *dantista*, I will look at how Curtius read Dante's own readings of medieval Latin texts as a means of understanding Dante as a vernacular author.

While Dante's relationship to medieval Latinity has long been a controversial topic, particularly with regard to the question of reading the *Commedia* as a sustained allegory, it was largely the work of Curtius, touching not on Dante's relationship to medieval Latin allegory but rather on his relationship to medieval Latin rhetoric, which has defined much of the discussion of the topic in German and Italian scholarship of the last fifty years. Parallel to Curtius's efforts to reconstruct the medieval Latin rhetorical context for Dante's *Commedia*, Robert Hollander's landmark scholarship on Dante's application of medieval allegory, supported by his electronic presentation of many of the commentaries on the *Commedia*, has broken new ground in seeing how the earliest commentators indeed read him in a theological context as defined by Thomas Aquinas.[4] Curtius and Hollander both seek a sustained intellectual context in which Dante's work can be interpreted, a context that medieval Latin traditions define. In this paper I wish to review the issues relating to Curtius's contributions to the issue of contextualization, and it is fitting that this article honor Robert Hollander in the context of Curtius studies because he was in point of fact the only colleague to encourage me in my research on Curtius in the early 1980s, research which led to the publication of my *Modernism, Medievalism and Humanism: A Research Bibliography on the Reception of the Works of Ernst Robert Curtius* (Tübingen, 1983), and to the subsequent renaissance of Curtius studies in Germany and elsewhere.

Most recent studies on Curtius's work on Dante lay stress on its autobiographical, emotional and subjective nature, and as such really avoid confronting the scholarly issues per se, perhaps because *dantisti* remain extremely skeptical about reading Dante from the perspective of medieval Latin traditions. While the autobiographical insights into Curtius's work are fascinating, for the time being this area of Curtius's pioneering work belongs to that realm *ov'è più bello tacer che dire*. For example, Willi Hirdt's 1986 essay "Ernst Robert Curtiius and Dante Alighieri" records the most important passages in Curtius's work on the Italian poet, but frequently ends up by downplaying Curtius's objective contribution to Dante studies: e.g., by claiming that Curtius's cataloging the rhetorical devices in the Francesca and Paolo episode of *Inferno* V "makes painfully clear, how this approach unavoidably and remotely skirts the work's content" (schmerzhaft deutlich, wie dieser Weg unvermeidbar und weit an der gehaltlichen Substanz des Werkes vorbeiführt),[5] and by situating his work in terms of personal academic rivalries, especially with Hugo Friedrich. Frank Rutger Hausmann follows a similar tack in his "Curtius, Hugo Friedrich et l'interprétation de Dante."[6] What Hirdt and Hausmann both indicate briefly is that the Curtius's insistence on situating Dante within overlapping medieval Latin traditions was self-consciously opposed to the approaches of Benedetto Croce and Karl Voßler, but neither author explores this opposition in any depth.

The complex issues revolve ultimately around a fundamental hermeneutic problem, in this case the assumption championed *mutatis mutandis* by both Voßler and Croce that it was not possible for their own contemporaries to read Dante's work as a late medieval reader—a fourteenth-century Florentine Catholic—would (presumably) have read it. They proposed an aesthetic and stylistic analysis of the *Commedia* based on the claim that Dante had successfully overcome medieval religious and scholastic thought, a position succinctly summarized by Voßler in 1925:

> To have overcome and united the two incomplete visionary styles of the Middle Ages—the religious, symbolic and mystical style of the Apocalypse, and the secular, moralizing, classifying and intellectualist style of allegory—this is in the world history of art the significance of the *Commedia*. It owes its international artistic value to this double victory.[7]

Voßler's disdain for allegory and religious literature was shared by many, both then and now. But it hardly met universal acclaim:

when Erich Auerbach entitled his 1928 study *Dante, Dichter der irdischen Welt*, best translated as *Dante, Poet of the Worldly* (not *Secular*) *World*, he was reacting specifically against the secular de-contextualizing of the *Commedia* by Voßler and his school. Auerbach's stress on the worldly stemmed from his interest in how the Incarnation influenced medieval Christian literature because the Christian notion of the Incarnation laid emphasis on the truth of the historical, literal level of any allegory. Put otherwise, allegory for Auerbach was a way of returning to history. Consistent with this interest, Auerbach wanted to restore the importance of historical truth within the specific context of fourfold allegory. What Voßler and Croce did would now be qualified (and rather properly so) as a "colonialist" gesture: just as Europeans stripped their African and Asian colonies of religious artifacts and displayed them more or less as trophies in various museums dedicated to European national glory, that is, ripped out of their original religious context to serve contemporary political fantasies, so too did Voßler and Croce rip Dante out of his own time in order to make his work fit into their own critical projections of what was ultimately "aesthetic." (While Croce was one of the best known liberal opponents of Mussolini, his anti-historical position on Dante was still influential in Fascist circles, as exemplified in the essays on Dante by the influential Fascist philosopher Giovanni Gentile, whose work on Sordello continues to be cited with praise.)[8]

    Much of what Curtius attempted to do in the field of medieval rhetoric was directed against this so-called "idealist" and stylistic interpretation of Dante. The fundamental thrust of Curtius's rich and detailed work on Dante is that the *Commedia* needs to be read first in the context of medieval Latin literature, a suggestion at which many *dantisti* bristled[9] in part because Dante's work had been read within the context of nineteenth-century nationalism, which posited a false opposition between vernacular and Latin culture in the Middle Ages. Dante became the national poet of a modern Italy locked in a constant political struggle with the Vatican, so that Dante's ideal of "quella Roma onde Cristo è romano" (*Purgatorio* 32, 102), an ideal harmonizing Latinity and Christianity, was not exactly "politically correct." In his work on Dante, Curtius pits himself against the essentially anti-historical, idealist position as open to political abuse, although Curtius himself, unlike Auerbach, had reservations about the importance of allegory for Dante. The enormous personal importance of Dante for Curtius as the great symbol of continuity between Antiquity and the Middle Ages has hitherto made such a strong impression on researchers that they have often lost sight of the two issues that animate Curtius's analysis of Dante's ties to medieval Latin literature: first, the very cut-and-dried question of rhetorical and topological borrowings from medieval Latin literature in the *Commedia* and second, the importance of reading Dante as objectively and as empirically as possible.

In his critique of Curtius, Peter Dronke once noted that "a poetic tradition is a wider concept than Curtius allows"[10] and argued that vernacular oral traditions of the "races, whether Romanic or Germanic" (a poor choice of words) preexisted "the stimulus of learned influence." This critique is not particularly helpful because Curtius was not against a wide concept of literary tradition per se, but insisted on empirical documentation and looked to earlier examples of Rhenish humanism as an answer to the contemporary political abuse of scholarship. In order to understand Curtius's reserve in appealing to Germanic and Romanic oral traditions, it is important to remember the contemporary context for his work. During the 1930s and '40s when Curtius was writing the essays that later were incorporated into *European Literature and the Latin Middle Ages*, the Romance linguist Walther von Wartburg was busy assembling the materials, both written and oral, for the various entries of his monumental *Französisches Etymologisches Wörterbuch*. Controversy has followed this work because its use of regional dialectical variants could potentially be abused to argue for Germanic substrates in the development of French, which in turn could be used, speciously, to argue that large areas of what is now Belgium and northern France really were *urdeutsch*. For example, the influential historian Franz Petri, responsible for impressive studies on the language boundary between French, and German, published a massive two-volume study on *Germanisches Volkserbe in Wallonien und Nordfrankreich* (1937, 2d ed., 1942) that was understood as scholarly support for the proposed annexation of Belgium and northern France into the Third Reich, following the well-known pattern of Nazi annexations in Poland and Czechoslovakia based on specious evidence from medieval sources.[11] The 1648 treaty for the Peace of Westphalia speaks of the United Provinces of the Netherlands as *Trac-*

*tatus pacis inter catholicam suam maiestatem et dominos or-
dines generales Provinciarum Unitarum inferioris Germaniae.*
"Germania inferior" was potential grist for the mill of Nazi annexation. When one realizes that the so Germanic-sounding city
name "Maastricht" originally comes from the Latin "Mosae Tra-
jectum" (the crossing over the river Meuse), it becomes clear that
competing claims of Latinity and *Germanentum* in the Rhineland
and surrounding areas are absolutely explosive. If Curtius felt an
aversion to appeals to *Volkstum*, it is more than understandable.

As a self-conscious Rhinelander and Alsatian, Curtius looked
back to early examples of Rhenish humanism, so that his sense of
tradition can be usefully compared to that of Erasmus. In a letter
written in October 1520 to Peter Manius, Erasmus rejected attempts by other humanists to identify him with a particular na-
tion, such as the claim made only a month earlier by Gerard
Geldenhouwer (Noviomagus) that Erasmus was the "immortal or-
nament of the Batavians and Germans" (Batauorum Germano-
rumque immortale decus). Erasmus noted that he was not yet certain whether he was a Batavian ("An Batauus sim, mihi nondum
satis constat"). If given a choice, Erasmus observes, he would prefer that individual regions and individual cities claim him, but not
France or Germany ("optarim ut non Gallia modo ac Germania
me sibi utrinque vindicarent, sed singulae regiones, singulae urbes
Erasmum sibi certatim assererent").[12] The treatment that Erasmus
claims for himself is the same kind of approach that Curtius took
to the various provinces of Europe: Curtius in speaking of tradition clearly recognizes regional variants with regard to Latin, and
cites Dante's *De vulgari eloquentia* as the classic proof of the kinship of the Romance languages (*ELLMA*, 30). The point is always
that these variants exist in creative tension with the tradition in
which they are situated and that Curtius's appeal to tradition was
squarely aimed at the abuse of "Germanic" traditions by contemporary scholars and their abandonment of history.

For this reason, to apply the criterion of originality outside of
the context of medieval rhetorical traditions is anachronistic and
comes close to an appeal to an "aesthetic" reading. Once the pri-
macy of the "aesthetic" (i.e., a modern aesthetic) is posited for
Dante studies, as Croce and Voßler recommended, historical context is simply discarded. Curtius's position was far from being
anti-aesthetic or even pre-aesthetic, as some critics claimed, but

the danger of an aesthetic reading lay, as Curtius pointedly noted, in its subjectivity. When Curtius spoke of aesthetics, he did so *en connaissance de cause*, for knew his Kant well and was influenced in his youth by Neo-Kantianism. In fact, one of his first scholarly publications was devoted to Kant's aesthetics in the *Critique of Pure Reason* ("Der Schematismuskapitel in der *Kritik der reinen Vernunft*," *Kant-Studien* 19 [1914], 338 ff.). Critics of Curtius who consider his scholarship as anti-aesthetic must reassess their position given Curtius's familiarity with Kantian aesthetics.

The direct relevance of Curtius's sensitivity to the role of subjectivity in scholarship—he was often fond of quoting Hugo Schuchardt's phrase "researching the researcher" (die Erforschung des Forschers)—to his research on Dante is clearly evident in his review of Hugo Friedrich's book on "legal metaphysics" [*sic*] in the *Commedia* (*Die Rechtsmetaphysik der Göttlichen Komödie, Francesca da Rimini*, Frankfurt, 1942). Curtius begins by noting that Voßler's "daring subjectivism" is held in check by Voßler's knowledge of contemporary Dante scholarship and of German intellectual historical research: "Voßler's interpretation of Dante shows at every step a bold subjectivism that is even today characteristic of the work of the youthful seventy-year-old, but it is constantly checked by consideration of Italian Dante research on the one hand, and of German intellectual history on the other."[13] By contrast, Curtius goes on to reproach Friedrich for having proposed an original but irresponsible analysis. As far as Curtius is concerned, Friedrich proposes a reading of Dante that paid little attention to previous scholarship on the influence of legal culture on Dante and to the historical interaction between jurisprudence and rhetoric in medieval universities. Friedrich was subsequently a more successful teacher than Curtius so that it is hardly surprising how much German scholarship on Curtius's relationship to Dante is a barely veiled defense of Friedrich.

"Subjectivism" in scholarship was one of Curtius's favorite targets. At the end of 1945, he published a kind of work-in-progress forward to his later *magnum opus*, in which he said:

After the end of the First World War there were many attempts at "new scholarship" which appealed to introspection [*Schau*, in the phenomenological sense] and "intuition" or other forms of illumination and declared war on the often cited [empirical] positivism.

> Many sought to re-cast the grand personalities of history accord-
> ing to the dogmas of the George-Circle . . . History was trans-
> formed sometimes into a novel, sometimes into a myth. For the
> largest part these attempts were aberrations whose implications
> we are only now able to measure, for they paved the way for the
> most extreme falsifications of history which took their fateful
> course since 1933. "There is no objective science, no objective
> scholarship" was taught then. Science and scholarship were to be
> racially oriented, ethnically directed and politically linked. This
> pack of lies must disappear.[14]

Curtius's increasing rejection of subjective elements in literary
scholarship led him to make a claim that *dantisti* would have preferred to ignore: "The *Commedia* shows stylistic and composi-
tional features which Dante could not have found already present
in the vernacular literatures but only in medieval Latin literature.
He composed in the form of a fiction a cosmological, moral and
theological pedagogical epic (*Lehrgedicht in epischer Form*).
Where did models for such an enterprise exist? Only in the medieval Latin literature written in France between 1150 and 1200."[15]

What Curtius would probably argue now, given the wonderful
electronic accessibility of so much medieval Latin writing, is that
Dante's *Commedia* must be read within the context of medieval
Latin "traditions" (to repeat Dronke's phrase). For example,
Geryon is described as "ver' che ha faccia di menzogna." Without
first consulting, for example, Gmelin's or Singelton's commentaries, one can quickly do an Internet search using the terms
"verum" and "facie veritatis," and a Latin proverbial phrase, at-
tributed to Martin of Braga, will pop up, "Mendacium facie veritatis occulitur." The text of Martin of Braga (or of another author,
the authorship of *Formula vitae honestae* is not exactly clear) is
somewhat different, but a quick check of Singleton's commentary
shows that Singleton had already (in pre-Internet days) identified
the following source text for Geryon: "crebro siquidem faciem
mendacii veritatis retinet, crebro mendacium specie veritatis occulitur." The question remains: was Dante inspired by a written
text or by an oral proverbial tradition? In matter of fact, Dante
probably moved in a bilingual erudite world where Latin and Italian coexisted, without tension, and were spoken and written side
by side, much as nowadays in western Europe English more and
more coexists with other European languages among academics.

This modern game of *sortes interretiales* (*per navigationem electronicam*, and long ago it was Robert Hollander who noted "it would be pleasant to have a computer program run on the *Patrologia*")[16] speaks volumes (or megabytes) about the coexistence of medieval Latin with the vernacular. There are passages in the *Commedia*—and not just the encounter with Cacciaguida where this multilingual situation is made explicit—where it often seems that Dante's Italian is barely distinguishable from a Latin subtext. Curtius, for his part, stressed that Dante's Italian was so close to Latin that it needed to be read in a continuum with Latin, and this suggestion helps us understand Dante's profound indebtedness to medieval Latinity. Giovanni Bertoldi da Serravalle (1350–1442, otherwise known as Johannis de Serravalle) translated the *Commedia* into Latin, and his Latin phraseology is useful in testing to what extent a medieval Latin "subtext" is often present in the *Commedia* for an author whose linguistic and literary competence in medieval Latin affords at least a base mark:

> In medio itineris vite nostre
> Reperi me in una silva obscura,
> Cuius recta via erat devia.

The standard Old Testament gloss for *Inferno* 1.1, "nel mezzo di cammin di nostra vita," has always been Isaiah 38:10, "in dimidio dierum meorum vadam ad portas inferi," [in the noon of my days I shall go to the gates of Sheol] but could there be another Latin subtext here, perhaps closer than the text from Isaiah? I would suggest that Dante's Latin subtext is perhaps not Isaiah, but Jerome's commentary on this passage from Isaiah (CL 0584, SL 73, lib. 11, cap [s.s.] 38), "unde in medio vitae cursu, et in errorum tenebris ducentur ad tartarum" [whence in the middle of life's course and in the darkness of wanderings, they will be led down to hell] especially because the connection to darkness is found in Jerome but not in Isaiah.[17] There may even be an allusion to Augustine's *Ennarationes in Psalmos* (CL 0283, Sl 38, Psalmus 22 [23], 4, l. 2), "nam et si ambulem in medio vitae huius, quae umbra mortis est?" [for even if I walk in the middle of this life, which is the shadow of death]. By the same token, does Dante's famous phrase in *Inferno* 1.7, "Tant' è amara che poco è più morte" [It is so bitter death is hardly more so] allude to Ambrose's phrase in *De bono mortis* (CL 0129, cap. 7, par. 28, pag. 729), "et tamen amarior vita quam mors?" [and yet how much bitterer is life than death?] (Giovanni de Serravalle's translation, *Tantum est amara quod ea vix amarior sit mors* might allude to Ambrose.) Since medieval preachers freely used texts by Jerome, Ambrose and Augustine, these phrases were clearly "in the air." Dante was not only a reader of medieval Latin, he was a speaker of this language who moved freely in its literature. Could it be that " una silva oscura" alludes to Ovid's *Metamorphoses* 6.521, where Philomela was raped after her rapist dragged her into a "dark hut in the old woods" (in stabula alta trahit silvis obscura vetustis)? By contrast, Giovanni de Serravalle did not use the phrase from Jerome or Isaiah, translating instead *in medio itinere vite nostre*, where to be sure the phrase *in medio itinere* is found both in classical sources and Jerome's commentaries. The most interesting problem in this search for a possible Latin subtext is the word *smarrita*, which in fact is a Gallicism of Germanic origin whose use here has important implications for why the *Commedia* must necessarily end with a prayer to the Virgin, but I am getting ahead of my argument.

The scholarly discussion of Dante's relation to medieval Latin has focused so narrowly on the question of Dante's allegory and the authorship of the Letter to Can Grande that it has missed the concrete linguistic proximity to medieval Latin culture. By contrast, Curtius avoided the issue of allegory in order to embed Dante firmly in the rhetorical traditions of medieval Latinity, but this approach is perhaps even more fruitful given the complexity of Dante's general allegorical practice. The question of Dante's use of allegory in the *Commedia* has been ignored in the old controversy of *Il Fiore*, where the superficial courtly allegory of the French original, with little or no biblical context, is carefully preserved. With all due respect to the proponents of Dante's authorship of this work, which I have challenged,[18] there is little question that the allegory of the *Roman de la Rose* is of far more superficial nature than that of the *Commedia*, regardless whether one strives to restrict Dante's allegory to moments or not, and it remains to the supporters of Dante's authorship of *Il Fiore* to explain how Dante could so radically change not only his understanding, but his application of allegory. Even as skillful a practitioner of allegory as Christine de Pizan was, especially in her *Epistre Othea*, took exception to any comparison between Dante and Jean de Meung. In probably the first known surviving comparison between Jean de Meung and Dante, Christine de Pizan wrote to Pierre Col on October 2, 1402 that if he really wanted an adequate depiction of paradise and hell, which he claims to find in Jean de Meung, he would be much advised to read Dante, who, Christine curtly observes, accomplishes this task more subtly in theological terms, more profitably, more poetically, and more effectively ("Mais se mieulz vuelz oïr descripre paradis et enfer, et par plus subtilz termes plus haultement parlé de theologie, plus prouffitablement, plus poetiquement et de plus grant efficasse, lis le livre que on appelle le Dant . . . la oyras autre propos mieux fondé plus subtilment, ne te deplaise, et ou tu pourras plus prouffiter que en ton *Romant de la Rose,*—et cent fois mieux composé; ne il n'y a comparison, ne t'en courouces ja.").[19] After the epistolary exchange of the "Quarrel of the *Rose*," and seemingly in order to strengthen her criticisms of the superficiality of the *Rose*'s allegory when compared to that of Dante's, Christine went on to write the *Epistre Othea* (one of the most influential works in late medieval and early modern England), which follows a rigorous allegorical format of presenting an image based on pagan mythology, a verse text, a gloss that always cites a pagan author and an allegory which always cites a Latin Father. One would be hard pressed to find a more consistently allegorical work—or a work closer in spirit to Dante's own practice of combining pagan and Christian authors, a practice which is perhaps the crowning leitmotiv of Robert Hollander's lifetime of Dante scholarship. In the prologue to her *Advision*, a virtual handbook of allegorical interpretation, Christine, with the Dante-*Rose* comparison always firmly in mind, invokes the Thomist notion of the *poetae theologi* when she speaks of the "poetes theologisans."[20] While it is unlikely that she knew the Epistle to Can Grande, she was responding to the fundamental link of medieval Latin poetry and theology in Dante as the ideal for poetic composition.

Nonetheless, the switch from the language of heaven to Latin to archaic Florentine in the speech of Cacciaguida illustrates concretely the continuum that existed in Dante's mind between Latin and Italian. This kind of practice conforms to Dante's own proclaimed, and often cited, ideal in *De vulgari eloquentia*, II, iv: "quantum illos proximius imitemur, tantum rectius poetemur" [the more closely we imitate them, the more correctly we will compose], echoed again in *Purgatorio* I.7, "qui la morta poesì resurga" [Here from the dead let poetry rise up]. Dante's use of Vergil as a source has been well studied, so that it requires little further scrutiny here. While Petrarch noted in a famous aside that Dante was "unequal" to himself when he composed Latin ("sibi imparem quod in vulgari eloquio quam carminibus aut prosa clarior atque altior assurgit"),[21] he does however demonstrate that medieval Latin and Italian coexisted in Dante's mind. In this context of Dante's relationship to medieval Latinity, it is striking how Dante has St. Bernard pray at the end of the *Commedia*. At the beginning of *Paradiso* 33, Dante wrote arguably one of the most beautiful prayers ever to have been composed in honor of the Virgin Mary, though he puts it in the mouth of St. Bernard, whose Marian devotion (all in Latin) was and is celebrated. Ever since Gilda Sappa exhaustively investigated the sources for this famous prayer in 1921,[22] and determined that there were numerous thematic parallels between St. Bernard's Marian works (*In nativitate Beatae Mariae* and his five sermons *In assumptionem Beatae Mariae*) but no verbal reminiscences in the strict sense demanded by *Quellenforschung*, Dante scholars have puzzled over this beautiful prayer.[23] St. Bernard in Dante prays to the Blessed Virgin in Italian using a language and imagery clearly taken from the writings of the good saint, with all of the required liturgical cadences and *topoi*, but if one searches the electronic databases of the Patrologia Latina and Corpus Christianorum, it becomes clear that Dante's diction and phraseology in Italian are absolutely original and can simply not be seen as calques on medieval Latin. St. Bernard's prayer does not cite St. Bernard's text (an interesting departure from the practice of self-citation in some medieval authors). Of course Dante knew perfectly well that he had written an original Italian devotional prayer, "closely imitated" on Latin models, but where the otherwise concrete verbal reminiscences are absent.

Yet Dante had also prepared his readers for this final prayer to the Virgin with his use of the term "smarrita" in *Inferno* 1.3, which anticipates the phrase near the end of the *Commedia*, "i' sarei *smarrito* / se li occhi miei da lui fossero aversi" [I should have been lost if my eyes had been turned from it] (*Paradiso* 33.77–78) as though Dante sought to underscore the allusion to the opening lines of *Inferno*. Eugen Lerch identified it as a Gallicism based on Old French *esmari*, "confused, lost, upset," which can be traced to Gothic *marzjan*, OHG *marrjan/merran*.[24] It is found most often in Old French Marian devotional works because, among other things, *esmarie* in the feminine singular rhymes perfectly with "Marie" (e.g., Regr N D 27,2 says "Biaus fius, a droit ai non Marie / car jou sui forment esmarie" [Fair son, I am rightly called Mary, because I was terribly lost] and ND Lo 512, "Douce dame sainte Marie / con ma pensee est esmarie," [Sweet lady, holy Mary, how lost is my thought]). Given Dante's sensitivity to the puns involved in Old French *amer*, he must surely have understood the connotation of *esmari*. Dante is confused as all sinners who turn to the Mother of God. It is the Blessed Virgin who will reveal to Dante the final *visio Dei* that expunges forever the profound confusion that marked his departure in *Inferno* 1. Giovanni de Serravalle missed the Gallicism completely with his translation "cuius recta via erat devia," and little wonder too, because there is no corresponding medieval Latin subtext.

Curtius's attempts to recuperate Dante's place in medieval Latinity, much like those of Auerbach as well, were clearly motivated as a response to the political, philosophical, and aesthetic abuse of the *Commedia* and mark a new direction in Dante studies. It is not necessary to repeat his detailed demonstrations of how Dante's rhetorical practice perfectly mirrors medieval Latin rhetorical practice because Dante's training, after all, was in medieval Latin rhetoric to begin with. What must however be stressed is that Dante took from medieval Latin traditions his cosmopolitanism, and that this attempt to make all the world his home is perhaps his greatest legacy. Before Dante, Hugo of St. Victor made the point emphatically in the *Didascalion*, III.19: "delicatus ille est adhuc cui patria dulcis est; fortis autem iam, cui omne solum patria est; perfectus vero, cui mundus totus exsilium est."[25] [He remains weak for whom his homeland is sweet, while he is strong for whom the whole earth is his homeland, and truly he is perfect for whom the whole world is an exile.] Dante surely must have had this passage in mind when he wrote the famous lines in *De vulgari eloquentia*, I.6.3: "Nos autem, cui mundus est patria velut piscibus equor, quanquam Sarnum biberimus ante dentes et Florentiam adeo diligamus ut, quia dileximus, exilium patiamur iniuste, rationi magis quam sensui spatulas nostri iudicii podiamus." [To me, however, the whole world is a homeland, like the sea to fish—

though I drank from the Arno before cutting my teeth, and love Florence so much that, because I loved her, I suffer exile un-justly—and I will weight the balance of my judgement more with reason than with sentiment." (tr. Steven Botterill, Princeton Dante Project)] It was in this same spirit that Erasmus considered the wisest, most philosophical attitude in dealing with affairs and men was to act to make the world the common property of all: "philosophikoteron est mea sententia sic de rebus et hominibus agere, ut mundum hunc communem omnium patriam esse duca-mus."[26] [My opinion is the most philosophical—that we must act regarding objects and humans as though we held this common world were the homeland of all.] By showing how medieval Latin-ity, above all in the works of Dante, strove to this end, Curtius re-vived one of the most powerful traditions in European culture.

## NOTES

1. Text and translation of the *Paradiso* are from Charles Singleton's edition, Bollingen Series LXXX (Princeton: Princeton University Press, 1982), 376–77. For the *Inferno* and *Purgatorio*, I have used the Petrocchi text printed with the translation by Jean and Robert Hollander (New York: Doubleday, 2000 and 2003).

2. *Juristische Buchproduktion im Mittelalter*, ed. Vincenzo Colli (Frank-furt: Klostermann; 2002). See also See Jean Destrez, *La pecia dans les manu-scrits universitaires du XIIIe et du XIVe siècle* (Paris: Editions Jaques Vautrains, 1935); and Graham Pollard, "The *Pecia* System in the Medieval Universities," in *Medieval Scribes, Manuscripts and Libraries: Essays Presented to N. R. Ker*, ed. M. B. Parkes and A. G. Watson (London: Scolar Press, 1978), 145–61; Louis J. Bataillon, Bertran G. Guyot, and Richard H. Rouse, eds., *La production du livre universitaire au moyen âge: exemplar et pecia*, Actes du symposium tenu au Collegio San Bonaventura de Grottaferrata, May 1983 (Paris: Centre na-tional de la recherche scientifique, 1991). John Ahern, "Hermeneutics and Manuscript Production in *Paradiso* 33," *PMLA* 97 (1982), 800–809, while mak-ing interesting observations about vernacular authors collecting the fascicules of their works, misses the more obvious medieval Latin context for Dante's re-marks.

3. Peter Dronke, *Dante and Medieval Latin Traditions* (Cambridge: Cam-bridge University Press, 1986).

4. *Allegory in Dante's "Commedia"* (Princeton: Princeton University Press, 1969).

5. Willi Hirdt, "Ernst Robert Curtiius and Dante Alighieri" in *In Ihnen begegnet sich das Abendland," Bonner Vorträge zur Erinnerung an Ernst Robert Curtius*, ed. Wolf-Dieter Lange (Bonn: Bouvier, 1990), 181–97, citation here, 188.

6. Frank Rutger Hausmann, "Curtius, Hugo Friedrich et l'interprétation de Dante" in *Ernst Robert Curtius et l'idée d'Europe*, ed. Jeanne Bem and André Guyaux (Paris: Champion, 1995), 57–67.

7. Karl Voßler, *Die Göttliche Komödie* (Heidelberg: Winter, 1925) 2:549: "Die zwei unvollkommenen visionären Stilarten des Mittelalters: die religiöse, symbolische und mystische der Apokalypse und die weltliche, moralisierende, klassifizierende und intellektualistische der Allegorie überwunden und vereint zu haben, das ist in der Weltgeschichte der Kunst die Bedeutung der "Komödie." Ihren internationalen Kunstwert verdankt sie diesem Doppelsieg."

8. The *Enciclopedia dantesca* has only a short entry on Gentile, and says nothing about his prominence in the Fascist regime. The secondary literature on the topic is remarkable for its lack of political courage. See Merle E. Brown, "Respice finem: The Literary Criticism of Giovanni Gentile," *Italica* 47 (1970): 3–27 and Giovanni Gullace, "Poésie et structure, Benedetto Croce et Giovanni Gentile interprètes de Dante," *Les Lettres Romanes* 26 (1972): 332–59.

9. Gino Rizzo, "Valore e limite del contributo de Ernst Robert Curtius agli studi danteschi" *Italia* 37 /1960), 277–86; Gustavo Vinaz, "Filologia e ambizioni storiografiche," *Studi medievali*, ser. 2, vol. 1 (1960): 195–202.

10. Peter Dronke, *Poetic Individuality in the Middle Ages, New Departures in Poetry, 1000–1150* (Oxford: Oxford University Press, 1970), 10.

11. Karl Ditt," Die Kulturraumforschung zwischen Wissenschaft und Politik. Das Beispiel Franz Petri (1903–93), *WF* 46 (1996): 73–176. Petri's involvement with the Kriegseinsatz der Geisteswissenschaften has been documented by Frank-Rutger Hausmann, *"Deutsche Geisteswissenschaft" im Zweiten Weltkrieg, Die "Aktion Ritterbusch" (1940–1945)* (Dresden: Dresden University Press, 1998).

12. Desiderii Erasmi Roterdami, *Opus Epistolarum* ed. P. S. Allen and H. M. Allen (Oxford: Clarendon Press, 1922), v. 4 (1519–21), 354, Letter no. 1147.

13. "Zur Danteforschung," *Romanische Forschungen*, 56 (1942): 3: "Voßlers Danteauslegung zeigte zwar auf Schritt und Tritt den kühnen Subjektivismus, der auch heute den Arbeiten des jugendlichen Siebzigers anhaftet; aber sie kontrollierte sich stets durch Berücksichtigung der italienischen Dantologie einerseits, der deutschen geisteswissenschaftlichen Forschung andrerseits."

14. "Nach dem ersten Weltkriege sah man zahlreiche Proben einer «neuen Wissenschaft», die sich auf «Schau», «Intuition» oder andere Formen innerer Erleuchtung berief und dem vielberufenen «Positivismus» den Krieg erklärte. Manche suchten große Persönlichkeiten der Geschichte nach der Dogmatik des Georgekreises umzuprägen. . . . Geschichte wurde mitunter zum Roman, mitunter zum «Mythos». Zum größten Teil sind das Verirrungen gewesen, deren Tragweite wir erst heute ermessen können. Denn sie haben der Geschichtsfälschung größten Ausmaßes den Weg gebahnt, die seit 1933 ihr verhängnisvolles Wesen trieb. «Es gibt keine objektive Wissenschaft», so wurde damals gelehrt. Wissenschaft sei rassisch, völkisch, politisch gebunden. Dieser Lug muß verschwinden." Now published in *Kritische Essays zur europäischen Literatur* (Frankfurt: Fischer, 1984), 434–35.

15. "Dante und das lateinische Mittelalter," *Romanische Forschungen* 57 (1943): 153–85, citation here 176: "Die *Commedia* zeigt stilistisch und kompositionelle Merkmale, die Dante nicht in den volkssprachlichen Literaturen,

sondern nur in der mittellateinischen vorfinden konnte. Er hat in Form einer Fiktion ein kosmologisches, moralisches, theologisches Lehrgedicht in epischer Form geschrieben. Wo gab es Vorbilder für ein solches Unternehmen? Nur in der mittellateinischen Literatur Frankreichs vom 1150-1200."

16. "Dante Theologus-Poeta," *Studies in Dante* (Ravenna: Longo, 1980), 67.

17. While I am convinced that Jerome's commentary on Isaiah rather than, or as well as, Isaiah's text is Dante's source, I have always been tempted by Notker Balbulus's celebrated phrase *media vita in morte sumus* (surviving in *The Book of Common Prayer* at the beginning of the service for the Burial of the Dead as "in the midst of life, we are in the midst of death," and in Martin Luther's hymn, "Mitten wir in Leben sind, / Mit dem Tod umpfangen").

18. *Dante and the «Roman de la Rose»: An Investigation into the Vernacular Narrative Context of the «Commedia»*, Beihefte zur Zeitschrift für romanische Philologie, Bd. 184, (Tübingen: Niemeyer, 1981), and "The *Fiore* and the *Roman de la Rose*," in *Medieval Translators and Their Craft*, ed. Jeanette M. A. Beer (Kalamazoo: Medieval Institute Publications, 1989), 265-83.

19. Christine de Pizan et al., *Le Débat dur le Roman de la Rose*, ed. Eric Hicks (Paris: Champion, 1977), 40-41. See my discussion of this passage in *Dante and the Roman de la Rose* (1981), 73.

20. As Curtius long ago pointed out in *ELLMA*, chapter 12, "Poetry and Theology," Dante's practice here, just as Christine de Pizan already recognized, corresponds to Thomas Aquinas's term *poetae theologi*, found in 1 Met 4,83 (*fuerunt quidam poetae theologi, sic dicti, quia de divinis carmina faciebant*) or 2 Met 1 (*fuerunt quidam qui vocauntur poetae theologi, sicut Orpheus, Hesiodus et Homerus, qui sub tegumento quarundarum fabularum divina hominibus tradiderunt.* All of Thomas Aquinas's works can now be consulted and searched on the Web at www.corpusthomisticum.org.

21. See Aldo Bernardo, "Petrarch's Attitude toward Dante," *PMLA* 70 (1955): 488-517 and Guido Billanovich, "Tra Dante e Petrarca" *Italia medioevale e umanistica* 8 (1965): 1-44.

22. Gilda, Sappa, *La preghiera di S. Bernardo nell'ultimo canto del Paradiso: commenta e preceduta da un breve discorso intorno a la Vergine Maria nella "Divina commedia"* (Mondovi: Torto e Moletta, 1921).

23. For an example of how utterly clueless many *dantisti* are regarding the importance of St. Bernard for Dante, see Raoul Manselli, "Bernardo di Chiaravalle," *Enciclopedia dantesca*, v. 1: 601-5.

24. Eugen Lerch, "Germanische Wörter im Vulgärlatein? *Werra, marrire, bastire*," *Romanische Forschungen* 60 (1947): 647-84, see especially 669. Lerch also notes Dante's use of *smarrimento* in *Vita Nuova* 25 and *Convivio* 2.11. In fact, Dante sees to have been one of the first authors in Italian to use this word which is now so common for the *Ufficio oggetti smarriti*.

25. *Hugonis de Sancto Victore Didascalicon de Studio legendi*, ed. C. H. Buttimer, (Washington, D.C.: The Catholic University of America Press, 1939), III.19, 69.

26. Desiderii Erasmi Roterdami, *Opus Epistolarum*, v. 2: 1514-17, ed. P. S. Allen and H. M. Allen (Oxford: Clarendon Press, 1910), Letter no. 480, 369.

# Did Langland Read
# the *Lignum Vitae?*

## Macklin Smith

Readers of *Piers Plowman* still wonder how William Langland became the poet they admire, but even historicists will concede that his poetic intelligence is inexplicable merely as a product of cultural learning.[1] As a poet, Langland was a prime doer who did well. He began with a new vision, worked obsessively on it for over twenty years, wrote his poem in at least three circulating versions, and became the only alliterative maker with a national audience. Passionately wrought, intellectually complex, rough-styled yet carefully crafted, *Piers Plowman* in its longer versions can be characterized as a multilingual, episodic personification allegory combining multiple genres within a framework of multiple dream visions. Its story offers a mimesis of possible personal salvation amidst incurable social evil.

Generically, *Piers Plowman* presents, in the main, a two-part sequence of dialogic *psychomachia* and visionary *meditatio* set within, and ultimately subsuming, its social satire. Will's initial *Visio* reveals a pervasively sinful world whose royal misrule, mercantile greed, ecclesiastical corruption, and common misery foredoom our best attempts at social reform. The only hope, Will realizes, lies elsewhere and inward. If he can learn in his *Vita* how personally, with grace, to do well, he may thereby find eternal life in heaven. Will's quest for Dowel is at first psychological, but his conversations with his kindred intellectual and imaginative faculties fail to yield any satisfying discovery. Only when the increasingly frustrated (and willful) Will learns humility and witnesses penitential healing can he converse with Anima, the unitary Soul, and find himself privy to contemplative visions of the life of

149

Christ. Ironically, such revelations are not just personal but social, historical, and indeed universal, yet the world remains blind to them. Only the individual Will, allied with Conscience and aided by Grace, can hope to awake to Truth.

There is no other medieval poem like *Piers Plowman*.[2] How might Langland have conceived its extraordinary generic scope, its complexity of theme, mode, and architectonics? In this essay, I shall argue that one important influence may have been Bonaventura's *Lignum vitae*. Langland's reading of this compact, contemplative Life of Christ might account for the quality of its lineation during Will's *meditatio*, preoccupied as it with triadic, chiastic, and parallelistic patterns suggestive of the Trinity, Incarnation, and Atonement. His reading would primarily account for what is essentially new in the B Version: its affective solution to intellectual errancy; its central image of the Tree of Charity; Will's threefold visions of the Christ's life; the Samaritan/Charity's Trinitarian analogies; Conscience's subsequent recapitulation of this *vita Christi* in terms of hierarchical triads; the *Vita*'s pervasive thematic focus on Dowel, Dobet, and Dobest, whose dialectic of progressive perfection is ultimately exemplified in Christ.[3] For Langland, whose talent and purposes predisposed him to risk radical modal juxtapositions and narrative incoherencies,[4] the *Lignum vitae* might also have seemed to offer both spiritual and artistic authorization: Bonaventura's presentation of the Life of Christ, like Will's interior visionary experience, is allusive, discursively incoherent, and theologically pointed, while conforming to a triadic, hierarchical scheme of theological mysteries. I imagine Langland's reading of the *Lignum vitae* between his composition of the A and B Versions, when it would have offered him both the narrative means whereby to extricate the Dreamer from his psychological impasse and the poetic means by which to reshape his already well-shaped lines in imitation of divine forms.

## LINEATION

Even at the beginning of his poetic career, Langland's lines display, in the thematic arrangement of their alliterative collocations, a conceptual brilliance not found elsewhere. Metrically, our poet follows most of the rules discovered by Hoyt Duggan and Thomas Cable,[5] but as George Kane and A. V. C. Schmidt have observed, Langland innovates in his invention of new alliterative patterns (to include the extended lines *aaalax, aaalaa, aaalxx*, and *aaalbb*) and, more radically, in his willingness to allow *non-coincidence* of required metrical stress and required alliterative chime.[6] The alliterative triplet may be expanded or redistributed in the line, and alliteration need no longer conform with stress. *Piers Plowman* displays, then, in comparison with other alliterative poems, expanded variety in the thematic array of its alliterating and/or stressed content words, a richer range of alliterative effect and new possibilities of counterpoint between stress and chime.

Both key innovations facilitate Langland's doctrinal pointing during his treatment of the *vita Christi*. The line immediately following Christ's death on the cross is an extended *aaalax*—

> The **day** for **drede** wiþdrou3 ‖ and **derk** bicam the **sonne**
> (18.60)

—whose initial triplet and excess of **d**-syllables, enacting the sun-darkening eclipse, feel ominous and melancholy, but whose chiastic frame of "day" and "sonne" figuratively enfolds the death of the Passion in its redemptive life. As Christ justifies the Atonement during the harrowing of hell, he utters two paired and emphatically parallel lines, each with alliteration on the littlest word in the language:

> And as **Adam** and **alle** ‖ þoru3 <u>a</u> **tree deyden**,
> **Adam** and **alle** þoru3 ‖ <u>a</u> **tree** shul turne to **lyue**
> (18.359–60)

The explicit typology of the two trees, whose fruits are death and life, may seem clear and simple enough, but the Adam/Christ typology is more subtly revealed through the alliterative sequence of "Adam," "alle," and "a," with its chiasmus of singularity, universality, singularity. In the first line, perhaps only the Tree of the Knowledge of Good and Evil is referenced; in the second, if the Tree of the Cross here reflects, by means of typical Langlandian word play, its origin in Unity, Trinity, and Alpha, the seemingly unobtrusive article looms huge. Like the death of Jesus, that which seems simply common is uniquely miraculous.

The brilliance of Langland's lineation is not, of course, restricted to matters theological. It pervades the poem's social satire, psychological dialogue, and handling of sin. Langland's lineation, however, is sadly understudied, and its pointedly doctrinal (and exemplarist, and Bonaventuran) features have gone almost unnoticed.[7] Stephen Barney has recently compared Langland's line favorably to Chaucer's, and in so doing he has joined Kane, Schmidt, and very few others in attending to the poem's poetry.[8] Many critics, while justly appreciative of Anne Middleton's demonstration that Langland composed and revised in episodic increments,[9] seem oblivious to the poet's alliterative craft in line-shaping. Thematically smart, emotionally intense, clever yet clear, in multivalent tension with the ongoing syntax, his lines often communicate an episode's fundamental rather than ancillary meaningfulness.

Readers who ignore Langland's lineation are like cartographers unwilling to examine landforms in multiple scale. Here, for example, is what Will first sees in the *Visio*:

> I sei3 a tour on a toft trieliche ymaked,
> A deep dale byneþe, a dungeon þerInne
> With depe diches and derke and dredfulle of si3te.
> A fair feeld ful of folk fond I þer bitwene
> Of alle manere of men, þe meene and þe riche,
> Werchynge and wandrynge as þe world askeþ.
> (Prol. 14–19)

The heavenly (and Trinitarian) tower on the hill manifests itself in a normative *aa|ax* line, with perfect thematic conformity between the alliterating staves and the fourth-stressed "ymaked." As we turn to the hellish deep dale, two successive lines alliterate on d; both have extra stresses in the first half-line, and the second has extended *aaa|ax* alliteration. If heaven is beautiful and orderly, hell is fearfully (and amusingly) cluttered. This miniature contrast is neatly framed chiastically by "I sei3" and "of si3te"—a small demonstration of Langland's skill, comparable to Chaucer's, with little words and throw-away phrases. The line summarizing the Field of Folk is a teasingly normative *aa|ax* line, with stresses on "feeld," "folk," "fond," and "-twene," and is thus rhythmically analogous to that characterizing the Creator's dwelling; but of course it is just as crowded as the dungeon beneath. In performance, it would be almost impossible not to honor the line's very special effect by stressing all five f-syllables. Note that the "extra" alliterations are not merely ornamental (like many in the works of the *Gawain* poet); nor are they thematic merely by virtue of their crowdedness. The secondary words matter: Creation is appropriately fair and abundant—or is it alluring and overcrowded?

For the remainder of the Prologue, the kinds of folk will be differentiated in many ways, but here they are differentiated, successively, in terms of poor and rich and working and wandering. Will has already described himself dressed like a hermit "vnholy of werkes," who "wente wide in þis world wondres to here" (3–4); so the folk's alternative activities of working and wandering are already negatively imaged in the condition of their beholder. After the Fall, of course, our exile and wandering through the world requires the necessity of work, so the last line in this passage is morally astute. But what does the world require? It requires what God also wills: that we labor within it to obtain our necessary sustenance, that we wander through it in search of salvation, and that we do works of charity as best we can as a condition of salvation. The accumulation of worldly wealth is not concordant with this spiritual goal. Hence the rich are excluded: "Of alle **man**ere of **men**, þe **meene** and þe riche." In this masterful line, we see that all kinds of people, including the poor, are linked by alliteration, stress, and paronomasia into one group. Sonantally and thematically, the "riche" (who rhyme with the previous "diches") cannot enter this unity.

How did Langland come to construct such lines?[10] I would suggest that there emerge in most ages a few poets of special talent who rise above their culturally received ideas, and that Langland exemplifies this phenomenon. However, even original poets are influenced—sometimes in unexpected and, as it were, original ways. Reading a new kind of book can turn such a writer's talent to fresh use. Given Langland's clerical status, nonuniversity education, apparently marginal vocation, London residence, evident intellectual curiosity, and range of interests from social welfare to moral psychology, it seems likely that as an emergent poet he would have sought out various kinds of books that his alliterative contemporaries disregarded. In this context, the evident fourteenth-century English diffusion of Bonaventura's modest yet structurally innovative and rhetorically powerful *meditatio* is intriguing. Some manuscripts containing the *Lignum vitae* had a provenance outside the Franciscan Order, and most group this work with homiletic and meditative materials that would have appealed to Langland. In some instances, the *Lignum vitae* even shares a binding with works used for the Harrowing of Hell episode: the *Gospel of Nicodemus*, and the Four Daughters of God allegory (in [pseudo-] Bonaventura's *Meditationes vitae Christi* or treated separately).[11] If the triadic, hierarchical formal schematics of the *Lignum vitae* influenced the shape of the B Version's *Vita* narrative, its numerological thematics may also have influenced the shape of some of the more theologically expressive lines in that textual space.

Like Dante (whom he did not know),[12] Langland displays, especially in the *Vita* passus, an appreciation of the essential formal idea of his verse medium. His is a line, after all, whose persistent rhythm entails three sonantally linked stresses terminating in a fourth, and whose normative three-into-one alliterative shape is also metrically symmetrical: duples figure in each half-line, duple duples in each line.[13] Now, whether such formal rhythms would have seemed suggestive to a poet writing about King Arthur or about the Siege of Jerusalem is open to question, but it can easily be imagined that a talented poet writing about the human soul, and about the Old and New Testaments, and about the Trinity, would have appreciated the shape of the English alliterative long line.[14] The correspondences between the shape of the line and the architectonic and thematic ideas in *Piers Plowman* will be clear from this list: its three realms, allegorically represented as toft, dale, and field; Will's quest for the triadic progressive perfection Dowel, Dobet, and Dobest; the three-tiered Tree of Charity; the tripartite *vita Christi*; the Four Daughters of God; the Cardinal Virtues; the division into *Visio* and *Vita* (with the *Vita* possibly tripartite);[15] in the B Version, the octave of dream visions, presented as four sets of two paired dreams, and with paired inner dreams.

For some readers, the actual narrative of *Piers Plowman*, episodic and digressive, may seem to weaken any authorial, scribal, or critical claims for overarching triadic and symmetrical design. Similarly, the typical effects of Langland's collocations—ironic, sardonic, strained, bitter, ferocious in their tensions and juxtapositions—may seem to belie a theologically motivated lineation. For example:

In **habite** as an **heremite, vnholy** <u>of werkes</u> (Prol. 3)
And han **wit** at **wille** to **werken** <u>if him liste</u> (Prol. 37)
I **sei3 somme** þat <u>seiden</u> þei hadde **ysou3t Seintes** (Prol. 50)
Siþ **charite** haþ ben **chapman** and **chief** <u>to shryue lordes</u> (Prol. 64)
Ac þe **parisshe preest** and þe **pardoner** <u>parten þe siluer</u> (Prol. 81)

But there is no essential conflict between a Christian faith in providential order and a Christian denunciation of sin. Langland displays, in one field, truth and falseness. As a Christian ironist, he
writes discursive incoherence into architectonic order, linguistic
conflict into symmetrically formed tropes and verses. Such are the
logical manifestations of an Augustinian (and Bonaventuran) poetic.[16]

## "Þat oon dooþ alle dooþ and ech dooþ bi his one"

Langland's most perfect line (16.183) illustrates the ideal form.
Piers speaks this line during Will's inner dream of the Tree of
Charity, where it characterizes the equal and cooperative powers
of the three staves supporting the tree. Allegorically, this line represents the Trinity. It is unique in its combination of stand-alone
syntax, indefinite diction, interwoven alliteration, flexible caesura,
and chiastic symmetry. It is, like so many of Langland's lines, con-
summately artful, but it differs from all others, and from *Piers
Plowman* generally, in its formal perfection, its balance, its stasis,
its remove from worldly particulars, its utterly abstract Realism.
This line translates, or transcends, such B-text equivalents as:

> *Deus pater, deus filius, deus spiritus sanctus* (10.246)
> Filius by þe fader wille and frenesse of spiritus sancti (16.88)
> *Spiritus procedens a patre & filio &c.* (16.223)
> So dooþ þe Sire and þe sone and also *spiritus sanctus* (17.212)

Such Latin or Latin-infused lines embody the verbal and doctrinal
authority of the Credo; they name the real subsistences, or persons, of the one divine essence. The English line communicates
not the proper names of the Trinity, but the quality of their individual yet united interactivity.[17] Although set within a human
temporal-spatial context of figural and figurative description, exposition, and narration, the line's singularly abstract statement

lacks even the sacred and doctrinally real (yet humanly conceived) metaphor of Father, Son, and Holy Spirit. Fleetingly, it expresses that "ungropable . . . ununderstandable" nature which *The Cloud of Unknowing* ascribes to the Godhead.

The line's diction[18] and syntax[19] can be construed variously, to produce these readings:

> *What one does all do, and each does on its own.*
> *What one does, all do and each does singularly.*
> *What the One does, All do and Each does by means of Oneness.*
> *The One does, all do, and each does—distinctly.*
> *The One does, All do, and Each does, as One.*

I take the line to mean all these, and more.[20] Insofar as it represents the Trinity,[21] it points to an essentially untranslatable mystery, whose essence it nevertheless attempts to mirror formally by means of its enfolding unitary chiasmus, its vocalic alliterative linking of plurality and singularity, and its coincident triadic internal alliterative repetition of the meta-verb "doop." The form of God is also revealed in three clauses and in rhythms of trisyllabic phrasing; in lineal self-sufficiency and wholeness; and in the self-referential, self-acting, self-reflecting, self-paralleling, and self-generating qualities of its chiastic signs. I can imagine this line as inspired by Augustine's syntax in *de Trinite* 6.12:

> *Ita et singula sunt in singulis et omnia in singulis et singula in omnibus et omnia in omnibus et unum omnia.*

> [So they are each in each and all in each, and each in all and all in all, and all are one.]

Augustine's sentence, however, is rhetorically but not numerologically theological. Langland would turn Augustine's stunningly abstract presentation into mimetic form.

But even supposing Langland to have been familiar with *de Trinitate* and to have known this sentence, his substitution "to do" for "to be," his translation, as it were, of essence into activity, must have a different source, one whose theology is more directly incarnational. In context, the staves Piers describes in this line are to be used by him, at Will's request, to knock down fruits from the Tree of Charity, precipitating the Fall and, soon, the Incarnation of Christ; the Trinitarian meaning of these staves will subsequently be explained by Abraham as pointing forward to the Passion and Resurrection. Langland's most perfectly nonworldly line participates, then, through analogy and concordance, in a conflux of psychological, moral, historical, ecclesiological, and theological processes. What happens during the Tree of Charity and Abraham/Faith episodes happens, quite literally, all over the place, internally and externally, then and now, temporally and eternally.

As Lawrence Clopper has noted, Langland's fluid typology in the fifth vision follows a decidedly Bonaventuran model:

> Bonaventura would not deny that the distinctions between typology, tropology, and anagogy are real any more than he would that the relations among the Persons of the trinity were; nevertheless, he is intent on asserting that in some mysterious way the threefold sense is but one, that it is identical in essence with the literal, and that each of the allegorical "senses" inheres in each and all of the others.[22]

Demonstrating Langland's conflation of historical and moral realities, Clopper cites these "novelties": Abraham/Faith and Moses/Hope as "personifications of completed figural relations; "the intrusion of a parabolic figure, the Samaritan-Charity, into the chronology when we expect the historical Christ to complete the typology"; the cross-referencing of Charity, the Samaritan, Piers, and Christ.[23] In addition, the figure of Will, who has previously struggled to recognize his proper psychological function, is now utterly engaged in the experience and communication of these realities. During the final four visions of *Piers Plowman*, Will's experience is at once moral, as the will of everyman, and historical, as it manifests itself in enacting Adam's sin, in witnessing the life, death, and resurrection of Christ, and in facing the tribulations of Antichrist at the Last Days.

Clopper's broader argument, that Langland was a disaffected Franciscan, seems to me unlikely despite the poet's admiration for St. Francis as an exemplar of saintly virtue, his interest in poverty, and his offended response to corruption in the Order.[24] Langland's antifraternalism, although bitterly sincere, is conventional, not topical enough to betray the views of a disaffected insider. Never-

theless, there are Franciscan resonances in *Piers*, the most basic of
which is, quite simply, the affective allegory itself: Will's penitential reformation through contemplating the *vita Christi*. But
Will's meditations on the life of Christ do not *feel* Franciscan; they
do not manifest themselves in sentimental lingering over the
sweet manifestations of God's mercy. Will does not kiss the feet of
the baby Jesus, but rather the Cross of Resurrection. Will's affective response—

> Ariseþ and reuerenceþ goddess resurrexion,
> And crepeþ to þe cros on knees and kisseþ it for a Iuwel
> For goddes blissede body it bar for oure boote . . .
>
> (18.427–29)

—is to God's work of salvation. As I read Langland's possible reading of Bonaventura's *Lignum Vitae*, the poet has taken from it its
triadic, hierarchical scheme, its Christocentric spirituality, and its
concision while rejecting the honeyed style of its meditations.
The influence is more conceptual than textual.

## The *Lignum vitae*

Bonaventura's work offers, uniquely within the *meditatio* tradition, a hierarchically organized, explicitly ramified presentation of
Christ's life. Like other examples of this emergent, extraordinarily
"popular" genre, it combines narrative, visualization, exposition,
and prayer to engage the reader (or listening audience) in affective
devotion. The arrangement of its matter, however, is neither in-
clusive, like a gospel harmony, nor temporally and spatially focused, like a Passion narrative. Nor does this arrangement reveal
the typically pastoral purpose of simplifying the central Christian
narrative and its affect for rudimentary penitential purposes.
Bonaventura selects events, images, themes, and moral lessons
from the Gospels so that their presentation will follow a theologically expansive yet spiritually focused contemplative program of
mystical union with Christ. The unifying image of the *Lignum
vitae*, within which its narrative, visualization, exposition, and
prayer are subsumed, is that of the Crucified Jesus. This image, at
once historical and eternal, human and divine, unites the threefold mysteries of Christ's Origin, Passion, and Glorification.

Bonaventura's methodology is conformative. To become one with God, the faculties of the human soul, of the image of God in man, must become fully engaged in contemplation of the divine image. Each chapter of the *Lignum vitae* typically entails a "progression from memory to intellect to will."[25] It treats an event in Christ's life by using quotation, narration, and visualization to engage the memory, exposition to engage the intellect, and exhortation and prayer to engage the will. This methodology is intriguing as a possible source for Will's own pattern of alternating visionary and expository experience between his inner dream of the Tree of Charity and his exhortation to prayer on Easter morning. Will, as that faculty properly moved to penance and prayer, as that faculty properly engaged in *kyndely* charity, has had grave difficulty (as he has confessed at length) communicating with his kindred faculties in the higher reason; it is only during his postpenitential *meditatio* on the life of Christ that he becomes receptive both to sacred historical memory, as seen in his visions, and to sacred exposition, as heard from Abraham/Faith, Moses/Hope, and the Samaritan/Charity.

If Langland read the *Lignum vitae*, he would have discovered therein not only the conventional Franciscan pedagogy in which imagination aids understanding, but a model and justification for presenting the life of Christ in a condensed, hierarchically ramified arrangement. Bonaventura's Prologue could not be more explicit in delineating these concordant triplets of ordinals, levels, and mysteries:

> Because imagination assists intelligence (*quoniam imaginatio iuvat intelligentiam*), I have arranged in the form of an imaginary tree the few passages selected from many, and have disposed them in such a way that, in the first or lower (*in prima et infima*) branches, the Savior's origin and life (*origo et vita*) are described; in the middle (*in media*) branches, His passion (*passio*); and in the top (*in suprema*) branches His glorification (*glorificatio*). The first (*in prima*) four branches have four quotations placed right and left in alphabetical order. So too with the second and third groups (*in secunda et tertia*) of branches. Growing from the tip of each branch hangs a single fruit. Thus we have, as it were, twelve fruits, in accordance with the mystery of the Tree of Life.
>
> (Prol. 2)[26]

Reading on, Langland would soon have found himself addressed in intimate imperatives and urged to form a mental picture of this tree (*describe in spiritu mentis tuae arborem*), to suppose its roots watered by an eternally gushing, Edenic fountain in the garden of the Church, and to suppose its twelve branches adorned with medicinal leaves and fragrant, variously hued flowers, as well as delicious fruits. Bonaventura explains that the Tree of Life has one Fruit "born of the virginal womb, and ripened on the tree of the cross to delectable maturity by the midday heat of the Eternal Sun, that is by Christ's love. It is the Fruit that is placed in the heavenly garden of Eden—God's table—as food for those who long for Him" (Prol. 3). Because the One God's conditions, powers, and acts are multiple, however, and so that the souls of the devout may accordingly be rewarded with a variety of consolations, twelve fruits are described.[27]

In Bonaventura's hierarchy, the one Tree, rooted in Eden, reaching to heaven, and bearing the crucified Jesus, images the triune incarnational mysteries of Origin, Passion, and Glorification. Each mystery in turn bears four fruits, which are divine attributes or virtues:

> DE MYSTERIO ORIGINIS
> 1 *Praeclaritas originis* (Brilliance of Origin)
> 2 *Humilitas conversationis* (Humility of Living)
> 3 *Celstitudo virtutis* (Loftiness of Power)
> 4 *Plenitudo pietatis* (Plenitude of Mercy)
> DE MYSTERIO PASSIONIS
> 5 *Confidentia in periculis* (Heroism in Trials)
> 6 *Patientia in iniuriis* (Patience under Mistreatment)
> 7 *Constantia in suppliciis* (Fortitude under Torture)
> 8 *Victoria in conflictu mortis* (Victory over Death)
> DE MYSTERIO GLORIFICATIONIS
> 9 *Novitas resurrectionis* (Wonder of Resurrection)
> 10 *Sublimitas ascensionis* (Sublimity of Ascension)
> 11 *Aequitas iudicii* (Equity of Judgment)
> 12 *Aeternitas regni* (Eternity of Kingdom)[28]

The taste of these fruits refreshes the soul; their nourishment in turn strengthens the soul who meditates on them "if he abhors the example of unfaithful Adam, who preferred the Tree of the Knowledge of Good and Evil to the Tree of Life."[29]

Each branch bears four leaves, and it is at this level of subordination that Bonaventura offers his meditations.[30] Thus, for example, under the first fruit of *Praeclaritas originis* occur meditations on (1) Jesus begotten of God, (2) Jesus prefigured, (3) Jesus sent down from Heaven, and (4) Jesus born of Mary. Under the seventh fruit of *Constantia in suppliciis*: (1) Jesus despised by all; (2) Jesus nailed to the cross; (3) Jesus linked with robbers; (4) Jesus made to drink gall. Under the tenth fruit *Sublimitas ascensionis*: (1) Jesus, leader of the host; (2) Jesus risen to heaven; (3) Jesus, giver of the Spirit; (4) Jesus, forgiver of sins.

The meditations typically combine brief narration of an event from the life of Christ, a scriptural quotation, a summary moralization, an affirmation of God's purpose, and a hortatory appeal to the reader's affection. Discursive commentary on a scriptural event is followed by personal and indeed intimate imaginative engagement. Under "Jesus sent down from heaven," Bonaventura begins by associating the six days of Creation prefiguratively with the Sixth Age of mankind inaugurated at the *plenitudo temporis* (Gal. 4.40), when Gabriel was sent to the Virgin. Bonaventura then presents the Incarnation as an awesome mystery explicated with carefully theological definition:

> After she consented to his word, the Holy Spirit descended upon her in the form of a divine fire in perfect purity, and the power of the Most High overshadowed her, to enable her to bear such fire. Instantly, by the operation of that power, a body was formed, a soul created, and both were united to the Godhead in the Person of the Son; so that this same Person was God and man, with the properties of each nature unimpaired (*qua operante in instanti corpus fuit formatum, anima create et simul utrumque Divinitati in persona Filii counitum, ut idem esset Deus et homo, salva utriusque proprietate naturae*). (1.3)

Now turning directly to address his putative contemplative, Bonaventura employs this apostrophe:

> (*O si valeres utcumque sentire . . .* ) If you could perceive the splendor and magnitude of this flame sent down from heaven, the refreshing breeze that came down with it, the consolation it poured forth; if you could understand the loftiness of Mary's elevation, the glorification of humanity, the condescension of divine

Majesty; if you could hear the Virgin singing her delight; if you could accompany her into the hill country and witness how the woman who had been barren embraced her and greeted her with words by which the tiny servant recognized his Lord, the herald announced the Judge, the voice proclaimed the Word—oh, surely then, together with the Blessed Virgin, you would most sweetly sing this holy canticle: "My soul magnifies the Lord . . ." (*Magnificat anima mea Dominum, etc.*); surely, then, with the infant prophet, you would joyfully and jubilantly adore the marvel of the virgin conception.

(1.3)

We shall not find this theological precision, or thematic control, or florid style, or apostrophe, or enthusiasm, or periodic syntax in Langland's version of the Annunciation.

For Langland, the *plenitudo temporis* is not fulfilled at the Annuncation, but at the Nativity—humanized, punningly, in reference to Mary's pregnancy, and further humanized in prefigurative reference to Jesus' just Joust against Satan, to the Christ-Knight on the Cross:

> And þanne spak *spiritus sanctus* in Gabrielis mouþe
> To a maide þat hiȝte Marie, a meke þyng wiþalle,
> That oon Iesus a Iustices sone moste Iouke in hir chambre
> Til *plenitudo temporis* tyme comen were
> That Piers fruyt floured and felle to be rype.
> And þanne sholde Iesus Iuste therfore bi Iuggement of armes,
> Wheiþer sholde fonge þe fruyt, þe fend or hymselue.
> The maide myldeliche þo þe messager graunted,
> And seide hendeliche to hym, "Lo me his handmaiden
> For to werchen his wille wiþouten any synne:
> *Ecce ancilla Domini; fiat michi secundum verbum tuum.*

(16.90–99)

In this passage, the Incarnation is treated not as a matter for theological definition and affective wonder, but as theologically rich *poetry*. The alliterative collocations are pointedly, and conventionally, doctrinal in their thematic links ("maide," "Marie," "meke"; "fonge," "fruyt," "fynd"; "Iesus," "Iuste," "Iuggement"), yet they communicate as well a familiar English homeliness. The maid Mary behaves, in parallel, both "myldeliche" and "hendeliche." Her consent, "to werchen his wille wipouten any synne," is at once precisely theological and teasingly erotic. The focus is on Mary's meekness rather than magnificence, yet Mary's meekness is highlighted in contradistinction to the heroism of Jesus's incarnate mission.[31] The entire passage, larger in import yet narrower in reach than its Bonaventuran counterpart, concentrates on the typology of Incarnation and Passion. To this end, Langland omits Bonaventura's elaborative treatment of the Visitation and of John the Baptist's *in utero* jubilation. Langland's lines contain no elegantly contemplative exaltation, but rather a lightly understated, richly allusive narration. In sum, the poetry hardly suggests the *Lignum Vitae* as a source *text*. Yet Langland's treatment shares with Bonaventura's a concise, almost allusive treatment of the event, and it differs utterly from the temporally coherent narrative treatment found in other Englished *vitae Christi*. Moreover, it contains one line whose collocations seem, intriguingly, to encapsulate Bonaventura's Prologue: "That Piers **fruyt floured** and **felle to be rype**."

The immediate reference, of course, is to the Tree of Charity just envisioned by Will. The above lines, in fact, inaugurate Will's visions of the life of Christ, and they immediately follow Piers's assault on Satan with "*Filius* by pe fader wille and frenesse of *spiritus sancti*" (16.88)—a line displaying unmistakenly Bonaventuran exemplarism. At this point Will has already requested that Piers "pulle adoun an appul" (16.73), and Piers has "caste to the crop" (75)—with one of his Trinitarian staves?—and shaken the very tree, facilitating the Fall just dramatized by Will. In one line (81), the patriarchs and prophets fall to the ground, to be seized by Satan, and this brings us immediately, and with theological economy, to the *plenitudo temporis*.[32]

The Tree of Charity is itself Bonaventuran. Rooted in Eden and reaching to heaven, it images the Trinity as an active moral power in salvation history; and Will's contemplation of it yields the life of Christ. That, surely, is its main meaning; yet, also like Bonaventura's tree, it yields many and various other meanings.[33] As in the *Lignum vitae*, much is made of its flowers, leaves, and fruits,[34] and of its three levels,[35] all of which have multiple significations; yet these are ruminations, *distinctiones*, on an essentially simple truth: Charity *is* a Tree (16.4) whose fruit is charity (16.9). Such Bonaventuran chiasmus, multifoliation, and redundancy recur again and again during Will's inner dream of Piers and Charity.

The Tree of Charity, also named Patience,[36] has three props, three tiers of branches, and three stages of growth; is attacked by the sins of the world, the flesh, and the devil; is protected by the Father, the Son, and the Holy Spirit; and finally, "þe Trinite it meneþ" (63). To define the props that support the tree is to define the tree itself (53–63). The props and the tree are both single and triadic. Many fruits grow on the tree, and a singular fruit (66) "hangeþ" on the tree. If one is tempted to conclude, merely, that Langland throughout this episode lacks control over his narrative, or that the sequence of impressions is simply dreamlike in its confusion, it helps to review almost any paragraph in the *Lignum vitae*, against which a similar complaint may be lodged.[37]

## WILL'S VISIONS OF
## THE LIFE OF CHRIST

Three such visions occur from Passus 16 through 19. These correspond to Bonaventura's three tiers insofar as they treat Origin and Life, Passion, and Glorification. Will's visions share Bonaventura's principle of selectivity in the *events* of Jesus's life and his interest in subordinating these events to higher theological mysteries. Just as the *Lignum vitae*'s leaves must be viewed hierarchically, as spatially and temporally distinct (and therefore piecemeal) entities, so Will's *vita Christi* visions shift focus suddenly, often without surface narrative coherence, as if leaping from ramification to ramification. Events, usually briefly narrated, sometimes alluded to by a Latin tag, sometimes locked in a single line, alternate with commentary. These events are selected for their theological aptness.

Many events treated by Bonaventura (such as the Transfiguration) are omitted in *Piers Plowman*, yet Langland at times seems to have selected the same ones as has Bonaventura. For example, in Passus 18 we find depicted, in quick succession, Jesus despised, nailed to the cross, linked with robbers, and made to drink gall. These very events are covered in discrete meditations under the Seventh Fruit (*Constantia in suppliciis*); they are recapitulated in this fruit's fourth meditation on "Jesus Made to Drink Gall," during an apostrophe to the Virgin Mary, as a rapid series of dolorous imaginings:

You were present at all these events, standing close by and taking part in them in every possible way. This sacred and most holy flesh you had so chastely conceived, so tenderly nourished and sustained with your milk, so often held in your arms and kissed with your lips, so often gazed upon with your bodily eyes, you now seen torn by the blows of the scourging, then pierced with the barbs of the thorns, then struck with a reed, then battered by hands and fists, then transfixed with nails, then attached to the wood of the cross and opened with a spear, then mocked in all possible ways, and, finally, made to drink vinegar and gall!

Might Langland have appropriated the sequencing of events under the *Lignum vitae*'s Seventh Fruit, and might he have taken the pace of these events in this apostrophe as a model for his own treatment? Quite possibly, but the point of such comparisons, again, is not to argue that Langland must have "followed" Bonaventura, or that Langland drew only on the *Lignum vitae* for his *vita Christi* visions. More important is the possibility that Langland has used the Bonaventuran model of hierarchical and typological, rather than chronological, coherence—a model elsewhere unavailable. In *Piers Plowman*, as in the *Lignum vitae*, the birth of Jesus anticipates the Passion, and the pain of the Passion—never contemplated with lingering, morbid fascination—anticipates the joy of Redemption. In lieu of sustained narrative treatment, both works perform quick typological leaps.

In Will's first *vita Christi* vision (16.90–165), all of the events illustrate the Origin and Life—and all anticipate the Passion. These are: Annunciation (90–99); Birth (100–102); Miracles of Healing (103–16); Jesus Acclaimed Messiah [and vilified by unbelieving Jews] (117–26): Overturning the Tables in the Temple (127–35); Last Supper, Judas's Kiss, and Betrayal (136–66).[38] Langland, in his relatively condensed version, omits much of the matter treated by Bonaventura, and emphasizes Jesus's castigation of the moneychangers, which Bonaventura sweetly omits. More importantly, Langland transposes the Betrayal, the first event under Passion in the *Lignum vitae*, into the final event of Jesus's human life. This difference has two important effects: it reinforces the emphasis on the teleological, Passion-directed meaning of Jesus's life, and it adds narrative momentum toward the climax on Calvary. Our reading experience throughout this vision is that of a fast-forwarded *Lignum vitae*. We witness Will witnessing, quickly, the story of salvation. All the events in this "sequence" are prefigura-tive; all illustrate a higher providential design; all are narrated so as to reveal how Origin and Life anticipate the Passion. As Jesus increasingly inserts prophetic speeches stressing his role as the healer of mankind, the builder of the New Temple, the conqueror of Death, the coherence of these events emerges as thematic, hier-archical, theological, poetic.

A more expansive understanding of Will's first *vita Christi* vi-sion is that, following immediately upon the Tree of Charity episode (which functions as a kind of Prologue analogous to that in the *Lignum vitae*), this vision constitutes itself as the first of three *human* manifestations of Christ's life; and that, as such, it is meant to be understood in conjunction with Will's subsequent vi-sions of Abraham/Faith, Moses/Hope, and the Samaritan/Charity. According to this model, Will first contemplates the whole Tree, in which are figured the Trinity, the human Trinitarian image of the soul, all salvation history, and the whole Life of Christ. Will then sees, briefly, a succession of authorized gospel events, and then, as commentary on these events, he learns about the history of humanity between Fall and Incarnation, and about the nature of God, as Trinity, and Unity, and Love. In other words, Will's first vi-sion of Christ in his humanity, although pointedly referencing, both literally and figuratively, the theological mystery of the Ori-gin and Life, is also set within a framework of discourse which ex-plicitly comments on their divine Origin and their place with in God's providential order.

Similarly, Will's second *vita Christi* vision (Passus 18) treats the Passion as a series of final *human* events—each also revealing di-vinity—followed by an allegorical commentary on, and dramatiza-tion of, the salvific power of these events. And just as the Origin and Life had earlier anticipated and prefigured the Passion, so here the Passion points to Glorification. The *visibilia* seen by Will are the Entry into Jerusalem (6–35); Trial (36–45); Jesus Despised and the Crown of Thorns (46–49); Crucifixion (50–55); Death, Earth-quake, Eclipse (56–77; Jesus Pierced by Longinus' Lance (78–91); False Jews Cursed by Faith (92–109). At this point Will withdraws into the deeper, mysterious darkness of *descendit ad inferna* (111) —analogous to his earlier inner dreams—and there witnesses the Harrowing of Hell (111–427).[39] Langland, if working directly from the *Lignum vitae*, has here transposed from its first chapter under

Glorification (*Iesus, triumphans mortuus*) the Harrowing of Hell and the Victory over Death. In any case, he has certainly relied on the *Gospel of Nicodemus* for his Longinus episode and various details in the Harrowing, and he has boldly transposed the Four Daughters of God allegory from its conventional placement (in [pseudo-]Bonaventura's *Meditationes vitae Christi*) in justification of the Incarnation to its new location at the climax of the Passion.[40]

Will's initial gospel-based vision of the Passion does not linger over the human suffering and death of Christ, the normally attenuated and cruelly coherent sequence of abuse and torture; instead, it emphasizes providential justice, mercy, and grace, the victory of incarnate divine power over mortal human sin. At Christ's willed death—

> *Consummatum est*, quod Crist, and comsede for to swoune,
> Pitousliche and pale as a prison pat deiep,
> The lord of lif and of light po leide hise eighen togideres.
> (18.57–59)

—the perfect mingling of pathos and power is expressed in the rhythmic pairing of normative *aa|ax* lines, one each for divinity and humanity; in following, uniquely six-stressed *aaa|axx* line, which sequences divine status and the final human mortal act; in the juxtaposition of qualifiers and simile (literal yet figurative); and even in the dictional descent from Scriptural Latin and universal Name, through recently French "comsede," to the emphatically common English "swoune."[41] Deep in hell, and emerging from the allegorical commentary, this same Lord of Light will blind Satan, embrace the captive souls in his light of love, and proclaim in theologically organized plain English his legal right:

> Lucifer loke ne my3te, so light hym ablente.
> And þo þat oure lord louede into his lighte he laughte,
> And seide to Sathan, 'lo! Here my soule to amendes
> For alle synfulle soules, to saue þo þat ben worpi.
> Myne pei ben and of me; I may þe bet hem cleyme.
> (18.325–29)

Will's third *vita Christi* vision concerns Glorification. As a showing of humanity, it is very brief indeed, manifested in the appearance of Christ Resurrected, at the beginning of Passus 19:

> and sodeynly me mette
> That Piers þe Plowman was peynted al blody
> And com in wiþ a cros before þe commune peple,
> And ri3t like in alle lymes to oure lord Iesu.
>
> (19.5–8)

Will's dialogue with Conscience immediately follows, soon evolving into Conscience's homiletic commentary on the names of Jesus and Christ—itself consisting mostly of a narrative *vita Christi* (26–199). There follows a vision of Pentecost, the Division of Grace, and the Establishment of the Church (201–336), but no sooner is the House of Unity constructed from the timber of the Cross than it is assaulted by the forces of Antichrist. For the rest of Passus 19, and during all of Passus 20, the general view is that of an unregenerate society misled by Antichrist's men. The poem thus seems to conclude pessimistically.

## CONSCIENCE'S *VITAE CHRISTI* AND PIERS THE PLOWMAN'S PARADIGM

However, Conscience's sermon offers a higher perspective than that possible from a standpoint within corrupt worldly institutions. Recapitulating Will's previous three visions, Conscience asserts that the true meaning—and ultimate definition—of Dowel, Dobet, and Dobest is to be found in Christ's life. "Jesus," and "Christ" (the human and divine names) denote, as Conscience explains, one and the same person, much as a one nobleman may attain three successive ranks and titles:[42]

> That knyght, kyng, conquerour may be o persone.
> To be called a knyght is fair, for men shul knele to hym.
> To be called a kyng is fairer, for he may knyghtes make.
> Ac to be conquerour called, þat comeþ of special grace.
>
> (19.27–30)

Following this analogy, Conscience focuses not on Christ's dual human and divine natures, but on the positive, comparative, and superlative goodness manifested in Christ's life (34–62): a knight during the Ministry; a king when crowned with thorns on the Cross; a conqueror over Death. This triad of progressive perfection forms a typology of unity, mirroring the typology of unity inherent in the mysteries of Origin, Passion, Glorification. As Conscience will soon make clear, the holy names refer to one person, God and man: Jesus, who was born and died like common, sinful humanity, is also the resurrected Christ.[43]

But meanwhile Conscience offers moral commentary on Will's vision of this resurrected Christ. Conscience links the suffering of the crucified Jesus with our common suffering of tribulations in this world. Both are cooperatively providential. Basic to Conscience's message is the consolation of this common, saving suffering, whose essential spirituality is expressed in the *Lignum vitae's* opening words: *Christo confixus sum cruci* (Gal. 2.19).

> Ac þe cause þat he comeþ þus wiþ cros of his passion
> Is to wissen vs þerwiþ, þat whan we ben tempted,
> Therwith to fi3te and fenden vs fro fallynge into synne,
> And se bi his sorwe þat whoso loveþ ioye,
> To penaunce and to pouerte he moste puten hymseluen,
> And muche wo in þis world willen and suffren.
>
> (63–68)

Conscience here urges the *imitatio Christi* of willing suffering as a means to final joy. To do well, according to Conscience, is to will to do what Christ has done. In referring to our need to suffer "muche wo in þis world," Conscience also characterizes the rule of Antichrist which pervades the concluding passus of *Piers Plowman.* When in the poem's final speech Conscience vows to undertake a new pilgrimage "to seken Piers þe Plowman," and when Will then, hearing Conscience cry after Grace, himself awakes, this conclusion means, I believe, that a life of willing suffering is indeed possible in this world of sin, and that this life will lead from "sorwe" to "ioye."

Conscience's second *vita Christi* narrative[44] communicates that faith and hope in divine justice that characterize Bonaventura's treatment of Glorification. It recapitulates the entire sequence of Christ's life *sub specie aeterni.* It treats the Nativity (70–74), the Gifts of the Magi (75–95), the Hidden Life of trials and fasting (96–107), the Miracle at Cana and later Ministry (108–39), Crucifixion, Death, and Burial (140–48), the Resurrection (149–53), Appearances to Mary Magdalen and the Apostles (154–82), the

Foundation of the Church under Peter/Piers (183–91), the Ascension (192), and finally the Rule of the King of Heaven (193–97) and the promise of Judgment to come:

> The goode to the Godhede and to greet joye,
> And wikkede to wonye in wo withouten ende.
>
> (198–99)

Analogous to the Samaritan's role in anticipating the Passion, and to the role of the Daughters of God in anticipating the Resurrection, Conscience's role as commentator on Will's vision of the Resurrection is to offer both consolation against the tribulations of Antichrist and clarity about the eternal, divine power manifest in the Christ's Glorification. If Will—and the reader—can remember Conscience's moral and, here, anagogic advice, maintaining faith in God's rule, then even the "wo in pis world" will all be understood as providential, and sufferable.

Not only does Conscience's homiletic commentary include a version of Glorification that affirms divine providence, but his organization of the Life of Christ conforms, once again, with the Bonaventuran scheme. The names of Jesus and Christ, and the progressive perfection of Dowel, Dobet, and Dobest, follow the chronology *and* hierarchy *and* typology of the theological mysteries:

| Origin | Passion | | Glorification |
|--------|---------|---|---------------|
| Dowel | Dobet | > | Dobest |
| Knight | King | > | Conqueror |
| *Jesus, filius Marie* | *Jesus, filius David* | > | *Christus resurgens* |

Within the Trinity, as we have seen, divine doing is self-contained, self-sufficient, and coequal: "Þat oon doop alle doop and ech doop bi his one." However, God's creation initiates time, and God intercedes temporally in human history, most centrally by becoming incarnate as man. Within its human chronology and embodied in human nature, the life of Christ is progressive, hierarchical, and perfected, and in this form it may be understood and imitated. With respect to the triadic *sequence* of theological mysteries, all three are providentially cooperative in the eternal intelligence of God; seen within their human chronology, however, the Origin and Passion can be seen as cooperative in the final causation of Glorification—calling to mind Clergie's memory of Piers's superior paradigm:

> And no text ne takeþ to mayntene his cause
> But *Dilige deum* and *Domine quis habitabit;*
> And demeþ that dowel and dobet arn two Infinites,
> Wich Infinites wiþ a feiþ fynden out dobest,
> Which shal saue mannes soule; þus seiþ Piers þe Plowman.
> (13.126–30)

According to Piers's paradigm, salvation is attained through the two "infinites" of charity and dwelling with God. Applied to Will's life, this paradigm in effect describes Will's situation after he has envisioned the Tree of Charity and come to dwell in the house of Unity, and it suggests that he may rightly hope for salvation.

As we have seen, the way to salvation in *Piers Plowman* is through the Will's *kyndly* love of Christ, and his triadic visions of the *vita Christi* are instrumental in his cultivation of charity. Under Conscience's tutelage, Will learns that his long quest for Dowel, Dobet, and Dobest has come to fruition in the triadic mysteries of Christ's life, and that he need only imitate that ultimate paradigm, cooperatively, by "muche wo in pis world willen and suffren" to find the Dobest of final joy. The form of Will's learning is *trielich ymaked* in a strikingly Bonaventuran manner, and was learned, as I believe, from the Lignum vitae.

## APPENDIX: THE *LIGNUM VITAE* IN MEDIEVAL ENGLISH MANUSCRIPTS

The *Lignum vitae* circulated widely in late medieval Europe, and ample evidence exists for its availability in England by the 1370s outside the Franciscan Order. It is usually found in miscellany manuscripts, where it finds company with various patristic, ascetic, contemplative, and homiletic works.[45]

In the Prolegomena to the Quaracchi ed., Vol. 8, xli–l, are listed 175 manuscripts containing the *Lignum vitae*, twelve of them from England. These are, at Cambridge, University Library Ff.VI.24

(15th c.) and Peterhouse 203 (15th c.); in London, Harleian 1801 (14th c.), Harleian 3227 (15th c.), Harleian 3995 (15th c.), British Library, Royal 11.B.iii (14th c.), Arundel 507 (14th c.), Cotton Vespasian E.1 (15th c.), and British Library Additional 15404 (13th c.); and at Oxford, Bodleian Canonici 328 (1445), Rawlinson C.116 (14th c.), and Laud Misc. 181 (14th c.). With the exception of Laud 181, inscribed as *"quondam fratrum montis S. Michaelis prope Moguntiam* (Maintz) *ord. Carthus.,"* we may assume an English provenance. Ephrem Longpré supplements the Quaracchi list with—in addition to a French poetic translation and a Latin synoptic version adapted to the canonical hours—another seven Latin transcriptions, one from England but of Venetian provenance.[46] To these we can add Manchester John Rylands Library Latin 153[47] and Bodleian Laud Misc. 402,[48] both English.

Medieval manuscript catalogues offer evidence of additional copies. *The Corpus of British Medieval Library Catalogues* so far lists four, including the above-cited Peterhouse manuscript, donated in 1440. No longer extant were two books containing the *Lignum vitae* in the library of the York Austin Friars, catalogued in 1372, and a third at Syon Abbey, probably not catalogued till the end of the fifteenth century.[49] All told, we know of at least 182 manuscripts, fourteen of these probably written in England.

Beyond the fact that the *Lignum vitae* was owned by Augustinian communities at York and Brentford in the late fourteenth and late fifteenth centuries, respectively, our knowledge of specific provenance is limited to six manuscripts. British Museum Additional 15404 is catalogued as having formally belonged to the Cistercian abbey of St. Mary of Camberon, in Hainault (Essex). Another book of Cistercian provenance is John Rylands Latin 153 (undated), from Byland Abbey (Yorkshire). Laud Misc. 402, written in thirteenth-, fourteenth-, and fifteenth-century hands, is catalogued as "from Durham"; another Durham book is the tri-lingual Arundel 507, which contains notations *"Ricardi de Segbrok, monachi Dunelmensis"* dated 1396. Royal 11.B.iii, in an early fourteenth-century hand, belonged to Bury St. Edmunds Abbey. Of Rawlinson 116, we have record only of its having been purchased from *"frater Johannes de Pacwode."*

Although we must imagine that the *Lignum vitae* was owned by Franciscan Friaries, no direct evidence confirms this. However, two manuscripts pieced together over time include sequences of Bonaventuran *opuscula* (Laud 181 and Cambridge Univ. Lib. Ff.VI.24), and the John Rylands book contains only Bonaventura (*Breliloquium, Intinerarium mentis ad Deum, De triplica via, Lignum vitae*). Whether such authorial sets are evidence of an "in-house" Franciscan culture or of a broader interest in Bonaventura's contemplative work is a matter of speculation. In either case, it is clear that the *Lignum vitae* enjoyed a fourteenth-century readership that included Benedictines, Augustinian Friars, and Cistercians, and that by the first half of the fifteenth century its audience had expanded to university students.

Most of the earlier *Lignum vitae* manuscripts are miscellanies. Aside from the exclusively Bonaventuran John Rylands Latin 153, the most unusual manuscript in terms of content is also the earliest: British Museum Additional 15404, a thirteenth-century quarto containing *Lignum vitae*, a life of Judas Iscariot, a life of Pontius Pilate, and Petrus Alphonsus's *Twelve Dialogues* [between a Christian and a Jew] *on the Superiority of the Christian Law*. The early fourteenth-century Royal 11.B.iii is especially important for *Lignum vitae* iconography in England: it contains the drawing of Christ Crucified on the Tree of Life, printed in the Quaracchi edition, Vol. 8, 68. Yet Royal 11.B.iii is a miscellany, including among its thirty-one items Peraldus, two miracles of the Virgin, the *Tractatus decustodia cordis*, Grosseteste's *Summa de decem mandatis*, several sermons, a table of the sacraments, extracts from Seneca, extracts from *Barlaam and Josaphat*, two hymns in French, a French treatise on the Fifteen Joys of the Virgin, notes on various texts to be included in sermons, and a medical recipe for an ointment called *gratia dei*; the *Lignum vitae*, in other words, finds its place here among a number of practical, homiletic works. One of the books catalogued by the York Austin Friars in 1372 held Richard of St. Victor's *Liber Benjamin*, the *Lignum vitae*, an excerpt from Walter Map's *De nugis curialium*, and Fulgentius' *Expositio sermonum antiquorum*; the other lists *"liber de ligno"* between Bartholomeus Anglicanus' *De naturis rerum* and the apocryphal *Gospel of Nicodemus*. Laud Misc. 402, combining texts written from the thirteenth to the fifteenth century, also includes the *Gospel of Nicodemus*, a number of Latin poems, and works by John Peccham, Hugh of St. Victor, Robert Grosseteste, and others.

The fourteenth-century Harleian 1801 inserts *"Meditatio sive Contemplatio Fratris Bonaventure, de D.N.J.C"* immediately after its sequence of Bonaventuran titles; it also contains works by Richard of St. Victor, Anselm, and Augustine, a Bernardine meditation beginning *"Multi multi sciunt, et seipsos nesciunt,"* and a French poem on "Merci, Verite, Justise, et Pes," In the fourteenth-century Rawlinson 116, the *Lignum vitae* finds its place with Anselm, John Chrystostom, Seneca, John Peccham's *Collationes de omnibus dominicus per annum, sive super Evangelia homiliae breves*, Aristotle, Bernard's *Sermo de "Missus est Angelus"* and *De quatuor virtutibus cardinalibu*. Finally, the fourteenth-century Arundel 507 features the *Lignum vitae* as its first work (written in part in a thirteenth-century hand). This is followed immediately by the English lyric, "Synful man loke vp and se," with subsequent items including an *Oratio ad D. N. Jesum Christum*, schemata of the seven works of the Passion and the Ten Commandments *in forma scala*, the Lignum vitae itself *eum expositione brevi*, an *Arbor vitiorum* and an *Arbor virtutum*, a history of the origin and discovery of the True Cross, in French, English treatises on the sins of the mouth, on cleanness, on the love of God, and on the Passion, a summary of Christian faith and duty (written about 1357, by John de Caterige, monk of York, in consequence of the Archbishop's order that the laity be instructed on Sundays in their vernacular tongue), some leonine verses, a narrative in French verse on the danger of incontinence, and works by Anselm, Rolle, and others.

The contents of these *Lignum vitae* manuscripts—homiletic, poetic, exegetical, schematic, and contemplative—would have appealed to many of Langland's clerical interests and aims in *Piers Plowman*. Langland certainly made use of several of the works appearing in them. The point is not that Langland read any of the particular manuscripts just described, but that the *Lignum vitae* was copied or collated along with other works congenial to his intellectual interests. The fifteenth-century manuscripts, also characteristically miscellaneous, continue to accommodate both the *Gospel of Nicodemus* (Cotton Vespasian E.1) and *Meditationes vitae Christi* (Syon manuscript #740). Although we need not imagine it, Langland could have found in one book three texts that inspired his B-continuation: the *Lignum vitae*, the *Gospel of Nic-*

*odemus,* and some version, probably in the *Meditationes vitae Christi,* of the Four Daughters of God allegory.

## NOTES

1. My topic here might seem situated far, far away from Robert Hollander's influence, for William Langland, whoever he was, never read Dante and can hardly be called a Humanist. Langland's inspiration came from Lady Holy Church, not Beatrice. Yet it was Professor Hollander, along with D. W. Robertson, Jr., and John Fleming, who taught me early on to value medieval studies and to love the great fourteenth-century poets. In an undergraduate Princeton course on Three European Masterworks, we read the *Commedia, Don Quixote,* and *Faust*—all in translation, of course, but the Dante came in Italian and English, and Hollander would read to us from time to time in *terza rima.* Although I had no idea what he was saying, his almost hedonistic devotion to the sheer *poetry* validated my own subjective response to literature. His cruel exam on Dante consisted of nothing but 100 identifications, teaching us that textual immersion—the literal sense—must precede all plausible allegorization, medieval or modern. Much later, in Professor Hollander's graduate seminar on Allegory, we read Prudentius, and I saw, during our broad investigation of the theory of allegory, some ways in which the *Psychomachia* responded textually both to Virgil and to Scripture. Robert Hollander thus guided and encouraged my thinking toward what would become my first book, *Prudentius' Psychomachia: a Reexamination.* For the past thirty years I have been reading *Piers Plowman* with pleasure, attention to detail, and curiosity about its intellectual and aesthetic coherences—a labor of love soon to find its conclusion in a book on Langland's poetics. I learned this threefold habit of reading from Robert Hollander.

2. All citations are from *Piers Plowman: The B Version.,* ed. Kane and Donaldson (London: Athlone Press, 1975). If Langland read the *Lignum vitae,* its influence would first become evident in the B-Text, which in turn would seem to manifest most clearly, in its design and lineation, such influence.

3. Engagement with the *Lignum vitae* might also have prompted several revisions within the *Visio,* such as the insertion of the "plante of pees" lines (1.152–68) into Holy Church's speech. Here the exquisitely rich yet compact conflation of figurative imagery—of linden leaves, needle (of compunction?), lightness, love, heaviness, and eating—in association with incarnational and sacramental reference seems Bonaventuran in style and import. When Holy Church newly compares, with wry theological wit, her legitimate holy lineage and her status as Bride to Lady Mede's illegitimacy (2.20–35), she perhaps directly anticipates the Tree of Charity (35), and her Latin line, *"Qualis pater talis filius: Bona arbor bonum fructum facit"* (27), usually understood as an odd combination of homely proverb and scriptural quotation (Mt 7:17), is surely Christological, and may allude to the *Lignum vitae* itself.

4. These include multiple dream visions, dreams within dreams; English-Latin shifts, episodic digressions, modal shifts like that into the Rat Parliament, and the sententious landmarks on the pilgrimage to Truth.

5. See Hoyt N. Duggan, "The Shape of the B-Verse in Middle English Alliterative Poetry," *Speculum* 61 (1986): 564–92; Thomas Cable, "Old and Middle English Prosody: Transformations of the Model," in *Hermeneutics and Medieval Culture*, ed. Patrick J. Gallacher and Helen Damico (Albany: New York University Press, 1989), 201–11.

6. The extended *a*-lines and "weak staves" (alliteration on function words) were both acknowledged as Langlandian by Kane and Donaldson in their Athlone edition. For an anatomy of Langland's alliterative practice, see A. V. C. Schmidt, *The Clerkly Maker: Langland's Poetic Art* (Cambridge: D. S. Brewer, 1987).

7. Lawrence M. Clopper briefly claims and illustrates the Bonaventuran, expemplarist poetic in *"Songes of Rechelesnesse": Langland and the Franciscans* (Ann Arbor: Michigan University Press, 1997), 128–32. Here he argues that "the verse form enables Langland to generate trinitarian 'names' at the line level," as for example in 2.134: "**Werchep** by **wisdom** and by **wit** after" (naming the Father, Son, and Holy Spirit).

8. Stephen A. Barney, "Langland's Mighty Line," in *William Langland's Piers Plowman: A Book of Essays*, ed. Kathleen M. Hewett-Smith (New York: Routledge, 2001), 103–17. The best appreciation is by George Kane, "Music 'Neither Unpleasant nor Monotonous,'" in George Kane, ed., *Chaucer and Langland: Historical and Textual Approaches* (London: The Athlone Press, 1989), 77–89.

9. Anne Middleton, "Narration and the Invention of Experience: Episodic Form in *Piers Plowman*," in *The Wisdom of Poetry: Essays in Early English Literature in Honor of Morton W. Bloomfield*, ed. Larry D. Benson and Siegfried Wenzel (Kalamazoo: Medieval Institute Publications, 1982), 91–122.

10. He was also an innovator in the use of running alliteration, such as the two **d**-lines here, sometimes for thematic emphasis, sometimes for semantic smearing, sometimes for mimesis—as when pardoners, parish priests, and their poor victims associate several lines in a row, till the silver is divvied up. When used by other alliterative poets, running alliteratation usually impresses itself as mere ostentation.

11. See Appendix.

12. Of the English Ricardian poets, only Chaucer read and used Dante. For example, St. Bernard's prayer in *Paradiso* 33 finds its way into the Prologue of the *Second Nun's Tale*, whose hagiographic maturity is made to contrast ironically with the Prioress's infantile Marian piety; the Wife of Bath borrows from the *Convivio* to assert her anti-male-authoritarian concept of nobility of character. Langland, I think, would have been puzzled by the convoluted style of Dante's Bonaventura, preferring Bonaventura in the original, but like Dante Langland pairs Dominick and Francis (15.421; 20.252). Langland would have applauded Dante's nostalgic idealization of St. Francis, his bitterness at the Order's current spiritual laxity and avarice, and his centrist position vis-à-vis

the radical Spirituals. And it goes without saying that he shares Dante's commitment to the potential sacredness of the vernacular. For Langland, "Latin" can mean both Latin, literally, and spiritual truth, both figuratively and in its English incarnations. As I shall demonstrate elsewhere, the prosody of Langland's phrasal groupings is indebted to Vulgate rhythms, and Langland even quotes Latin lines that alliterate in an English manner (e.g., "*Amen, amen, receperunt mercedem suam,*" 3.254) and composes macaronic lines with intellectually brilliant alliterative counterpoint (e.g., "*Consummatum est,* quod Crist, and comsede for to swoune," 18.57).

13. Here I refer to normative stress repetitions, which produce a rhythm of paired content words, not to the differentiation of *a-* and *b-*lines with respect to their phrasal rhythms. See Duggan, op cit.

14. A point briefly noted in Claud A. Thompson, "Structural, Figurative, and Thematic Trinities in *Piers Plowman,*" *Mosaic* 9 (1975): 105–14.

15. Robert Adams argues that the B-rubrics *Visio, Vita de Dowel, Dobet, Dobest* are scribal, not authorial, in "The Reliability of the Rubrics in the B-Text of *Piers Plowman,*" *Medium Aevum* 54 (1985): 208–31; but see the rejoinder by Lawrence M. Clopper, "Langland's Markings for the Structure of Piers Plowman," *Modern Philology* 85 (1987–88): 245–54. As Clopper states in "Langland's Trinitarian Analogies," *Medievalia et Humanistica* NS 9 (1979): 102, "it is clear that Langland has divided his poem into four sections and that each of these sections contains two paired visions." See also Clopper, "The Contemplative Matrix of Piers Plowman B, *Modern Language Quarterly* 46 (1985): 3–28.

16. In "Langland's Mighty Line," Stephen Barney comments accurately on the poet's proclivities toward rhythmic imbalance, dictional density, and strenuous energy. Barney quotes some lines that "contradict" the poet's usual practice and "display something like a static balance" (109), but does not attempt to explain this range of difference. With Lawrence Clopper, I assume an Augustinian ontological hierarchy and a Bonaventuran exemplarist typology informing Langland's poetic art. For a persuasive discussion of non-Franciscan Augustian intellectual currents that may have affected Langland's thinking, see John Chamberlain, *Medieval Arts Doctrines on Ambiguity and Their Place in Langland's Poetics* (Montreal: McGill-Queen's University Press, 2000).

17. Note that of the four (representative) Latin lines quoted here, only 10.246 presents a purely nominal formulation; most suggest, through terms like "by," "*procedens,*" "doop," the divine *activities* of generation and procession, linking them to the divine interactivity expressed in our English line. Indeed, the single "doop" in 17.212 applies to all three persons, tying it to the triadic "doop" in 16.183.

18. "Bi" means *by means of,* of course, but also *unto* (as in the proximate lines 185 and 188: "a persone by hymselue"); it can suggest agency, proximity, and authority. "Alle" is both quantitative and qualitative, plural and singular. It means *every* individual collectively, but also *whole, entire, complete,* or *universal.* "Oon" and "one" are the same term, which can mean, as here, both *one* and *own.* Again, the ideas of *singularity, wholeness, oneness* are covered by this word. The indefinite pronoun "oon" can also be construed as a noun, indi-

cating the first whole number. The indefinite adjective "one," meaning *own*, can function too, through word play, as a numerical adjective *one* (with elliptical noun) or as the number *one*.

19. With pleasant economy, "doop" is both third person singular and third person plural—just as God is either singular (*dixit*), plural (*faciamus*), or both (Genesis 18). "Doop" is both transitive and intransitive, and "Pat" can function either as a relative pronoun or as a demonstrative adjective. The conjunction "and" can segregate two main clauses, or join them to the same object, or introduce a third.

20. Sensitive to such uncertainties, A. V. Schmidt translates: "All perform the same actions that each performs severally, and yet each one acts entirely by himself"; see William Langland, *Piers Plowman: A New Translation of the B-Text*, trans. A. V. C. Schmidt (Oxford: Oxford University Press, 1992), 194. The syntax can also be read as self-revising, with a temporarily experienced zeugmatic turn on "alle." Although the syntax of the whole line logically annuls it, this reading communicates a flash of theological truth: *Pat oon doop alle*. . . . The One God does all, creates all, enables all, acts on behalf of all.

21. While the *line's* import is Trinitarian, its reference to the three staves propping up Charity probably derives from the popular *Arbor crucis Adae* narrative, which traces the wood of the Cross from the Tree of Life. From three seeds of the Tree of Life spouted the cedar, the cyprus, and the pine, figuring the Father, the Son, and the Holy Spirit; and from these trees were cut "iii roddes of a yerd in length," which later "appiered" to Moses, in token that he should lead his people to the Promised land; and these "iii roddes shewen the Holy Trynite"; etc. I quote from a fifteenth-century prose edition of this story (extant earlier in poetic form); see Betty Hill, "The Fifteenth-Century Prose *Legend of the Cross before Christ*," *Medium Aevum* 34 (1965): 203–22.

22. Lawrence M. Clopper, "Shifting Typologies in Langland's Theology of History," in *Typology in English Medieval Literature*, ed. Hugh T. Keenan (New York: AMS Press, 1992), 227.

23. Clopper, "Shifting Typologies," 229.

24. Lawrence M. Clopper, *"Songes of Rechelesnesse,"* passim.

25. Patrick K. O'Connell, "The *Lignum vitae* of Saint Bonaventura and the Medieval Devotional Tradition," (PhD. diss, Fordham University, 1985), 212. I am particularly indebted to O'Connell's clarification of the structural importance of Bonaventura's embedded poem; see note 28.

26. Citations are from *S. Bonaventurae Opera Omnia*, Vol. 8 [*Opuscula varia ad theologiam mysticam*] (Quaracchi, 1898), 68–87; and *The Works of Saint Bonaventura*, Vol. 1 [*Mystical Opuscula*], trans. José de Vinck (Paterson: St. Anthony Guild Press, 1960), 97–144.

27. The scriptural source is Apoc. 22.2: "In the midst of the street thereof, and on both sides of the river, was the tree of life (*lignum vitae*), bearing twelve fruits, yielding its fruits every month, and the leaves of the trees were for the healing of the nations" [Douay]. Bonaventura's *Lignum vitae* is hardly apocalyptic, nor are its fruits mensural; but meditations on the Last Judgment and Eternal Rule occur at the end *De mysterio glorificatio*, and the theme of heal-

ing is pervasive. The "healing of the nations" is very likely evoked in Passus 20, where Contrition is "sik" (335), where the false friars can offer no "phisik" (342), and where terms for disease, medicine, and healing proliferate. As we shall see, Conscience at this stage of the poem has already narrated a version of the *vita Christi* that gives special prominence to the Judgment.

28. These are my translations. The degree of abstraction in Bonaventura's titles at this level of the hierarchy is compromised by de Vinck through insertions of "His." As Bonaventura descends/particularizes from the level/region of fruit to leaf, he introduces the name of Jesus into his titles; within the forty-eight meditations themselves, the *vita Christi* is further particularized as text, event, detail.

29. Will's general curiosity (mocked by Anima and other authorities), his initial wandering "wide in þis world wondres to here" (Prol. 4), and his long quest—prior to his vision of Charity—for the *meaning* of Dowel, may all be regarded as emulations of Adam's preference.

30. Langland would no doubt have appreciated that the architectonic form of the *Lignum vitae* is itself poetic, an expansion of Bonaventura's fifteen-quatrain poem. Its framing stanzas, quoted in the Prologue, provide, first, the conflation of spiritual imagery which the Prologue elaborates—

> *O crux, fructex salvificus,*
> *Vivo fonte rigatus,*
> *Cuius flox aromanticus,*
> *Fructus desideratus.*

—and last, a summary of the seven Gifts of the Holy Spirit with which the Epilogue concludes. The lines of its twelve interior quatrains comprise the titles for the quadrate leaf-clusters of *meditationes* associated with the particular fruiting branches of the Tree of Life. For example, the first fruit on the *Praeclaritas originis* is subdivided into chapter headings following this stanza:

> *Iesus, ex Deo genitus,*
> *Iesus, praefiguratus,*
> *Iesus, emissus caelitus,*
> *Iesus, Maria natus.*

The repetition of the Holy Name throughout the interior twelve stanzas emphasizes the tree's substantial unity while the qualifying adjectives and participles, following an *abab* rhyme scheme, delineate its differentiated historical and moral manifestations. The *-atus b*-rhyme, repeated throughout the poem, mirrors the conformity of all the fruits to the one Tree.

31. In other words, Langland is not indulging in the sort of Marian piety that Chaucer would satirize in *The Prioress's Tale;* nor is he working with the tradition of Aelred of Rievaulx's *De institutione inclusarium* or the *Ancrene Wisse.* Will is depicted as having a wife and a daughter, and Will Langland is not particularly interested in virginity.

32. Compare *Lignum vitae* 1.3.

33. In Prol. 4, Bonaventura describes his methodology as responsive to the multiplicity of Christ's conditions (*eius multiplices status*) and the great variety of consolations offered by His works (*opera multiformibus consolationibus*). Individual chapters of the *Lignum vitae* deal not only with the events of Christ's life but with sins, virtues, sacraments, penitential practices, Scriptural types, and other topics.

34. As a dedicated horticulturist, Piers can scarcely stop pointing to the leaves, flowers, and fruit on the tree under his care. In his initial description of Charity in Passus 16, he uses these words in lines 9, 11, 26, 28, 29, 31, 35, 39, 40, 45, 47 (punningly), and 49.

35. The three fructifying levels of the Tree of Charity refer allegorically, as Piers explains (67–72), to the three degrees of perfection (Marriage, Continence, Virginity). Its leaves, flowers, and fruit are also interpreted in moral terms by Piers, who refers to the Tree's successive leafing, flowering, and fruiting as vulnerable to the winds of the World, the Flesh, and the Devil, against which he can wield the Trinitarian staves of the Father, the Son, and the Holy Spirit.

36. "Patience hatte pe pure tree . . ." (16.8). Patience is a central personification in the Penance allegory preceding the *vita Christi* visions, and the word is of course etymologically one with the Passion. In this sense, Charity's alternative name of Patience can be understood as an allusion to the *Lignum vitae* itself, and the allegory of Charity, in all its convolution, would seem to assert a Bonaventuran conformity of human morality with divine work.

37. David Aers, in *Piers Plowman and Christian Allegory* (London: Arnold, 1975), 79–84, usefully summarizes the responses of exegetical critics to the Tree of Charity, and characterizes their attitude as one of irritation, "as if [Langland] is incapable of expressing rather more than two ideas simultaneously" (81).

38. This vision ends on Maundy Thursday. Although the Passion is mentioned prominently at its conclusion (162–66), this reference is appended as a subordinate clause. A similar visionary coda occurs at the end of Passus 18, as Will awakens to the Resurrection. In both cases, these codas reinforce the anticipatory meaning, the typological import, of the visions themselves.

39. At the end of Passus 18, Will awakes to the bells of Easter dawn; his reverencing of the Cross of Resurrection occurs not in this dream vision, but in the waking interval.

40. The source is Ps. 84.11: *Misericordia et veritas obviaverunt sibi; Iustitia et pax osculatae sunt.* The Debate of the Four Daughters of God originates as a personification allegory with St. Bernard's Sermon I on the Annunciation, but was best known in the fourteenth century from *Meditationes vitae Christi*, ch. 2, which follows the Intercession of the Angels to God on Our Behalf and precedes the Life of the Virgin before the Incarnation. Langland would almost certainly have known this work, but he could also have encountered the Four Daughters in Guillaume de Deguilleville's *Pèlerinage de Jhesucrist* or as a discrete allegory. The fourteenth-century Harleian 1801 includes with the *Lignum vitae* and other works both "*Meditatio sive Contemplatio Fratris Bonaventure, de D.N.J.C* " and a French poem on "Merci, Verite, Justise, et Pes."

41. Compare *Lignum vitae* .28, where *consummatum est* (John 19:30) is pointedly linked not just to the *end* of suffering but to the *fullness* of suffering, the mission of redemption itself.

42. This *clarification* of number and degree is notable in the context of the proliferation of friars "out of noumbre" very near the end of the poem; "Heuene hap euene noumbre and helle is wipouten noumbre" (20.269–70). See also Will's confusions over the many names for the unitary soul, Anima (15.16–46).

43. Conscience's exposition recalls Repentance's prayer, which incorporates a *vita Christi* in the form of the Creed. Repentance's petition pairs divinity and humanity, using ancillary vocalic alliteration to stress their (and our) first-person plurality: "That *art oure* fader and *oure* broper, be merciable to *vs*" (5.504). And:

> O felix culpa, o necessarium peccatum Ade *&c.*
> For poru3 pat synne pi sone sent was to erpe
> And bicam man of a maide mankynde to saue,
> And madest piself wip pi sone vs synfulle yliche.
> (5.483–86)

44. The two *vitae* provide a chiastic frame for Conscience's core moral wisdom expressed in 19.63–68. The use of chiasmus pervades all levels of discourse in both *Lignum vitae* and *Piers Plowman*. Just as Origin and Glorification frame Passion, so many of Bonaventura's sentences and *meditationes* find their ends in their beginnings. Just as "oon" and "one" frame "alle" and "ech" in *Piers Plowman*'s most perfect line, so do many of its speeches, episodes, and larger units display chiastic frames. Book's prophetic speech (18.229–59), itself a *vita Christi*, is located at the core of Will's central *vita Christi* vision—a chiasmus within a chiasmus. Piers's instructs Will to contemplate Charity "on top and on roote (16.22); the Field is situated "betwene" the Tower and the Dungeon. For a useful discussion of chiasmus, see Timothy Bahti, *The Ends of the Lyric* (Baltimore: Johns Hopkins University Press, 1996); Bahti comments, "Inversions of directions down and up, and of motions away and toward, are explicitly and repeatedly deployed within the Christian thematics of death and resurrection, damnation and salvation, life as exile and an afterlife as a return home, and so on" (246).

45. Unless further noted, all of the manuscripts discussed below are described in printed catalogues with the exception of Arundel 507 and Royal 11.B.iii, which may be accessed electronically through the British Library Manuscripts Catalogue (http://molcat.bl.uk/msscat/). The Harleian catalogues were commanded by King George III; many of the others date from the nineteenth century, but all of the printed and electronic catalogues provide good provisional lists of the works copied in the *Lignum vitae* manuscripts.

46. *Archivum Franciscanum Historicum* 26 (1933), 552, note 3. See Seymour de Ricci, *A Handlist of Manuscripts in the Library of the Earl of Leicester at Holkamhall* (Oxford, 1932), 14; the provenance of this fifteenth-century manuscript is Venetian, probably from the monastery of San Salvatore.

47. David N. Bell, *An Index of Authors and Works in Cisterian Libraries in Great Britain* (Kalamazoo: Cistercian Publications, 1992), 51.

48. Noted by K. W. Humphreys, *The Friars' Libraries*, 69; see n. 47.

49. See *The Friars' Libraries*, ed. K. W. Humphreys (2000), *Syon Abbey*, ed. Vincent Gillesie (2001), and *The University and College Libraries of Cambridge*, ed. Peter D. Clark and Roger Lovatt (2002), all published by the British Library in association with the British Academy. Updates to this project are forthcoming, and can be searched at Richard Sharpe's list, http://www.history.ox.ac.uk/sharpe/.

# Classical and Vernacular
# Narrative Models for Art Biography
# in Vasari's *Lives*

JAMES H. S. McGREGOR

IN HER SPLENDID BOOK ON VASARI'S *LE VITE DE' PIU ECCELENTI PIT-tori, scultori e architettori*, Patricia Rubin sums up a widely held view:
"The notion of writing a series of lives," she says,

> was probably derived from the famous book of philosophers' lives by the third-century historian Diogenes Laertius ... Association with this prototype equated artists with philosophers and their manual skill with an intellectual discipline ...[1]

Dependent on a classical model for his linking of biographies, Vasari also followed classical precedent in the form of individual lives.

> The structure of the individual Lives follows a sequence of topics that had its origins in classical biography, notably Plutarch, and that had been widely adapted by Renaissance authors both in writing lives and in eulogistic orations.[2]

It is undeniable that the *Lives* are a progression of parallel biographies with recognizable links to Diogenes Laertius and Plutarch among other classical writers, but it is also true that their subject, artists and their works, is unrepresented in either text. While recognizing this fact, Vasari scholars have not fully acknowledged both the novelty and intractability of the artist's life as a biographical subject within the conventions of the classical tradition. As a consequence the sufficiency of these and other classical models

183

for Vasari's project has not been adequately considered. My aim in this article is to spell out how Vasari went about matching an artist's life pattern with that of a classical philosopher as he added to the model of Diogenes Laertius's biographies the vernacular narratives about artists by Dante and Boccaccio. More specifically, I want to show how these vernacular models helped Vasari succeed in promoting the artist's "manual skill" to the level of an "intellectual discipline." This is not an obvious or inevitable transformation, and simple "association" with a classical prototype could not have ensured success. (Had the model been perceived as inappropriate, in fact, it could only have ensured mockery and failure.) In considering this transformation, it is also important to bear in mind the special character of classical philosophy and its close and particular relationship with biographical writing.

## CLASSICAL PRECEDENTS AND PREJUDICES

Philosophy in the ancient world was not a specialized discipline focused on abstract problems as it is today. In Greece and Rome philosophy identified and publicized an ideal pattern of living that was exemplified in the life of its founder. The philosopher's own writings or, as in the case of Socrates and a few others, those of his followers explained and defended an "examined life" that was lived publicly, rationally and self-consciously. As Alexander Nehamas has noted, ancient philosophers "are both the characters their writings generate and the authors of the writings within which their characters exist. They are creators and creatures in one."[3] The philosopher's unusual role as author of his own life linked classical philosophy and the genre of biography closely. The exemplary life pattern of the philosophical founder was uniquely suited to the narrative demands of biography.

In the classical tradition, however, a wide gap separated the philosopher and the artist. The most complete classical discussion of art and artists known to Vasari and the generations before him was the Elder Pliny's *Naturalis Historia*.[4] Books 33–36 of that encyclopedic work dealt incidentally with Greek artists as part of an extensive discussion of the natural materials that ancient art made use of. Pliny regarded artists as superior craftsmen, not intellectuals of any sort and certainly not philosophers. In his view the greatest artists were those who had invented techniques for transforming natural materials into objects that benefit mankind.[5]

> Pliny viewed the artist as an artisan (artifex) who by Nature has been granted an insight into an art (ars, techne) and has been enabled to execute works from the material that from Nature's hand inherently possesses a potentiality that permits it to be made into a work of art.[6]

This essentially manual activity had at one time been highly respected by the Greeks and restricted to free men, but this was no longer the case in Pliny's day; indeed he "concedes that painting was not an occupation for decent people."[7] Plutarch shared Pliny's misgivings; in the "Life of Pericles," he wrote, "even if a thing charms us, it is nevertheless not necessary to desire to emulate its creator."[8] Both Plutarch and Pliny provided important guidance for Vasari, as they did for earlier Renaissance writers on art like Ghiberti, but they could not aid him in equating the painter's work or status with that of the philosopher. Their classification of art as manual work, their acceptance of the artist's social inferiority and his subjugation to the material that Nature provided ruled out such a transformation.[9] The classical tradition most important to Vasari did not show him how to make art the equivalent of philosophical thinking or writing.

Vasari had to turn elsewhere for guidance in giving the distinctive feature of the artist's life—the art objects he creates—some form of narrative expression. His advisor on the second edition of the *Lives*, Vincenzo Borghini, reminded him of principles he had already applied in the 1550 edition:

> Il FINE di questa uostra fatica non e di scriuere la vita de pittori, ne di chi furono figluoli, ne quello che e feciono dationj ordinarie; ma solo per le OPERE loro di pittori, scultori, architetti; che altrimenti poco importa a noi saper la vita di Baccio Agnolo o del Pontormo.

> [The PURPOSE of your labors is not to write the lives of painters, nor whose sons they were or what their ordinary activities were, but only through their WORKS as painters, sculptors, architects.

Because otherwise it is of little importance to us to know the life of Baccio d'Agnolo or Pontormo.][10]

This focus on the artists' lives "through their WORKS" required that the art object become intellectual rather than material work, but it required much more than that. It was also crucial for Vasari's task that the art object be reshaped into an illustrative action or gesture that was characteristic of its creator. Only then could art work play its featured role in Vasari's *Lives*, where as Rubin reminds us (5), "artists prove their character, their excellence or *virtù*, through their creation of objects."

Great innovator that he undoubtedly was, Vasari did not solve this problem of art biography alone. He did not single-handedly make the artist's life pattern conform to that of the philosopher or make art into an intellectual product. Instead he called on a vernacular literary tradition that had pioneered the transformation of art works into narratives that exemplified character. To fit art biography to the norms of his classical models, Vasari turned to an Italian tradition that began with Dante and Boccaccio and continued through the *novellieri* or vernacular short-story writers.[11] While Vasari's biographies are examples of Renaissance classicism, then, that classicism was enabled by a vernacular tradition of writing fictions about art. Vasari scholars have always recognized the importance to Vasari of earlier vernacular writers as sources, but as far as I know, no one has suggested that Vasari relied on them to solve the essential problem of art biography.

## THE DESIGN OF GIOTTO'S O

Rubin identifies Vasari's *disegno* as the key concept that he relied on to transform the artist's life into one that conformed to the life pattern of the philosopher: "As a word, disegno means intention or plan. For artists it was a link between idea and execution" (242). In her view, disegno is Vasari's version of the philosopher's "intellectual product":

> Philosophically impure, Vasari's highly charged definition of disegno sets the transcendental Platonic "idea" with its relation to beauty in a pragmatic Aristotelian framework that justified and explained the interdependence of sense and intellect. (242)

In the general discussion of Painting in the introductory chapters to the *Lives*, Vasari identifies *disegno* as the fundamental concept linking the arts. He sees it as analogous to the conception in the mind of God which preceded and shaped the Creation.[12]

Rubin is right to identify *disegno* as a crucial concept in the adaptation of the artist's life to the philosopher's life pattern. This identification, however, though it is correct in substance, still fails to explain how the transformation was achieved. It simply re-states the problem in different terms. It is now *disegno* rather than "philosophy" that must become part of narrative. We still must ask how Vasari transfered *disegno* from an abstract concept at the level of "intention or plan" into an action that could be narrated, a story that could be told. This transformation involved these cru-cial elements:

1. *Disegno* had to be transformed from a concept or intention into an action.
2. *Disegno* had to be individualized so that it represented a particular painter rather than all painters in general or the underlying concept of painting.
3. *Disegno* had to be given narrative form so that it could play a part in the unfolding plot of each life.

The much-examined story of Giotto's "O" illustrates very dra-matically how Vasari transformed his fundamental concept into a principle of narrative. As Rubin notes (308), at the point where it occurs in the life of Giotto, Vasari shifts from one biographical topic to another. There is no break in Vasari's story, however, nor does he present the anecdote as an isolated narration. Instead he ties his famous story explicitly and causally to the preceding dis-cussion of Giotto's work at Assisi and makes it the springboard for the actions which follow. Given the quality of Giotto's work in Assisi, Vasari writes,

> Non è maraviglia se quell'opera qli acquistò in quella città e fuori tanta fama, che papa Benedetto IX da Trevisi mandasse in Tos-cano un suo cortigiano a vedere che uomo fusse Giotto e quali fus-sero l'opere sue, avendo disegnato far in San Piero alcune pitture.[13]

[It is no wonder that the work acquired for him so much fame in that city and beyond that Pope Benedict IX, having decided to commission certain pictures for St. Peter's, sent a courtier of his from Treviso into Tuscany to see what kind of man Giotto was and what his works were like.]

Despite the fact that the episode is a fiction and one that is generally believed to be Vasari's own invention, it is grafted into Giotto's life story as if it provided evidence of his expanding reputation and the cause of his subsequent success. In Vasari this and every other biographical *topos* loses its separate rhetorical identity and becomes a key element of plot.

At the center of the episode Vasari narrates Giotto's response to the Papal courtier's request for a drawing:

> ... andato una mattina in bottega di Giotto che lavorava, gl' espose la mente del papa, et in che modo si voleva valere dell'opera sua et in ultimo, gli chiese un poco di disegno per mandarlo a Sua Santità. Giotto, che garbatissimo era, prese un foglio, ed in quello con un pennello tinto di rosso, fermato il braccio al fianco per farne compasso, e girato la mano, fece un tondo sì pari di sesto e di proffilo, che fu a vederlo una maraviglia. Cio fatto, ghignando disse al cortigiano: "Eccovi il disegno". Colui, come beffato disse: "Ho io a avere altro disegno che questo?" "Assai e pur troppo è questo," rispose Giotto. ... Il mandato, vedendo non potere altro avere, si partì da lui assai male sodisfatto, dubitando non essere uccellato.[14]

> [going one morning to the shop where Giotto was at work, he told him the Pope's intention and how he wished to make use of Giotto's work, and in the end he asked for a little drawing to send to His Holiness. Giotto, who was very courteous, chose a sheet of paper and a brush which he dipped in red ink; then fixing his arm at his side to make a compass and turning his hand, he drew a circle so perfect in section and circumference that it was a marvel to see. Having done that, he said to the courtier with a grin, "Here is your drawing." Unsure whether he was being mocked, the courtier said, "Am I to have another drawing besides this?" "That is enough and more than enough," Giotto replied ... The messenger, seeing he was to have nothing else, went away dissatisfied, suspecting that he had been made a fool of.]

Unlike his messenger, the Pope and others recognize Giotto's excellence:

il papa e molti cortigiani intendenti conobbero per ciò quanto Giotto avanzasse d'eccellenza tutti gl'altri pittori del suo tempo.

[The pope and many knowledgeable courtiers understood from this how much Giotto exceeded in excellence all the other painters of his time.]

Inspired solely by the drawing, the Pope brings Giotto to Rome and awards him several prestigious commissions.

By his focus on actions, Vasari brings *disegno* out of the conceptual sphere and into the narrative plot: Giotto *draws* the O, and as he does, he turns *disegno*—the word itself in its various forms appears six times in a half page of text—from a concept into an activity.[15] The courtier *mistrusts* the O; the papal courtiers *understand* and *appreciate* the O. While it has not been so identified in the literature, this anecdote is a paradigm of the way Vasari concretizes *disegno* and makes it play a critical role in a particular biographical narrative. The courtier sees Giotto's drawing only as a *beffa*, a joke at his expense, but the "intendenti" we are told, see beyond its deceptive surface; for them it is a "maraviglia" and a potent statement about its maker.[16] Following the lead of these authoritative interpreters, readers decode the O as a sign of Giotto's superior abilities. As such, the anecdote exemplifies the biographical imperative as Vasari understood it and as Borghini restated it: to narrate the life through the art.

It is well known that Vasari did not invent this episode completely; he based it on a famous passage in Pliny.[17] In that text the painter Apelles comes to visit the painter Protogenes. Finding him absent, Apelles tells his maid. "If he asks who was looking for him say it was this person," and he draws a narrow line on a canvas in the painter's studio. Seeing the subtlety of the line, Protogenes correctly guesses that Apelles had been his visitor. He draws a still thinner line on top and disappears. Returning, Apelles accepts the challenge and draws a third line so thin that there is no imaginable room within it for another. Protogenes accepts defeat and rushes off to find Apelles at the port. Their collaborative work is retained as an example to future painters. Having survived for generations, it is destroyed in a fire at Augustus's house on the Palatine.

Sometimes the act of recognizing echoes of a classical text like Pliny's creates confusion rather than enlightenment. Knowing that a classical precedent exists, readers may assume that Vasari is simply imitating or even copying that earlier work. Rather than let interpretation come to rest on this act of recognition, however, the reader must press on to discern the similarities and differences between Pliny's text and Vasari's imitation. Several key elements of Vasari's story are indeed present in Pliny—the line that stands in for a painter's signature and indicates his supreme virtuosity is the most important. Other parts of the story of Giotto's O are Vasari's own inventions or significant variations on Pliny's themes, and they give his text dimensions and resonances that the original lacks. In Pliny, the episode is an anecdote. One of several told about Apelles, it illustrates the artist's skill but is not causally or chronologically tied into his life story. Vasari, as I have noted, binds his story firmly within the surrounding narrative both as a consequence of what comes before and as a springboard for the action that follows. Vasari also treats the theme of competition very differently. Pliny's Apelles and Protogenes compete directly with each other. Vasari's Giotto is pitted against other painters too, but only in the mind of the beholders—Giotto is not in the presence of another painter—and the sample figure he draws is independent and self-enclosed. Giotto addresses his gesture to the authoritative judgment of the papal court.[18]

The Papal messenger is Vasari's most important innovation, not just because he is an interesting character in his own right, but because his actions clarify the meaning of the episode and help to distinguish Vasari's purpose from Pliny's. The messenger's analogue in Pliny, Protogenes' maid, is a necessary but purely mechanical character who says nothing and leaves no record of her impressions. Her low status in the Roman social world renders her insignificant, and in the art world Pliny represents she is mute. Vasari's messenger, on the other hand, is crucial both to the distinctive tone and the underlying message of his text. The messenger's suspicion that he is being tricked and his inability to appreciate Giotto's mastery act as a foil to the superior understanding of the *cognoscenti*. The messenger has no sure grasp on Giotto's motive for painting and presenting the O, and he is bewildered by Giotto's confidence that the O will be *understood*. He falls back on the notion that Giotto's drawing is not a meaningful gesture but a joke, though he can not be sure of that either. Not only does he fail to decipher Giotto's message, he can not decide whether the O contains a message. It is not that he *mis*-interprets; he is like a novice literature student who can not confidently grasp the possibility of interpreting. The papal courtiers on the other hand correctly recognize that the O is a message, and they understand that its subject is Giotto himself. They read the O correctly as biographical information.

These more knowledgeable courtiers are successful interpreters. Their authoritative judgment alerts the reader that the O should be regarded as a hermeneutic or semiotic object: that it means or signifies something.[19] To say that art is hermeneutic or semiotic is to say that it makes statements that can (and must) be decoded. Giotto's gesture makes a statement about Giotto that knowledgeable viewers and readers will comprehend. (To others it will remain opaque.) Vasari's attention to the audience of art, art's content, and its status as a hermeneutic object here separates him dramatically from Pliny. Pliny understands Appeles' or Protogenes' art in aesthetic (both as an appeal to the senses and as a bit of technical bravura) and agonistic terms; he does not ascribe meaning to it. Art in general is to be appreciated for its usefulness, its beauty, and for the virtuosity of its creator. Vasari, on the other hand, portrays art here as meaningful and establishes biography as a valid key to interpretation of the symbolic in art.

While he practices connoisseurship, appreciates, understands, and admires technique and virtuosity, these are not the grounds on which Vasari built this narrative. This episode rests instead on art that is understood as a sign that conveys a message. This fundamentally hermeneutic feature, which distinguishes Vasari's presentation of art from Pliny's ideal, links him to a Christian semiotic tradition with roots in St. Augustine's *De Doctrina Christiana*; the messenger might be compared to the literalist Augustine imagines, who fails to see what a finger is pointing toward and sees only the finger.[20] Vasari transformed Pliny's anecdote into a revealing biographical gesture, narrative in form, comic in tone, and responsive to authoritative interpretation. In what follows, I will argue that Dante, Boccaccio, and the vernacular tradition they sparked guided Vasari in his transformation of Giotto's O into a significant biographical gesture.

## NARRATING ART:
## THE VERNACULAR TRADITION

Through paradigmatic sculpted scenes on the terrace where pride is purged in *Purgatorio* 10–12, Dante presents visual art as the representation of eloquent gestures.[21] In a sequence of scenes these gestures make increasingly complex statements, yet Dante keeps pace. He understands each successive scene correctly even though his own senses have misgivings. In his mind the gestures are so clear that they invite and sustain an almost judicial examination of their truthfulness. This crucial sequence of scenes begins with an Annunciation:

> L'angel che venne in terra col decreto
>   De la molt' anni lagrimata pace,
>   Ch'aperse il ciel del suo lungo divieto,
> Dinanzi a noi pareva si verace
>   Quivi intagliato in un atto soave
>   Che non sembiava imagine che tace
> Giurato si saria ch'el dicesse "Ave!";
>   Perché iv' era imaginata quella
>   Ch'ad aprir l'alto amor volse la chiave;
> E avea in atto impressa esta favella
>   "Ecce ancilla Dei", propriamente
>   Come figura in cera si suggella.
>
> (*Purg.* 10. 34–45)

> [The Angel who came to earth with the decree of peace
> that had been wept and yearned for all those years,
> which opened heaven from the long-standing ban,
> appeared before us so vividly engraved
> in gracious attitude
> it did not seem an image, carved and silent.
> One would have sworn he said: 'Ave,'
> for she as well was pictured there
> who turned the key to love on high.
> And in her attitude imprinted were
> the words: "Ecce Ancilla Dei"
> as clearly as a figure stamped in wax.][22]

The clarity with which the reader visualizes this scene has little to do with anything Dante actually describes; the poet relies instead on our knowledge of the iconography of the Annunciation to ground our visualization of the scene. Dante asserts that the images before him had power to communicate very particular words. Ostensibly expressed through the gestures and postures of the figures he sees, these words are actually quoted in the text: "Ave," the beginning of the Archangel Gabriel's address to Mary, "Ave Maria gratia pleta: Dominus tecum . . . ," and Mary's final response, "Ecce ancilla Domini, fiat mihi secundum verbum tuum." (Luke 1:28, 38). A canto later (*Purg.* 11:95) Dante calls this eloquent art "visibile parlare," visible speech, an identification that is heavily underscored by his own reliance on words rather than the gestures that would suggest them.

Dante presents these eloquent images as if he were part of their audience rather than their creator; and he treats them as objects so transparent in their intention that their hermeneutic content is unmistakable.[23] Dante emphasizes the clarity of the scenes and their unquestionable meaning by two insistent expressions. "One would have sworn," as Hollander's translation has it, that Mary and the angel spoke because of the humility impressed on her "as a figure stamped in wax." Both these metaphors suggest very restrictive definitions of truthfulness: the first is as certain as a statement that is affirmed by swearing an oath; the second suggests a document authenticated by an official seal. Making such unconditional affirmations would show a correct understanding of the figures' gestures and the statements they make. Yet the stone remains silent, the sculpted figures only *appear* to speak as Dante's use of the conditional mode ("giurato si *saria*") underscores.

In the scene that follows, Dante amplifies the tension between intelligibility and literal truth: between art as a hermeneutic object sustaining valid interpretation on the one hand and art understood with stubborn literal-mindedness as mute material. Building on the conditional he used in the previous scene, Dante describes a discord between his own senses that poses the (unrealized) threat not of misinterpretation but of meaninglessness. The literal threatens to deprive the work of interpretability and hence of its essential character as visible speech. In this more complex scene, David dances before the Ark of the Covenant while a crowd looks on.

> Dinanzi parea gente; e tutta quanta,
>   Partita in sette cori, a' due mie' sensi
>   Faceva dir l'un "No", l'altra "Sì, canta."
> (*Purg.* 10.58–60)

[The foreground, peopled by figures grouped
in seven choirs, made one sense argue "No"
and the other: "Yes, they sing."]

Dante echoes this sensory discord in the terzina that follows:

> Similemente al fummo de li 'ncensi
>   Che v'era imaginato, li occhi e 'l naso
>   E al sì e al no discordi fensi.
> (*Purg.* 10.61–63)

[In the same way, the smoke of incense
sculpted there put eyes and nose
in discord, caught between yes and no.]

In both scenes, the so-called "lower" senses—in the first case the ears and in the second the nose—are literally right. The choir does not chant audibly, nor does the incense have an aroma. This literalness is underscored by the repeated use of "yes" and "no," as if the senses were called upon to give exact testimony of their impressions. But in the larger dimension, the literal-minded senses are wrong: we know that the choir does sing.[24] The divergent understanding of Dante's senses and his mind underlie the discordant views of Vasari's messenger and the knowledgeable papal courtiers. Like the messenger, the senses see some sort of imposture while the mind and the knowledgeable courtiers see a message requiring interpretation.

For Dante, art transforms itself from material product into intellectual artifact when it elicits understanding. As visible speech rather than mute material, art makes statements that can be affirmed in the strongest possible language. These statements appear to be transparent: the gestures that encode them seem so unmistakable in intent that the act of interpretation is almost completely swallowed up in the mere act of observation. But these gestures are hermeneutic all the same and the scenes do require interpretation. The presence of the lower senses makes this point. The ear and the nose, which simply record data, are incapable of confirming what the eyes see. Their contribution to Dante's argument is to demonstrate that what the eye thinks of itself as merely *seeing* is in fact something that the eye and mind together *infer*. On their own, these lower senses, like Vasari's courtier, cannot take the step from observation to interpretation. Art requires understanding and failures of understanding can easily occur.

It is no great leap from establishing art as statement to an evaluation of artists by the quality of their statements. While Dante implies the possibility of such an evaluation, he offers no examples. The few artists, including Giotto, who appear in the *Commedia* are mentioned *en passant*. While artists are scarce, poets abound, and given Dante's characterization of visual art as *visibile parlare*, his treatment of poets in the *Commedia* establishes a model for depicting artists. Throughout the *Commedia*, as Teodolinda Barolini has described, Dante meets and converses with a large company of poets.[25] Since Dante sees each of these men as potential models, either negative or positive, no occupational group is better represented in the *Commedia*. Dante judges poets as he judges everyone else, but what he judges in poets is not their life story itself but their lives as exemplified in their art. He treats their poetry as biographical confessions. The most striking negative figure is Bertran de Born, who pays the price for writing poetry that divided a father and son by having his head severed from his body (*Inferno* 28.118–42). Similarly the gnarled sentence-structure and convoluted punning of Pier della Vigne provoke his suicide just as the Christian Virgilianism of Statius's *Thebaid* leads its author to salvation. In short, while Dante fills his poem with characters who are poets, the poet's soul that is revealed to eternal judgment is his poetic output, not his life story. It is, as Borghini advised, the narration of the life "through the works."

Dante's reading of poetry as biographical statement sets the stage for Boccaccio and the novella tradition that succeeded him. In that tradition art is personal statement, and artists, like Dante's poets, are judged on the quality and veracity of their statements. While the concept is Dante's, it remains for vernacular prose writers to establish the conventions of judging artists by the quality of their statements in art. Of these Boccaccio is primary. His celebrated comic story of Giotto and Forese da Rabatta (*Decameron* 6.5) builds on Dante's depiction of art as visible speech, but it uproots the topic from the realm of high comedy and sets it squarely in the regime of farce where it will remain almost without exception throughout the long reign of the novella tradition. Despite this generic transformation, Dante's underlying concepts remain active: art is a personal statement, and properly understood it is hermeneutic. Of course, such art can always be improperly understood as mere material, and Boccaccio founds a tradition in which failed interpretation becomes the most commonly exploited raw material for the comic novella.

Boccaccio's Giotto story is the best known and most widely discussed art novella.[26] On a trip to the countryside the painter Giotto, whom the story depicts as very homely, and an equally unattractive contemporary, the brilliant legal scholar Forese da Rabatta, are surprised by a sudden downpour. In mildewed rain capes and moldy hats borrowed from a peasant, they ride through drenching rain and splattering mud. When the rain lets up, Giotto starts telling a story. Instead of listening to the story, Forese begins looking Giotto up and down, and he suddenly interrupts the narrative to ask:

> "Giotto a che ora venendo di qua alla 'ncontro di noi un forestiere che mai veduto non t'avesse, credi tu che egli credesse che tu fossi il migliore dipintore del mondo, come tu se'?"
>
> (6.5:14)

> [Giotto, if a stranger who had never seen you before happened to meet us right now, do you think he would believe that you were the best painter in the world, as you are?"] (my trans.)

Giotto is not fazed by the interruption to his story; he immediately shifts gears and responds:

> "Messere, credo che egli il crederebbe allora che, guardando voi, egli crederebbe che voi sapeste l'abici."
>
> (6.5:15)

> ["Sir, I think he would believe it if, seeing you right now, he could believe that you knew your a-b-c's."][27]

Rather than represent visual art in this story through a description of an art object and Giotto's reaction to it, Boccaccio makes Giotto himself the story's subject. This requires him to transform Giotto's art from a visual to a narrative one, and so Giotto makes statements that stand in for his art. Rather than listen to these statements—Giotto's story—Forese becomes preoccupied with Giotto's appearance. He breaks in to comment that no one looking at Giotto would guess that he is the greatest painter in the world. Giotto replies that no one *looking* at Forese would think him literate. This interchange is a comic version of the dissension between the lower senses and the mind's eye in Dante. (For purposes of his narrative, however, Boccaccio has to reverse the order of the senses—here the ear that listens is the higher sense and the eye the lower.) Forese personifies Dante's lower senses and prefigures Vasari's hapless messenger.

We cannot judge Giotto on the quality of the story he tells, because we have no idea what that is. We can, however, judge his response to Forese's interruption. That response is easier to understand if we set it against the more typical Renaissance art novella.[28] In general, these stories preserve the distinction between the intellectual and the sensual that is fundamental in Dante. The artist represents the intellectual, his audience the sensual. While the intellectual as the higher faculty should properly assume control over the sensual, what happens in the typical art novella is an oblique version of that norm. The intellectual artist assumes control over the sensual in fact, but the control he asserts is exploitative and unenlightening. The typical novella artist allows the audience to persist in illusion and makes use of that illusion for material benefit.[29]

Seen against that background, what Giotto does in Boccaccio's story is a demonstration of his superior character. Giotto's story represents the activity of the intellect; Forese's focus on mere externals is sensual and misdirected. Giotto, however, breaks the hold of the external by reminding Forese not only of the painter's genius but of Forese's own genius as well. Giotto's statement shows his character: since it is better to undeceive Forese than to allow illusion to persist, he earns our positive moral judgment. Giotto enacts the essential character of his art as Boccaccio defines it earlier in the story. There he credits Giotto with

Avendo egli quell'arte ritornata in luce, che molti secoli sotto gli error d'alcuni, che più a dilettar gli occhi degl'ignoranti che a compiacere allo 'ntelletto de' savi dipingendo, era stata sepolta . . .

(*Dec.* 6.5, 6)

[having returned that art to the light which for many centuries had been buried under the errors of those who cared more to please the eyes of the ignorant with their painting than to satisfy the intellects of the wise . . . ]

## CONCLUSION

Vasari did indeed model his *Lives* on classical biographies, but he needed help in transforming the painter's material product into intellectual work and into revealing personal statements that would fit the formal demands of those literary models. He learned much of what he needed from vernacular fictions. He kept something of their comic tone, but even when his work was at its most serious, the principles remained the same. In the story of Giotto's O and, I would argue, in general, Vasari viewed art as hermeneutic; it was visible speech that its creator submitted for judgment. Transforming the artist's manual labor into a statement about its creator made artistic biography culturally and theologically significant. This is the important groundwork that the novella tradition established for Vasari. While offering him a wealth of delightful anecdotes as art historians have long recognized, it also did the far more important work of midwifing his transformation of classical models into texts that incorporated the values of his own era.

## NOTES

1. Giorgio Vasari *Le Vite de' più eccelenti pittori scultori e architettori nelle redazioni del 1550 e 1568*, Rosanna Bettarini, ed. with Commentary by Paolo Barocchi (Florence: Sansoni, 1967). Patricia Lee Rubin, *Giorgio Vasari: Art and History* (New Haven: Yale University Press, 1995): 5.

2. Rubin, *Giorgio Vasari*, 5.

3. Alexander Nehamas, *The Art of Living* (Berkeley: University of California Press, 1998): 3.

4. Pliny, the Elder, *Naturalis Historia* with an English translation by H. Rackham (Cambridge: Harvard University Press, 1938–63)

5. "In dealing with the several subject matters of the *Naturalis Historia* Pliny often indicates who was the first to make a given discovery or the first to bring it about. According to the Greek pattern there must be a beginning, an *arche*. Every *ars* has a *primus inventor*, and insofar as possible in the chapters on art in Books 34–36 *inventores* are singled out." Jacob Isager, *Pliny on Art and Society* (London: Routledge, 1991), 36. See also E. Sellers and K. Jex-Blake, *The Elder Pliny's Chapters on the History of Art* (Chicago: Argonaut Publish-

ers, 1968.) Rubin describes Vasari's knowledge and use of Pliny, pp. 147–51. See also G. Becatti, "Plinio e Vasari," Studi di storia dell'arte in onore di Valerio Mariani (Naples: Libreria scientifica, 1971): 173–82; G. Tanturli, "Le biografie d'artisti prima del Vasari," Atti 1974, 275–98.

6. Isager, *Pliny*, 105

7. *Nat. Hist.* 35:22; Isager, 105, 118.

8. Quoted in Ernst Krist and Otto Kurz, *Legend, Myth and Magic in the Image of the Artist* (New Haven: Yale University Press, 1979), 42. Speaking of Greek sources in general, they note (42), "Only a sample of such opinions need be given here to round out the material contained in the biographies. In spite of the fact that they portray painters and sculptors and architects as the friends of princes, they succeeded neither in banishing doubts about the social position of artists nor in bringing about a fundamental revaluation of the artists's achievements."

9. "The evidence of such an attitude is found in the writings of a Lucian or a Seneca. 'One venerates the divine images, one may pray and sacrifice to them, yet one despises the sculptors who made them,'" Krist and Kurz, *Legend*, 41.

10. In a letter quoted by Rubin p. 192 n. 10, quoting Frey II, cdlix, p. 102; emphasis in original. Translation mine. All subsequent translations are mine unless otherwise noted. The commonly recognized form of Baccio d'Angiolo's name has been used in the translation.

11. Writing about art and artists is common in the vernacular story tradition. After Boccaccio there are important texts by Sacchetti, Manetti, Grazzini, Bandello and Doni.

12. See Rubin, 214.

13. Bettarini/Barocchi, *Le Vite* Vol 2a: 103–4. In the 1550 edition, the word "grido" was included; it was dropped in the 1568 edition. *Grido,* as Rubin notes p. 309, n. 112, reflects Dante's "ora ha Giotto il grido" (*Purg* 11.95).

14. Bettarini/Barocchi, *Le Vite* Vol 2a: 104. Having missed the point of Giotto's performance, the papal courtier ("cortigiano") is demoted to messenger ("mandato").

15. avendo **disegnato** far in San Piero alcune pitture . . . , avuto **disegni** di loro . . . , un poco di **disegno** . . . , Eccovi il **disegno** . . . Ho io a avere altro **disegno** . . . gli altri **disegni** . . . , (Bettarini/Barocchi, vol 2a: 103–4).

16. Paul Barolsky, *Michelangelo's Nose* (University Park: Penn State University Press, 1990), 136, sees the O as "emblematic of Giotto's disegno or design; indeed, it is the embodiment of the artist's michelangelesque 'giudizio' or judgment."

17. *Naturalis Historia* 35, 36, 81–83. On this episode, see also Krist and Kurz, *Legend,* 96. Rubin, *Giorgio Vasari,* 309, overstates his indebtedness: "Vasari translated a story from Pliny into a Tuscan anecdote."

18. Pliny appeals indirectly to the authority of Augustus when he makes the fabled painting a part of the emperor's collection, but in Vasari the connection between painting and authoritative judgment is explicit and active.

19. The fact that it is a letter of the alphabet reinforces this identification.

20. Augustine, *De Doctrina. Christiana*, Prologue, 3.

21. The literature on *Purgatorio* 10 is extensive. A compact bibliographical survey is offered in n. 3, p. 10 of James T. Chiampi, "Visible Speech, Living

Stone, and the Names of the Word," *Rivista di Studi Italiani* 14 (1996): 1–12. On Dante and Art in general, see the Forward and collected articles in *Dante Studies* 94 (1996): vii–112.

22. Texts and translations of Dante are from the *Purgatorio*, with translation by Jean Hollander and Robert Hollander, *Purgatorio* (NY: Doubleday, 2003).

23. This collapse of interpretation and vision, which erases the distinction between sign and signification, may in Dante's view make the art of *Purgatorio* 10 worthy of its divine creator.

24. In the Vulgate text, however, from which Dante takes the word "choir," there is no mention of singing, though they convey the Ark "in jubilo, et in clangore buccinae" (2 Sam 6: 15). Dante apparently expects choirs to sing.

25. Teodolinda Barolini, *Dante's Poets: Textuality and Truth in the* Comedy (Princeton: Princeton University Press, 1984). See also Rachel Jacoff and Jeffrey T. Schnapp, eds. *The Poetry of Allusion: Virgil and Ovid in Dante's* Commedia (Stanford: Stanford University Press, 1991).

26. Rubin discusses this novella, *Giorgio Vasari*, 293–96. Part of my discussion here parallels that in my article "The Immateriality of Art in some Italian Renaissance *Novelle*," *Arizona Studies in the Middle Ages and Renaissance 5 (2001): Material Culture and Cultural Materialisms in the Middle Ages and Renaissance,* 75–88. See also Victoria Kirkham, "Painters at Play on the Judgment Day, *Dec.* 9.8," *Studi sul Boccaccio* 14 (1983–84): 256–77; Paul Watson, "The Cement of Fiction, Boccaccio on the Painters of Florence," *MLN* 99 (1984): 43–64; Andrew Ladis, "The legend of Giotto's Wit and the Arena Chapel," *Art Bulletin* 68 (1986): 581–96. See especially Andrew Ladis, ed., *Giotto as Historical and Literary Figure* (New York: Garland, 1998); and Paul Barolsky, *Michelangelo's Nose* (University Park: Pennsylvania State University Press, 1991) and his *Giotto's Father and the Family of Vasari's Lives* (University Park, Pa. : Pennsylvania State University Press, 1992).

27. The Italian text is taken from *Decameron*, ed. Vittore Branca, *Tutte le opere di Giovanni Boccaccio*, vol. 4 (Milan: Arnoldo Mondadori, 1976); the translation is my own.

"The significant thing here is that Forese looks instead of listens, which in a story where art is replaced by narrative spells misapprehension and failure. When he looks without listening, he makes a far more serious mistake than simply misunderstanding or misinterpreting Giotto's story—whatever that may have been; he also forgets who he is. Forese and Giotto are, after all, just the same. Each is ugly and poorly dressed, disfigured by rain and so on, but each is also a genius in his own profession. To see Giotto only as grotesque means forgetting not just that he is the greatest painter in the world, but also that Forese, the forgetter, is a genius as well. Forgetting Giotto brings with it a forgetting of Forese's own most significant and characteristic abilities. Giotto's pointed remark, however, brings Forese back to a consciousness of his true self." McGregor, "Immateriality," 84. See Rubin, *Giorgio Vasari*, 293, and Barolsky, *Michelangelo's Nose*, 24–25.

28. See n. 11.

29. For example, Sacchetti's tale 169 about the painter Buonamico.

# Griselda on Stage:
## Maggi's *Griselda di Saluzzo*

### Janet Levarie Smarr

Boccaccio's tale of Griselda was the most widely known story from the *Decameron*; its placement as the very last tale of the collection gave it a rhetorical emphasis that Petrarch mentions in the letter containing his translation. That Latin translation contributed to spreading the tale internationally, and was followed very soon by new versions of the story—drawing from Boccaccio or Petrarch or both—in French, Catalan, Spanish, and English.[1] The position of the story as the ultimate in a series of competing examples of magnanimity encouraged an extremism in the behavior of its main characters that has made it one of the most disturbing of Boccaccio's stories.

This very extremism undermines the moral clarity of its example and causes serious ethical questions, as scholars have pointed out.[2] Is Gualtieri's behavior really "wise" or is it "mad bestiality"? Is he to be considered a figure for God[3] or a Satanic tempter?[4] Is Griselda's behavior truly admirable or even tolerable? Is Griselda unusually strong, or patient, or just passive?[5] Can she possibly love Gualtieri and actually want to return to his side? What can motivate either character to such unnatural behavior? Which of these two characters (if either) exemplifies the day's topic of "magnificence"?[6] If Griselda is unique and inimitable, how can she serve as a model for others?[7] If the opening word of the *Decameron* is "umana" [human] and its guiding principle "ragione" [reason], how do we fit into this the dehumanizations of "matta" [mad] and "bestialità" [bestiality] on the one hand, and of inimitable sainthood on the other?[8] Finally, what is most at stake here: a relationship of husband and wife, or of ruler and subject, or of deity and human?

Robert Hollander, in his discussion of this tale, rejected the long-dominant reading of Griselda and Gualtieri as either moral examples or allegorical figures, and suggested instead that we take seriously Dioneo's framing remarks dismissing the exemplarity of the story. Citing other supportive scholars, he suggested that we view Griselda and Gualtieri both as narcissisticly uncompromising people, manifesting exhibitionism and tyranny rather than virtue and wise government.[9] The tale's inhuman excessiveness, in this view, becomes the clue to its moral impossibility. Other recent scholars, nonetheless, continue to argue that the story, no matter how immoral it seems now, was read in its time and for centuries after as offering positive moral examples.[10]

These issues have given rise not only to a rich critical commentary, but also to centuries of rewritings. Although many literary imitations do envision the tale as somehow offering moral examples, the array of rewritings, like that of scholarly assessments, manifests the continuing struggle with its interpretive problems. Raffaele Morabito, the foremost scholar in tracing the *fortuna* of this tale, suggested, quite credibly, that the very ambiguities of the story have been a key to its widespread retelling across many centuries and languages: "proprio grazie a tale possibilità [di associare al racconto significati morali diversi], il pubblico potenziale della storia nelle sue varie versioni fosse ampio e differenziato"[11] [thanks precisely to such a possibility (of associating different moral meanings to the tale) the public potential of the story in its various versions was broad and diverse]. Rewriters continually engaged with this material because they felt the need to make clearer and more plausible sense of it.

What is even more astonishing, however, is the popularity of this story with playwrights, for it is a remarkably undramatic narrative. It covers a span of at least thirteen years, during most of which time very little happens, although dramatic actions do cluster at the beginning and end: the debate about marriage and the unexpected choice of bride, and then the final scene of revelations. Two events in between—the taking away of the children—are nearly identical, a repetition that would be dull in the theater. When Griselda is sent home to her father, she simply returns to her old routines; nothing happens there worth staging. Most fundamentally, the entire story is without dramatic conflict, for Griselda acquiesces at once to Gualtieri's every demand.[12] As we are permitted only the slimmest access to her thoughts or feelings, even the conflicts that we might expect to be going on within her are brushed aside from the tale into brief parenthetical phrases. Like Gualtieri and the narrator, we are at a loss to understand exactly what motivates her behavior.

Although we do get some brief insight into Gualtieri's perspective—his astonishment, his reflection that Griselda's previous interactions with her children rule out mere apathy as an explanation of her willingness to relinquish them—, we are left in the dark about his own motivations. The narrator says merely that a new or strange idea occurred to the marquis to test his wife with intolerable provocations. Gualtieri's explanation at the end comes out of the blue and makes no sense: he has in no way taught Griselda how to be a wife; and the lesson about acceptance to his people was equally unnecessary, given their apparent happiness with Griselda before the tests began. Who are "the people," and what is the nature of their relation with Gualtieri: are they the common folk or the people at court,[13] and are they really actors in or merely an audience for the events of the story? That is, are the political reasons Gualtieri gives for his decisions based on real political pressures or purely a pretext? Can a dramatist somehow make his excuses plausible? For if Gualtieri has been so cruel for no good reason, why should the audience consider Griselda's return to this monster a reward and a happy ending? Has the story produced a lesson worth learning?

Finally, given the inhumanity of both main characters, how is a play to create a human drama to which audiences can relate?[14] In Boccaccio's sparse tale, there is no one with whom we can readily empathize. We are not invited to feel complicit or intimate with either of the two main characters: the presentation of Gualtieri is framed by negative comments; Griselda is inscrutable and explicitly inimitable. The "people" might represent the audience beyond the stage; yet, readily manipulated and wavering with every breeze of change, they appear contemptible and irrelevant. If the audience is locked out from all paths of empathy, how can the play be emotionally effective?

Dramatists thus had a double, interrelated, set of problems to negotiate: how to interpret the moral issues, but also how to turn this undramatically constructed story into good theater. Nonetheless, Griselda plays began to appear already around 1400, continued with increasing frequency through the Renaissance into the eighteenth and nineteenth centuries, and even enticed two twentieth-century dramatists. In all, more than three dozen plays have been inspired by this story, more probably than for any other *Decameron* tale.[15] At least sixteen plays had appeared before 1700, in French, German, English, Spanish, and Italian.[16] The eighteenth century saw a dozen Italian musical dramas more or less closely adapted from Zeno's 1701 librettto.[17] Halm's nineteenth-century reworking inspired at least another eight or nine imitations in German, French, Italian, and English. Two Germans dramatized the story anew in the early twentieth century.[18] Since then, the material has apparently come to seem either uninteresting or unworkable to playwrights.

One question that presents itself immediately is: why did this particular tale have such theatrical success? Attempts have been made to answer this question from different angles: Morabito points to the broad circulation of early source material in and beyond the *Decameron*; the inclusion of the tale into chronicles and volumes about memorable women contributed to wide acquaintance with the story.[19] From the perspective of performance history, it fulfilled some of the needs of eighteenth-century musical drama for tales with a pathetic heroine but a happy ending, a love interest but no bawdiness, a morally educative theme, and the opportunity for a wide range of emotional expression. Thus, despite its problematic characters, "*Griselda* was one of Zeno's most popular librettos, being set by some fifteen different composers in the first two decades of the eighteenth century and used frequently throughout the century."[20]

A second question asks not why but how: given the odd desire to stage this story, how could dramatists render it theatrical? Obviously the motivations and qualities of the main characters are one major concern; but so too is the problem of plot: for example, of making something interesting happen while Griselda is back in her father's home, or of dealing with the dull repetition of the child theft. Time is another problem: how much time can pass during the play, and how is that time to be distributed across the acts? Finally, there is the general question of what this story is about, a question often answered not only by the characters themselves but also by the addition of other characters and story lines to draw out a theme or make a point. What might make an audience care about this material? What might they be invited to ponder?

Hans Sachs in the sixteenth century stuck so closely to Boccaccio's narrative (with some additional material from Petrarch)[21] that his play has rightly been called a "dialogization" rather than a drama.[22] Later Renaissance dramatists tended to add new materials that comment on the main action, e.g., conversations among servants or townspeople, or parallel plots, such as Dekker's domestic alternatives: a henpecked husband with a domineering wife, and a young lady whose observation of the two opposite marriages leads her to foreswear marriage altogether.[23] In mid-seventeenth-century Milan, before *Griselda* became a hit with the musical theaters, Carlo Maria Maggi wrote a remarkable *Griselda di Saluzzo*, in which the original tale is similarly complicated with additional characters, events, and lines of action.[24] These additional materials will be analyzed chiefly for what they make of the main story.

Written and first performed around 1650 but not published until 1700, Maggi's *Griselda* was known to Apostolo Zeno, whose own *Griselda* (1701) borrowed some of its features.[25] Zeno's text became in turn the major source for other adaptors during the eighteenth century, Goldoni being the most famous. Maggi's play, then, launched a century and a half of Italian stage Griseldas, although Zeno's sentimentalization changed the direction of development. My aim is to consider how Maggi attempted to resolve both the particular difficulties that any dramatist would need to address in using this material and the narrative's inherent problems of moral assessment and meaning. Obviously we cannot infer from his solutions what he thought Boccaccio meant, but only what he thought would make sense for his own theatrical endeavor. Nonetheless, I propose that, unlike previous dramatic renditions, Maggi's treatment supports Hollander's negative reading of both main characters.

Carlo Maria Maggi was an unwed youth of twenty, just completing his doctorate of law, when he composed his *Griselda* at the urgent behest of Bartolomeo Arese, senator of Milan, later president of the Senate, one of Maggi's most important mentors and patrons.[26] After becoming president, Arese would appoint Maggi to a lifetime post as Secretary of the Senate. The Arese family was interconnected by marriage with the Borromeo family; and the Borromeos' Teatro Isola Bella became one of the recurring venues for Maggi's theatrical writings. He continued to write for aristocratic theaters until 1675, including a series of dramas for music beginning in 1666. His pieces were often performed for state occasions at the government palace, sometimes after having proven themselves at the Isola Bella.[27] In short, the very young author of *Griselda* was aiming to please the established leaders of Milan from whom he hoped for (and received) support for his career. The sonnet accompanying his play addresses the play itself as a Griselda, humbly wending its way "rozza" and "incolta" [rough and uncultivated] to the Arese-Borromeo palace. He bids it suffer humbly the accusations of the judicious, but also "non curar se poi ti morde il volgo" [Don't worry if the commoners criticize you]. Although Maggi became most famous for the satirical comedies of manners and dialect monologues of his last decade, and is thus usually described as addressing his theater to the bourgeoisie, obviously that was not the case for this early drama.[28]

The play was enough of a success that Maggi started to polish it for publication, but other business intervened: marriage, a professorship of Latin and Greek at the Scuole Palatine and the University of Pavia, a government career, and a prolific outpouring of poetry and drama. Near the end of his life, a visiting gentleman from Genoa urged him to get the *Griselda* printed;[29] we can infer, therefore, that the play was still circulating, possibly also being performed, even though it remained unpublished until just after Maggi's death.

*Griselda di Saluzzo*, though a youthful piece, was completely compatible with the lifelong concern of Maggi's theatrical writings: to steer Italian theater away from lascivious sport towards standards of good taste and morally educative entertainment. The Jesuit-run Collegio dei Nobili, a school for Milan's aristocratic youths established in 1684, was to become another of Maggi's most frequent theatrical venues, thanks to his own Jesuit education, his friendship with some of the Jesuit teachers, his professorial bent, and his vision of theater.[30] We can expect, then that Maggi would use the *Griselda* to offer a pious morality, and that he would depict Gualtieri in a manner complimentary to his noble and powerful audience. While these expectations are not entirely wrong, Maggi surprisingly seems to have used the play also to explore his ambivalent reactions to Machiavelli's *Prince*, in the context of concerns about Italy's political situation and his own relationship to those in power.[31] As a result, neither Gualtieri nor Griselda are presented unequivocally as positive figures.

Unlike earlier dramas on this story, Maggi begins near the end of the tale; although Maggi was not concerned to limit the action to one day only, he needed —and later playwrights agreed—a more dramatic concentration of events.[32] The first act begins with Griselda's arrival at the home of her father Giannolo, to whom she recounts her years with Gualtieri, how he took away her daughter to be killed long ago and has now received a papal annulment of the marriage and sent her home. By skipping the initial scenes of arguments about marriage and of wooing, such as we find in earlier plays, Maggi moves away from the marriage theme to the darker theme and tone of the injustices of the powerful.

After the first few scenes in the country, the rest of the play is set at court; but the first half of the first act has already framed that court as a locus of crime and intrigue. The court is "insidiosa" [treacherous], and Gualtieri's acts consist of "gran misfatto" [great crime] and "inumani imperi" [inhuman commands]. Griselda openly blames Gualtieri, not heaven or fortune, for what she has suffered. The first new arrival from court is an assassin; he has been told that his orders came ultimately from Gualtieri, but another courtier appears with contrary orders. Violent and mutually interfering plots at court have invaded the countryside. Griselda is rescued from the assassin only to be called back to court to bear further pain and humiliation.

Maggi avoids a tedious duplication by giving the couple only one child, the daughter necessary for Gualtieri's supposed remarriage. But there is a third woman too, Violante, clearly set in antithesis to Griselda; and through her and her brother's mouths Machiavelli enters the play. The two halves of act 1 begin each with a long solo, first by Griselda, then by Violante. Where Griselda thinks nostalgically of the past, Violante is plotting the future. Viewing Gualtieri's apparent disdain for Griselda, she has seen an opportunity to insert herself into Griselda's position. Gualtieri, to test Griselda's jealousy,[33] has been misleadingly affectionate to Violante. Thus, like Griselda, Violante is shocked by Gualtieri's announcement of his impending marriage to a new girl. Griselda too had been courted amorously by the marquis before being suddenly replaced. We respond sympathetically when

Violante's brother Ridolfo describes Gualtieri as capricious and fickle (II.iii. 214). Violante's reaction, however, is opposite Griselda's. Griselda ended her half of the act with the lines: "Vi seguo ubbidiente / Ovunque mi traete, avversi fati / Benché farvi pietade omai dovria / La sofferenza mia" [I follow obedient wherever you drag me, adverse fates, although by now my suffering should cause you pity] (I.v.202).[34] In contrast, Violante, when everything is going badly for her, declares (III.i.231): "Avvilita non già, se disperata, / Delle più crude imprese / M'armerò contro al fato" [Not yet laid low, though desperate, I will arm myself against fate with the cruelest undertakings.] She intends, like a Machiavellian prince, to master fortune with violence rather than to suffer meekly. Turning to a kinsman of Gualtieri's for aid in her plotting, she urges, "Ugone, ecco fortuna / Tutta la treccia sua ci lascia in pugno" [Ugone, see how fortune is leaving her whole forelock in our fist] (II.xvi.229).[35] She readily embraces both violence and fraud as means to her end.

It is not only the villain who chooses such means, however; for deceit is not simply a moral evil; it is also a political necessity. We first see Gualtieri on stage not as a loving husband, not as a husband at all, but as a shark among sharks in the political intrigues of court: as he encounters Violante and Ridolfo, his almost immediate aside lets us know that, suspecting their ambitions, he is dissimulating in order to await the right moment to strike at their treason. So too Ugone, Gualtieri's kinsman and political supporter, feigns love for the equally feigning Violante in order to spy on her brother's plans. Guido, the sincerely desperate lover of the supposed new bride, is deceiving the court about his identity and aims. Even Griselda, when approached by Guido to form an alliance against the new marriage, feigns a sympathetic complicity while planning to inform Gualtieri against him.[36] She plainly thinks her own deceit of Guido a moral action that will defend the ruler against Guido's subversive intent. The court is a place where no one can be innocent of deceit.[37] The density of asides in the final scene of act 1 (and elsewhere) indicates the number of hidden and interfering agendas lurking behind the friendly phrases of courtliness.

Ugone seconds his deceit with force, surrounding the city with soldiers because, as he explains, "Con l'arti stesse, onde poter s'ac-

quista, / Con le stesse mantiensi" [Power is maintained with the
same arts by which it is acquired] (II.xv.229). In this view, a Machiavellian one to match Violante's, there is no difference between
Violante and Gualtieri except success.[38] If she plots in act 3, scene
ii, to poison Gualtieri's new bride, we are merely reminded of
Griselda's parallel lament in act 1, scene 2, that Gualtieri poisoned
her at the start of their marriage: "Con superbo fastidio / De' miei
casti diletti / I primi sorsi avvelenò Gualtieri" [with haughty disdain Gualtieri poisoned the first sips of my chaste pleasures]
(I.ii.194), a poison less fatal but more successful at reaching its target.[39] Violante not only contrasts with Griselda, she also parallels
Gualtieri.

More generous behavior clearly does not pay in such an envi-
ronment. Ridolfo and Violante lament in Machiavellian terms
the treachery of Guido, whom they had helped gain entrance at
court: "Furon sempre dell'alme / Troppo lenti legami i benefici"
[Benefits have always been too weak a bond of souls] (II.iii.214).[40]
Again it is not only ambitious villains who see the world this
way. The sympathetic Guido further exemplifies this truth when
he trusts Griselda to be grateful to him for saving her from the assassin; thus he is both betrayer and betrayed in relationships
where helping others is evilly repaid even by relatively sympathetic characters.[41] Ridolfo has learned from this to value Machiavelli's advice:

> Soli di gran fortuna, ingegno e forza
> Sono cardini veri.
> Un grande stato in amistà non speri.
> (II.iii.214)

[Only craft and force are the true hinges of great fortune. Let a
great state not place hope in friendship.]

Violante builds further on her brother's Machiavellian precepts
with a warning against half-hearted actions:

> Grandi e fieri consigli
> Altri mai non imprenda, o mai non lasci.
> Chi comincia una volta ad esser empio,
> Se per viltà s'arretra, ei divien tosto
> Della sciocchezza sua misero esempio.
> (II.iii.214)

[Great and lofty counsels—never learn others or abandon these. Whoever once begins a wicked deed, if he stops short from cowardice, soon becomes the wretched example of his own folly.][42]

But Ridolfo is not willing to commit himself wholeheartedly to their plot.

Beginning to sound like Griselda, he cautions his sister: "Al dominar, la sofferenza è guida" [Patient suffering is the guide to domination] (II.iii.214). The word "sofferenza" evokes Griselda, who ended her first long stage presence with "la sofferenza mia" (I.v.202). But Violante calls it cowardice or baseness in her brother that "tu soffrendo giaci / E sotto il giogo il collo pieghi e taci" [you lie suffering and bend your neck under the yoke in silence] (215). She holds in contrast: "Conquistar non si può senz'ardimento" [One cannot conquer without boldness] (III.ii.233). Griselda may be compelled as peasant to respond in this patient way; a nobleman should not.

On one hand, we recognize that Violante is the play's worst villain, and that Ridolfo is right to renounce her course of impetuous vengeance. On the other hand, the question at stake between brother and sister is itself Machiavellian: not which course is morally correct, but which means best leads "al dominar." Ridolfo will prove Violante's Machiavellian point, that by doing evil halfheartedly he obtains neither success nor exculpation.

Griselda's example will demonstrate that by patient suffering one may unexpectedly end up on top; but she was not aiming at power. We have been shown that Machiavelli was right about not expecting gratitude, for generous gestures win nothing but betrayal. We have been shown that Machiavelli was right that fraud and force are just as necessary for Gualtieri in hanging onto power as for Violante in attempting to gain it. Nor does the play make an effort to highlight Gualtieri's legitimacy. Ugone's express aim in act 2 (vi.217), as he explains that his bedtalk with Violante will give him access to Ridolfo's plans, is not to uphold the legitimate government but to ruin his political rival. Only the use of spies and the willingness of rival courtiers to report on each other keeps Gualtieri in control of events. From the perspective of Griselda's father, Gualtieri does not deserve to rule.

If Gualtieri's combination of deceit and violence are necessary in his relationships with ambitious courtiers, what about in his relationships to his wife and daughter? Were they necessary there too? The excuse of political necessity—that he needed to prove to his vassals the true nobility of their ruler's wife—is mentioned briefly in the final scene, but the play has done nothing to prepare us for it. Rather, the *argomento* had already suggested that he wanted capriciously to test Griselda and later to see whether she would be jealous. Furthermore, his quick reference to the political excuse is surrounded at greater length by a different and more psychological motive. Reminding Griselda of her promise to obey his every wish, he confesses that once he had begun to test her as a demonstration to his subjects, he began to wonder how far she could be pushed:

> E perchè ognor sua sofferenza invitta
> Vinse le mie speranze e'l rigor mio,
> Volli provar con le fierezze estreme
> Quanto può soffrendo un petto forte.
> (240)

[And because her patient suffering, remaining always unconquered, surpassed my hopes and my harshness, I wanted to test with extreme cruelty how much a strong breast can put up with.]

The initial testing became a competition that Griselda was winning, and Gualtieri, like a gambler, became obsessed with the game. At the end, he seems even willing to let her kill herself until her father intervenes with his protest. Griselda's very patience has provoked Gualtieri's cruelty.[43]

Gualtieri does claim in one aside at the midpoint of the play (II.viii.221) that his feigned anger and scorn at Griselda are struggling against his true pity; this is our only clue not to take his character at face value. But as he spends only that one scene alone together with Griselda and only two others with her in a large crowd (at the ends of acts 1 and 3), we do not see much of their relationship, which has slipped from the center of attention. In what we do see, he is unremittingly cruel, and from Griselda's opening narrative, we gather that Gualtieri has been feigning scorn for their entire married life.[44] Most of the interactions of this couple, however, have taken place before the play begins; and both Gualtieri and Griselda disappear almost entirely during the second half of the play. What we witness then is the consequent con-

fusion and pain of everyone, and an alternate course of action that
Griselda might have taken if she had Violante's character.[45] The
main conflict of the play is not between Gualtieri and his subjects,
nor between Gualtieri and Griselda, nor within Griselda herself;
rather, it takes place in the minds of the audience as they ponder
the contrast between Griselda's and Violante's responses to Gualtieri's actions.

The link between the two themes or plot lines, domestic and
political, is Ridolfo's line, already cited, that one wins by patient
suffering, a Christian sentiment enforced by Griselda's reference
to martyrdom (I.ix.208). We see the two main women as exempli-
fying two paths to glory. But is Ridolfo right to think of Christian
suffering as a means to winning political, not spiritual, victory?

This question appeared repeatedly in Maggi's abundant political poetry.[46] One sonnet openly attacks Machiavelli:

> "Fu maligno scrittor chi fe' gl'inganni
> Arti di regno, ed infamò gl'imperi.
>     Quei che ingrandir desian su gli altrui danni,
> Vergogna e ambizion fa menzogneri,
> Il colorir fallacie è da tiranni,
> È da giusti regnanti esser sinceri."[47]

[He was a malicious writer who made deceits the arts of ruling,
and defamed dominion. Shame and ambition turn into liars those
who desire to grow great by means of others' harm; coloring false-
hoods is the mode of tyrants; just rulers should be sincere.]

Nonetheless, Maggi shared Machiavelli's intense desire to see
Italy freed from its ruling invaders, and the recognition that internal conflicts were preventing Italy from the united action necessary to achieve this freedom.[48] While repeatedly condemning
hypocrisy, Maggi vacillates between urging Italians to fight and
urging them rather to turn to God and await his aid. Sometimes
he sounds like Violante reproaching her brother: "Non val che
Italia a' piedi altrui si penta, / E, obliando il valor, pianga il des-
tino" [It is not worthy that Italy bows to another's feet, and, forgetting valor, bewails its destiny] (43). Threatened by new wars
between the Spanish and the French for control of Milan, Maggi
writes ruefully, "Disarmata ragion loco non trova / Con chi sol
pensa ad ingrandir di Stato" [Unarmed reason holds no place with

one who thinks only of augmenting his State] (44) and in a different poem:

> Pensa . . . che disarmata ogni preghiera è tarda.
>     Gran desio di regnar pianti rifiuta;
> Con spartana virtú Sparta si guarda:
> Libertá supplicante é già perduta.
>
>                                             (44)

[Think . . . that every disarmed prayer is late. Great desire to rule rejects lamentations; Sparta is guarded with Spartan valor: a suppliant liberty is already lost.]

At other moments, however, he takes a more Griselda-like position, awaiting the pity of heaven and, to hasten divine mercy, urges his fellow Italians to repent and pray. He is foolish who "Vuol pace in terra e non lo fa col cielo" [wants peace on earth and does not make peace with heaven] (38); it is "perverso . . . / Voler soccorso e non cercar perdono" [perverse . . . to wish for help and not to seek pardon] (57). Perhaps God will protect Italy from ruin if we pray humbly in true penitence (58).

We might note that the Griselda in Maggi's play does not in fact pray or repent.[49] She simply suffers and endures. She has given up expecting things to get better. Her father Giannolo, though hardened by a long life of labor and poverty, protests that even after all these years he continues to sink from bad to worse. He too, while blaming Gualtieri, does not expect relief. The restoration at the end of the play takes everyone by surprise but evokes no thanks to heaven—nor, for that matter, to Gualtieri. It is too long overdue for Griselda or her father to feel like thanking anyone. Gualtieri has simply been called at last to his proper obligations.

Even if Maggi saw the Griselda story as an opportunity to develop his thoughts about how to respond to the pressures of politics, why did he give treason and treachery so large an emphasis? True, Gualtieri is deceiving everyone, but treachery—much less treason—does not strike most readers of Boccaccio as a major theme of the tale.[50] Perhaps Maggi, in contemplating the story and trying to understand Gualtieri, pursued the line of allusion that leads from Dioneo's description of Gualtieri to Dante's *Commedia*. Scholars have noticed the connection between Boccaccio's allusion to Gualtieri's "matta bestialità" and Dante's use of the phrase in *Inferno* 11, 82–83, where Virgil outlines to Dante the structure of hell, divided according to Aristotle's *Ethics* into sins of incontinence, malice, and "matta bestialità."[51] That three-part scheme would associate the phrase—and therefore Gualtieri—more specifically with Dante's region of fraud and treachery. A second appearance of these two words, near each other though not side by side, seems to have gone unremarked and serves to strengthen this specific connection. In *Paradiso* 17, 64–69, Cacciaguida tells Dante that the Florentines will falsely accuse Dante of treachery, though guilty of it themselves:

> che tutta ingrata, tutta *matta* ed empia
> si farà contro a te; ma, poco appresso,
> ella, non tu, n'avrà rossa la tempia.
> Di sua *bestialitate* il suo processo
> farà la prova, sì ch'a te fia bello
> averti fatta parte per te stesso." [my emphases]

[which shall then become all ungrateful, all *mad* and malevolent against you, but, soon after, their brows, not yours, shall redden for it. Of their *brutish* folly their own conduct shall afford the proof, so that it will be for your fair fame to have made you a party by yourself.][52]

Since Dante is told in this scene that he will have to leave "ogni cosa diletta / più caramente" [everything beloved most dearly] and go into exile, did Boccaccio think of Dante when he wrote about Griselda's losses and exile? She too is unjustly exiled and suffers innocently from the treachery of someone in a special relationship of obligation to her, the lowest form of treachery in Dante's Hell; in her case too, she will ultimately be justified against those who have falsely condemned her. This intertextual reading, if Maggi did pursue it, supports a damning view of Gualtieri.

Giannolo, in an outburst that precipitates the resolution of Maggi's play, finally speaks his protest openly to Gualtieri: "In che t'offese mai questa innocente? . . . Questo misero padre in che peccò / Che ne' suoi giorni estremi / Tu gli traffiga il core / Con perdita sì dura? . . . Che sarà mai che mova / Cotesto cor, se non ottien clemenza / Vecchiezza ed innocenza?" [How has this innocent woman ever harmed you? . . . How has this wretched father sinned, that in his final days you pierce his heart with so cruel a bereavement?

. . . What will ever move that heart of yours if old age and innocence obtain no mercy?] (III.v.239). Giannolo's outcry is admirably
honest in this court of lies, but he can afford to utter it only because he is an outsider, old, and has nothing left to lose. He is, like
Dante, a party of one.[53] Yet his outburst is astonishingly effective.

The question of how an ethically serious and pious intellectual
is to relate to the politics of his society would obviously have been
in Maggi's thoughts, whose incipient career depended (like Griselda's) on pleasing a few very powerful men. How far might he be
willing to obey? How much should he speak up against perceived
injustices? Against the slings and arrows of outrageous fortune, in
what course of action might virtue consist? The last of Dante's
speaking sinners is an ambitious aristocrat,[54] and Dante had repeatedly railed at shepherds that act as wolves.[55] Maggi's poetry
similarly criticizes the rulers of Europe: "Voi, cui le gregge umane
il ciel commise / Per custodia fedel, non per macello" [You to
whom heaven committed the human flock for faithful guarding,
not for slaughter] (39–40). In his reading of Boccaccio's tale and its
Dantean echoes, Maggi seems to have thought especially about
the cruel betrayal of trust between rulers and subjects, the powerful and the helpless.

Violante's choices of behavior, fueled by desire and anger, lead
to failure. What kind of alternative does Griselda offer, and what
motivates her passive suffering amid all this intensity of malicious action? The first motive to be mentioned in the play is the
love that Gualtieri initially aroused and to which, as his wife, she
remains faithful despite his cruelties. In her opening scenes she recalls the brief moment when Gualtieri seemed affectionate, and
near the very end but still before her restoration, she calls him
"Adorato Gualtieri." Zeno and his followers tended to make sentimental married love a central focus of their drama. Maggi manages, however, to create a fairly plausible character by avoiding excessive emphasis or idealism on this score and by adding other
understandable if not entirely exemplary motives.

Second is egoism, the pride that Hollander and others have suggested undermines the ethical exemplarity of the *Decameron*'s
final ten tales.[56] After giving up the last remaining hopes at the end
of act 1 (even death has eluded her), Griselda claims a sense of
pleasure in the glory of sheer pointless suffering, in the constancy
of despair:

Sarà gloria al mio martire
Sofferir senza speranza;
Perché è sol vera costanza
Sofferir per sofferire.
                    (I.ix.208)

[It will be the glory of my martyrdom to suffer without hope; for
the only true constancy is suffering for the sake of suffering.]

At the beginning of act 2 as she makes preparations for Gualtieri's wedding, she imagines herself on stage, preparing the scene
not for someone else's wedding but for her own performance: "Or
Griselda s'affanna /Ad apprestar più vaga e più superba / Delle
tragedie sue la scena acerba" [Now Griselda labors to make more
lovely and more grand the bitter scene of her tragedies] (II.i.209).
Toward the end of act 3, about to drink knowingly the poison that
Violante has prepared, she invites her audience to watch: "e tu
sleal Ridolfo, / Tu, Violante indegna, / A questo di mia morte / Sì
bramato spettacolo e sì caro / Pur saziate i dispietati lumi" [And
you, disloyal Ridolfo, and you, unworthy Violante, now satiate
your pitiless eyes with this long-awaited and desired spectacle of
my death] (III.v.239). She wants her suffering to be a spectacle.
This is a proud humility that, with more psychological realism
than moral exemplarity, seeks to flaunt its very abjection.[57]

Thirdly, and perhaps most sympathetically, she manifests a ter-
rible weariness. Already at the beginning of the play, she announces:

Vengo, o paglie paterne,
Con l'affannato fianco
A riposar su voi l'animo stanco.
                    (I.ii.196)

[I come, o paternal straw, with worn out flank to rest on you my
weary spirit.]

But such rest is made impossible. In her opening speech in act 2
(i.209), she confesses that the conflict between "dispetto e sofferenza" [resentment and patient suffering] has left her "Sì affati-
cata e stanca, / Che alla fin mal distinto / Dal vincer sì penoso è
l'esser vinto" [so weary and exhausted that in the end it is hard to
distinguish such a painful victory from being vanquished]. In the
play's final scene, commanded to sing at the wedding despite her

sorrow, Griselda chooses as her theme "Più non spero" [I no longer hope] repeated in its final line "fuor di speranza" [beyond hope] (235). Patience is the necessary virtue of despair. As Violante's plot to poison the wedding cup is discovered, and Gualtieri asks Griselda who should drink from it, she eagerly requests it for herself (236). Thus weariness makes her twice beg for death: from the assassin in act 1, and from the poison in act 3. Her weariness leaves her nearly silent during the drama's conclusion, too tired and bewildered to utter words of joy.

In shock, Griselda says nothing after the final revelations except briefly to interrupt Gualtieri's tirade against Ridolfo with her first-ever "No" to her husband:

> No, perdona, o Gualtieri.
> Quest'alma mia che ne' sofferti guai
> Vinse il proprio dispetto,
> Della vendetta ancor fugge il diletto."
> (241)

[No, excuse me, Gualtieri. This soul of mine that in its suffered woes overcame its own resentment, still shuns the pleasure of vengeance.]

Has she been inspired to speak up by the astonishing effectiveness of her father's protest? Her phrasing is an equally effective reproach to Gualtieri, who was about to act like Violante, delighting in violent revenge.

If Griselda sees herself as the chief spectacle, the only character who describes himself as the audience, and with whom the audience is clearly invited to identify, is Griselda's old father Giannolo. Not only does he receive, like us, the background information of Griselda's opening speech, but also he returns with an unexpected long solo presence on stage near the end of act 2, lamenting that Gualtieri has invited him to the palace to be the spectator of a performance he does not wish to see:

> E vuol l'empio ch'io sia
> Degli spietati strazi
> Della misera figlia
> Spettatore infelice.
> (II.xv.228)

[The wicked man wants me to be the unhappy spectator of my wretched daughter's pitiless torments.]

Perhaps Maggi feared that by this point his own audience would be getting restless with a play so full of cruelties.[58] Giannolo's helplessness is the audience's helplessness to affect the actions of the play or even to avoid watching; but it is also the helplessness of the common people under a ruler who is thoughtless of justice. Not even the humility of Giannolo's hut has defended him from the "superbo rigor" [proud harshness] that drags him on downward from even the lowest level. His hard life and long years have rendered him relatively impervious to the cruelties of fortune, but he protests that in his case patient suffering is leading nowhere and never ending. We may argue that although both he and Griselda see the performance at court as a tragedy, it will end with surprising good fortune. However, Maggi entitled his entire play, last scene notwithstanding, "tragedia."[59] The final scene simply fails to undo or excuse the long misery of unjust domination. The play ends with young Guido's joy at the prospect of marrying Griselda's daughter, but it is much easier for him to bury bitter memories in bliss than it will be for any of the older characters. It is the younger generation that will enjoy a new and happier era.

Maggi, I would argue, has interpreted Boccaccio's final story in a manner fairly close to Hollander's. Rejecting the hints of religious allegory, and setting aside the debates about marriage that attracted dramatists around 1600, Maggi turned the tale into a meditation on how one should respond to the vicious injustices perpetrated by a ruling class, local and international, whose treacherous ambitions not only embroil courtiers in endless intrigues but also afflict the innocent subjects hoping vainly to live in peace. He makes Gualtieri totally unadmirable, and Griselda's sufferance more helpless, weary, and indulgent in self-glorifying fantasy than actively virtuous. Although Griselda's "sofferenza" is held up as better than Violante's "furor," the end of the play suggests a better middle ground between abjection and fury, which Giannolo discovers and Griselda learns: it is the risky but honest protest that addresses the ruler directly and publicly, reproaching his injustice and advising an end to violence, a protest and exhortation that Maggi made over and over in his political poetry.[60]

## NOTES

1. Christine de Pizan's *La cité des dames*; Bernat Metge's "Walter e Griselda," the anonymous "Castigos y dotrinas que un sabio daua à sus hijas," and Chaucer's "Clerke's Tale," all close to 1400. On the diffusion of this tale throughout Europe, see Käte Laserstein, *Der Griseldisstoff in der Weltliteratur*. Forschungen zur neueren Literaturgeschichte, LVIII (Hildesheim: Gerstenberg Verlag, 1978); R. Morabito "La diffusione della storia di Griselda dal XIV al XX secolo" in *Studi sul Boccaccio* XVII (1988): 237–85; *La circolazione dei temi e degli intrecci narrativi: il caso Griselda*, ed. R. Morabito (L'Aquila-Roma: Japadre, 1988); *La storia di Griselda in Europa*, ed. Raffaele Morabito (Rome: Japadre, 1990).

2. For reviews of the arguments and interpretations of Boccaccio's story with useful bibliography, see Giulio Savelli, "Struttura e valori nella novella di Griselda," *Studi sul Boccaccio* 14 (1963): 278–301; Michel Olsen, "Griselda, fabula e ricezione," in Morabito ed., *La storia di Griselda in Europa*, 253–64, esp. 255–56; Thorsten Greiner, "Una matta bestialità? Zur Deutung von Boccaccios Griselda-Novelle," *Zeitschrift für Romanische Philologie* 111:4 (1995): 503–22, esp. 505–7; Robert Hollander, *Boccaccio's Dante and the Shaping Force of Satire* (Ann Arbor: The University of Michigan Press, 1997), 136–59; his notes, as usual, cover most of the bibliography on the topic. But see also, since then, Olivia De Masi, "Un ipotesi per un'interpretazione della novella di Griselda, *Decameron* X.10" *(Pre)publications* 156 (1997): 3–7.

3. Suggested first by Petrarch; see also Charles Haines, "Patient Griselda and *matta bestialitade*," *Quaderni italianistica* 6:2 (1985): 233–40.

4. Giuseppe Mazzotta, *The World at Play in Boccaccio's Decameron* (Princeton: Princeton University Press, 1986), 124–25: Gualtieri casts himself as God, but we see him also the Satanic tempter of Job-like Griselda; moreover, his very attempt to play God casts him as Satan.

5. T. K. Seung, *Cultural Thematics. The Formation of the Faustian Ethos* (New Haven: Yale University Press, 1976), 207, 211–13, suggests that only a character passive to the point of masochism can cohabit with the "excessive self-centeredness" of the assertive individual emerging in European thought. Any interpretation, however, that sees Griselda as a positive example, whether of humility, patience, constancy, fortitude, or faith, posits an exceptional strength of character.

6. Savelli, "Struttura e valori," 278–79, asks "se sia davvero la novella di Griselda o non sia invece quella del marchese di Saluzzo," and notes previous scholars who discussed this issue. See also Francesco Tateo, "La Novella di Gualtieri?" in Raffaele Morabito, ed., *Griselda I: La Circolazione dei temi e degli intrecci narrativi: il caso Griselda. Atti del convegno di studi, L'Aquila, 3–4 dicembre 1986* (L'Aquila: Japadre Editore, 1988), 35–38.

7. Millicent Joy Marcus, *An Allegory of Form. Literary Self-Consciousness in the Decameron*, Stanford French and Italian Studies, 18 (Saratoga, CA: Anma Libri, 1979), 98–108, argues that Boccaccio intentionally sows confusion in order to undermine our expectation that the story will provide a lesson or *exemplum*.

8. Haines, "Patient Griselda," 239–40, probes the connection between the last tale and the *Decameron*'s opening word.

9. *Boccaccio's Dante*, 136–59; Hollander cites Momigliano, Bergin, and Bonadeo in support of his negative reading of the main characters. See also Claude Cazalé Berard, "Filoginia/misoginia" in *Lessico critico decameroniano*, ed. Renzo Bragantini and Pier Massimo Forni (Torino: Bollati Boringhieri, 1995), 135–37.

10. See, for example, Victoria Kirkham, "The Last Tale in the *Decameron*" in *The Sign of Reason in Boccaccio's Fiction* (Florence: Leo S. Olschki, 1993), 249–65.

11. Raffaele Morabito, *Una sacra rappresentazione profana. Fortune di Griselda nel Quattrocento italiano*. Beihefte zur Zeitschrift für romanische Philologie, Band 253 (Tübingen: Max Niemeyer Verlag, 1993), 13.

Similarly on page 1: "Tuttavia proprio nell'ambiguità e nella contemporanea esplicita indicazione di un possibile valore morale che, tramite il riferimento allegorico o simbolico, superi la particolarità delle vicende dei personaggi, ha radice la fortuna che alla storia arrise, cospicua, nelle eta successive."

12. Gabriele Muresu, "Goldoni e il melodramma: il rifacimento della *Griselda* di Apostolo Zeno," *La parola cantata. Studi sul melodramma del Settecento* (Rome: Bulzoni, 1982), 22: "appare chiaro che la novella di Boccaccio, se non a patto di profonde modifiche strutturali, non sembra essere facilmente 'teatrabile'," not only because of the small number of characters, but mainly because of "l'assenza di un intreccio vero e proprio."

13. Boccaccio seems to mean the common people, but Petrarch made them courtly advisors.

14. Eric Cross, "Griselda," *The Late Operas of Antonio Vivaldi 1727–1738* (Ann Arbor: The University of Michigan Press, 1981), v. I: 148–50, comments on the problem that the two main characters created for musical drama: neither Zeno "nor any other playwright could do much with these two illogical people" (150).

15. This paper is the beginning of a longer project investigating Griselda on stage.

16. Seventeen if we count Dekker's *Honest Whore, Part I*, in which the genders are reversed.

17. These are listed in Maria Teresa Muraro, "Primi appunti sulla fortuna del Boccaccio nei libretti per musica," *Studi sul Boccaccio* 5 (1968): 265–73. See also Annalaura Bellina "Boccaccio nel teatro musicale italiano: Ragion did mercatura e ragion di stato," in *Boccaccio e Dintorni. Miscellenia di studi in onore di Vittore Branca*, II. Biblioteca dell'"Archivum Romanicum" Series I, Vol. 179. (Firenze: Leo S. Olschki Editore, 1983), 289–93; Gabriele Muresu, "Goldoni e il melodramma: il rifacimento della *Griselda* di Apostolo Zeno," esp. 13n.; Anna Maria Iorio, "La diffusione settecentesca della *Griselda* italiana" in Morabito, ed., *Griselda I: La Circolazione dei temi*, 57–66; Walter Tortoreto, "Griselda nel teatro musicale della prima metà del Settecento" in *Griselda I*, 107–24.

18. Gerhardt Hauptmann's *Griselda*, as a modern work (1906), shifts from moral to psychological and sociological frameworks. Ludwig Berger's *Griseldis*,

*ein Volksstück* (1920) imitates Hauptmann but veers into a more metaphysical direction. Already in the nineteenth century, the tale required major reformulation by Halm, whose Griselda ultimately rejects her husband.

19. Raffaele Morabito, *Una sacra rappresentazione profana*, 1–3.

20. Cross, "Griselda," 150.

21. The discussion among court advisors about Gualtieri's need to marry comes from Petrarch, as noted by Laserstein, *Der Griseldisstoff in der Weltliteratur*, 66.

22. Laserstein, 69. Sachs's *Griselda* is "nicht dramatisiert . . . nur dialogisiert."

23. Her conclusion is thus Gualtieri's original "wisdom" of unwillingness to marry; however, the play's final comments jovially encourage her to reconsider.

24. I am using the text in Carlo Maria Maggi, "La Griselda di Saluzzo. Tragedia in 3 atti." in *Scelta di Poesie e Prose*, ed. Antonio Cipollini (Milano: Ulrico Hoepli, 1900), 189–242. Two earlier plays in Italian are *Una sacra rappresentazione profana*, ed. Raffaele Morabito, dated by Morabito to the fifteenth century; and Galeotto Oddi, "Griselda tragicommedia del balì" written c. 1620 but not published—and possibly unperformed—until the edition by Jacqueline Malherbe and Jean-Luc Nardonne in *L'Histoire de Griselda, une femme exemplaire dans les littératures européenes*, 2: *théatre*, ed. Marie-Françoise Déodat Kessedjian et al. (Toulouse: Presses Universitaires du Mirail, 2001), 359–468. It is unlikely that Maggi would have known either of them.

25. For the dating of Maggi's play, see Raffaele Morabito, "Per un repertorio della diffusione europea della storia di Griselda," in Raffaele Morabito, ed., *Griselda I: La Circolazione dei temi*, 16. For Zeno's knowledge of and debt to Maggi, see Laserstein, 146 and 148.

26. Antonio Cipollini, citing Muratori, in "Commemorazione," in Carlo Maria Maggi, *Scelta di Poesie e Prose*, ed. Antonio Cipollini (Milano: Ulrico Hoepli, 1900), 189n. The first *Vita di Carlo Maria Maggi* was published by his adoring friend Muratori shortly after Maggi's death: Lodovico Antonio Muratori, *Vita di Carlo Maria Maggi* (Milan: Giuseppe Pandolfo Malatesta, 1700). For a brief and less personal biography, see also *www.canzon.milan.it/letteratura_milanese%5Cmaggi.htm* or the identical *www.anticacredenzasantambrogio milano.org/carlo%20maria%20maggi.htm*. There are also useful references to Maggi in the chronology of Milanese events at *www.storiadimilano.it/cron/dal1676al1700.htm*. Another chronology of specifically theatrical events in Milan during the seventeenth century appears in *La Scena della Gloria. Drammaturgia e spettacolo a Milano in età spagnola*, ed. Annamaria Cascetta and Roberta Carpani (Milan: Vita e Pensiero, 1995), 731–54; however, it does not mention Maggi's *Griselda*.

27. Glenn Pierce, "Evidence of transition in the early works of Carlo Maria Maggi: the melodramas," *Canadian Journal of Italian Studies*, 3:3–4 (1980): 203–4.

28. For Maggi as a dramatist of the bourgeoisie, see Pierce, "Evidence of transition," 193–222; and Dante Isella, "Il teatro milanese del Maggi o la verità del dialetto," *I Lombardi in rivolta. Da Carlo Maria Maggi a Carlo Emilio Gadda* (Torino: Giulio Einaudi editore, 1984), 25–47. Maggi's late comedies were

written after a gap of several decades devoted to nontheatrical writing. Pierce, "Evidence of transition," 217–20, interprets this gap as a sign of Maggi's loss of interest in—even growing fristration with—aristocratic theater. Cipollini's "Commemorazione" in Maggi, Scelta di Poesie e Prose, 26–27, comments that Maggi's theatrical work, while increasingly broad in its appeal, remained very popular with aristocratic audiences throughout his life.

The little that has been written about Maggi in the last century (despite his great fame c. 1700) has focused almost entirely on his late comedies and writings in dialect: e.g., Ireneo Sanesi, Storia dei Generi Letterari Italiani (Milan: Dottor Francesco Vallardi, 1935), 2:214–26; Mario Apollonio, Storia del teatro italiano (Milan: Biblioteca Unversale Rizzoli, 2003 [originally 1946], 2: 322–35; Walter Binni, L'Arcadia e il Metastasio (Florence: La Nuova Italian, 1963), "La commedia del Maggi" 169–75; Franco Ferrucci, "The Milanese Theater of Carlo Maria Maggi," Italian Quarterly 8:32 (1964): 28–41; Antonio Petrella, "Carlo Maria Maggi's Theory of Comedy," Italian Quarterly 47–48 (1969): 223–37; Glenn Pierce, "Carlo Maria Maggi and the Bosinada," Forum Italicum 13:4 (1979): 480–95; and of course Dante Isella's edition of Carlo Maria Maggi, Il teatro milanese, Turin: Nuova raccolta di classici italiani annotati, 1964.

Glenn Pierce, "Evidence of Transition," and Roberta Carpani, "La storia sanata. Il libretto di 'Il trionfo d'Augusto in Egitto' di Carlo Maria Maggi,'" in La scena della gloria: drammaturgia e spettacolo a Milano in età spagnola, ed. Annamaria Cascetta and Roberta Carpani, La città e lo spettacolo 4 (Milan: Vita e Pensiero, 1995), 329–77, have analyzed also some of Maggi's earlier melodramas. However, I am unaware so far of any discussion of the Griselda.

29. Muratori cited by Cipollini in Maggi, Scelta di Poesie e Prose, 189n.

30. Isella, I Lombardi in rivolta, 35; Gianfranco Damiano, "Il Collegio gesuitico di Brera: festa, teatro e drammaturgia fra XVI e XVII secolo," in La scena della gloria, esp. 503–6.

31. Perhaps this is less surprising when we recognize the political aspect of drama by contemporaries known to Maggi. Glenn Pierce, "Evidence of transition," 195–96, points out that both Carlo Torre and Tommaso Santagostino wrote dramas advocating the view that rulers govern by the consent of the people and not by divine right. These plays, however, date from 1666 and 1670, when Maggi was writing his melodramms, but considerably after his Griselda.

32. Hans Sachs, Lope de Vega, and Dekker et al., had begun with the debates about marriage and the choice of Griselda. Zeno and his followers picked up Maggi's idea of starting near the end and even limit the events to one exhausting day.

33. Maggi offers this motivation only in the "argomento" preceding the play proper.

34. The third number refers not to the lines, which are unnumbered, but to the page. Zeno would replace "la sofferenza mia" with "la costanza mia;" Maggi is less idealizing.

35. See Machiavelli's Prince, chapter 25, on the need to deal boldly with Fortune.

36. Thus Guido's praise of her kindness gains a dark irony; we know that she is not as kindhearted as he thinks.

37. Maggi, who eventually wrote his own treatise of advice for young noble-women and gentlemen, already echoes (consciously or not) the sentiments of Giovanbattista Giraldi Cinzio's *L'uomo di corte* (1565), who sheepishly advises his young nobleman, after a section on the importance of truthfulness and the evils of dissimulation, that he will have to feign his responses to the other courtiers in order to defend himself prudently from their deceits [Walter Moretti ed. (Modena: Mucchi, 1989), 64].

38. Machiavelli discusses the importance of both force and deceit, and of success as the determining factor in how one is judged, in chapter 18 of *The Prince*.

39. Roberta Carpani, "La storia sanata," 373, notes Maggi's propensity to symmetrical scenes in another of his plays, the *Trionfo d'Augusto*.

40. For Machiavelli's comments on benefits as an unreliable bond, see chapter 17 of *The Prince*.

41. Zeno makes the daughter's young lover into a sweet and noble youth; Maggi's version of both youngsters is less honorable: they actually attempt to flee together and are caught.

42. Machiavelli discusses the successful use of audacious crime and cruelty in chapter 8 of *The Prince*.

43. Similarly in Dekker's *The Honest Whore, I*, the endlessly patient Candido provokes everyone around him, including his wife, to try his patience. Appropriately, the final scene takes place in a madhouse. De Masi, "Un ipotesi," 5, suggests this competition already in Boccaccio's tale: "una sorta appunto di gara di resistenza psicologica. Infatti riconoscendo in Griselda una presa di coscienza della necessità di una conseguente opposizione alla crudeltà del marchese, si giustificano i reiterati e sempre più accaniti assalti di ferocia psicologica da perte di questi, fino alla resa."

44. In fact, it is that apparent scorn for Griselda that planted the seed of Violante's and Ridolfo's ambitious hope. Indirectly, then, Gualtieri is responsible for their subversive plots.

45. This alternative is no doubt inspired by Dioneo's final remark, but whereas previous dramatists (Dekker, Lope de Vega) developed this remark by offering Griselda alternate men, Maggi shows us instead what Griselda herself could have been. Violante couples the promiscuity of Dioneo's suggestion with resentment and a thirst for vengeance.

46. Unfortunately, I do not know the dating of individual poems, but many of these themes recur.

47. Maggi, *Scelta di Poesie*, ed. Cipollini, 72. Subsequent citations of Maggi's poetry are from this edition.

48. Much of the political poetry in *Scelta di Poesie* concerns these issues.

49. Cf. Hans Sachs's Griselda, who prays to God at every turn.

50. Savelli, "Struttura e valori," 291, remarks that Boccaccio's tale "è sostianzialmente novella d'inganno," but he associates it with the genre of "beffa" rather than the theme of political treachery.

51. See Vittore Branca's notes to his edition of the *Decameron, Tutte le opere di Giovanni Boccaccio*, 4 (Verona: Mondadori, 1976), 1154. See also Singleton's notes to *Inferno* 11 in his edition of *The Divine Comedy*, Bollingen Series LXXX (Princeton: Princeton University Press, 1977), vol.1, esp. 175.

52. The text and translation are from Charles Singleton's edition, 3:190–91.

53. Giulio Savelli, "Struttura e valori," 297–98, suggests that Griselda might have represented for Boccaccio or his contemporaries the new bourgeois intellectual reflectively detached from politics. Did Boccaccio similarly think of her as an image for Dante's noble—though more imposed than voluntary—detachment from the infernally ungrateful and treacherous society around him? Perhaps Savelli's word "distacco" [detachment] has the wrong implications; Dante certainly remained political to the core.

54. Ugolino had even forged alliance with the Visconti, former rulers of Maggi's Milan. Italy's own native tyrants were not better than the subsequent invaders who replaced them.

55. E.g., *Paradiso* 9:132 and esp. 27:55–57.

56. See note 9. The idea that our efforts to be virtuous manifest the sin of pride was a topic fairly, widely discussed in the era of Reformation and Counterreformation between Boccaccio and Maggi. See, for example, the discussions in Marguerite de Navarre's *Heptameron*, and John J. Conley, *The Suspicion of Virtue: Women Philosophers in Neoclassical France* (Ithaca: Cornell University Press, 2002).

57. Savelli, ""Struttura e valori," 289, comments on this feature already present in Boccaccio's story: "la teatralità sempre in agguato rischia di vanificare ogni azione liberale o magnifica immeschinendola: . . . Il fine di operare liberalità e magnificenza, 'con ogni studio,' è infatti quello di erigere a se stessi un monumento attraverso l'altrui ricordo delle proprie virtù."

58. Carpani, "La storia sanata," 368, observes Maggi's tendency to identify himself with lower-class characters. He also points out, 375, the local public taste for drama mixed with humor, and the failure of a play too relentlessly tragic.

59. Cf. Goldoni called his *Griselda* a "commedia."

60. Ferrucci, "The Milanese Theater," 30, describing Maggi's worldview as "suffused with a Christian pessimism," suggests that: "As far as actual political behavior is concerned, Maggi limits himself to advising through his characters a prudent silence, for the situation does not seem to offer any real possibility of escape." This is clearly not the case for the young Maggi and his *Griselda di Saluzzo*.

# Cock and Bull Cosmologies: Reading the Post-Enlightenment Universe

Nicholas Rennie

Affirming that the universe is a book written "in lingua matematica" (in the language of mathematics),[1] Galileo advocates simplicity as a key principle for making sense of a cosmic text that has come to appear chaotically at odds with itself. As his *Dialogue Concerning the Two Chief World Systems* argues, a geokinetic account of the motions of the planets corresponds to empirical evidence with greater simplicity than do the Aristotelian, geocentric theories, and is therefore also more probable.[2] This is the argument that Salviati and Sagredo, whom Galileo calls "two great luminaries" of his age,[3] help make against the muddled innocence of the *Dialogue*'s third interlocutor, Simplicio. However, the *Dialogue* also undermines its standard of simplicity by a rhetorical sleight of hand undertaken with the Church's vigilant censors in mind: what Galileo offers is a "hypothesis" that is not "absolutely" superior to traditional conceptions, but merely preferable with regard to the "arguments of some professed Peripatetics."[4]

The equivocation between geocentric and heliocentric philosophies is partly interesting, in post-Copernican literary writing, inasmuch as it figures as a problem of selecting, interpreting, and evaluating texts. Whereas the notion of a Book of Nature might reasonably imply the existence of a definitive hermeneutic code (*Il saggiatore* defines this as the language of geometry),[5] Galileo's reference to probability also implies that choice of the right code can be a matter of some uncertainty. Furthermore, the question will arise whether a definitive hermeneutic key may even be imagined to exist. The poet of *Paradise Lost* remains undecided whether the sun is at the "centre, or eccentric" (Book III, l. 575), but if it is not for humans or even angels to know such things, there is no doubt that these truths are nonetheless permanently inscribed in the "Book of God" (Book VIII, l. 67).[6] On the other hand, how do later poets of the cosmos posit a textual frame of reference once the Book is made to compete with other books? Milton's poem, which begins by announcing its intention to "justify the ways of God to men" (Book I, l. 26), refers to an overarching order within which all chaos is subsumed. In the work of Leibniz, Pope, Rousseau, Voltaire and their contemporaries, the "long" eighteenth century will return obsessively to the problems of the relation between chaos and order in its debates over the reality and nature of theodicy.

Here, I focus on a selection of passages by Leopardi and Goethe —two very different writers from distinct cultures and traditions, whose work is nonetheless in both cases deeply rooted in the seventeenth and eighteenth centuries' poetic and philosophical concerns. In doing so, I wish to suggest some ways in which literary writing, at the end of the Enlightenment, reflects on the cosmic relation between order and its opposite as a problem of reading. How and what do these writers read when their work is cosmography? Who does the reading, and with what authority?[7]

If in Freud's view Darwin inflicts the second "blow" to human narcissism after Copernicus,[8] Leopardi has already prepared the way. In the *Operette morali* (*Moral Essays*), first published as a complete edition in 1827,[9] the narrator of the "Cantico del gallo silvestre" (Canticle of the Wild Cock) cites the targumic image of a wild cock that stands on the earth with its feet and touches the heavens with its beak and crest (*PP* 2:161; *ME* 170).[10] The figure takes form silently and mysteriously as a backdrop to the text's introductory and inconclusive inquiry into the myth's origins and contours. We are told, in fastidious detail, how the story—whose original title is transliterated as "Scir detarnegòl bara letzafra"— has been transmitted by way of an old parchment, one inscribed with an obscure pastiche of ancient languages ["in lettera ebraica, e in lingua tra caldea, targumica, rabbinica, cabalistica e talmudica" (in Hebrew characters, and in a language compounded of the Chaldean, Targumic, Rabbinical, Cabalistic and Talmudic)] that the narrator has translated with great effort and in consultation with an assortment of scholars (ibid.). From this enigmatic composite of writings comes the apocalyptic wisdom of the totem-like creature, whose words take up the rest of the text. It announces that every part of the universe is directed toward death; and just as the reigns of the greatest kings and emperors have been forgotten, of the whole world and indeed of all created things there will eventually remain not a trace: "un silenzio nudo, e una quiete altissima, empieranno lo spazio immenso" (*PP* 2:165; a naked silence, and a most lofty calm, will fill the immensity of space [*ME* 173]). Gone is the Pythagorean harmony of the spheres, which the Moon, in another of the *Operette*, says she cannot hear (*PP* 2:46; *ME* 71). Gone too are humanity and its works, along with the universe itself, whose mysteries, as the closing words of the "Canticle" inform us, will pass away without ever having been understood. There remain only the words of the Wild Cock, whose authority as a prophet of doom is as enigmatic at the end of the piece as its textual genealogy is at the beginning.

It is in the lighter style of an Aesop or La Fontaine that the protagonists chat in the sketches to an unfinished Leopardian dialogue between a Horse and a Bull. To an astonished Bull, the Horse explains that an animal called "man," a being similar to the monkey but now long extinct, once subjugated its fellow creatures, and indeed considered itself master and telos of the world (*PP* 2:237–45). As the Horse goes on to say, humans assumed that the sun, moon, and stars, though "infinitely" larger than they and their lands, rose and set only to serve them (*PP* 2:239). The two animals marvel at the follies of this extinct creature, but do so, in part, because they share in them: the Horse and Bull are each convinced that the world was made, respectively, for horses and bulls (*PP* 2:237, 239). These conceits find their way into Leopardi's "Dialogo di un folletto e di uno gnomo," in which an imp and a gnome reflect sardonically on the anthropocentrism—and geocentrism— of a now extinct humankind (*PP* 2:33–37; *ME* 59–61). Here too, these considerations reflect the certainty that the universe is in fact centered around those who speak in the dialogue.

Elsewhere in Leopardi's *Operette*, an individual human being learns about the universe and humanity's position in it by conversing with the natural world directly: an Icelander hears from a personified Nature of her indifference to the human race; Copernicus is summoned to an audience with the Sun, during which he is told to inform the world that the Sun refuses to continue revolving around it.[11] By contrast, in that existence presided over by the Horse and Bull, the Imp and Gnome, or the Wild Cock, these creatures are left to report on humanity's past or impending demise. These elucidators of the constellations are no heroes of Enlightenment—neither the "Tuscan Artist" Galileo of *Paradise Lost* (Book I, l. 288), nor that Newton celebrated in Pope's epitaph as an instrument of divine illumination,[12] but a coterie of dubious, even openly moronic nonhumans. Their pronouncements suggest that the human universe ends, not in the grandeur of a tragically apocalyptic finale, but possibly only in mindless chatter. This is true not only of the dialogue between the Bull and the Horse, who each show themselves to be all too human in putting their respective species at the center of the dehumanized world, but of the Cock as well. As the parchment's translator writes, the avian prophet may possess reason; alternately, it may only have been trained to parrot human language—the narrator adds that he does not know by whom (*PP* 2:161; *ME* 170). Both the figure's towering proportions, and the possibility that what the translator has rendered "in volgare" [in the vulgar tongue (*PP* 2:161; *ME* 170)] is in fact nonsense, strengthen the Babelic associations of the Wild Cock's composite speech. The mythic creature may speak words of wisdom; or perhaps its utterances are like that of Dante's Nimrod, whose words in *Inf.* 31.67 Robert Hollander has described as a "fallen Hebrew," or language of confusion, one that parodically mimics the language of understanding of St. Paul in 1 Cor. 14:18–19.[13]

Yet if the worlds depicted in the Leopardian stories are bleak, they are particularly so because it seems that such tales are all that is left in a universe that has lost any reliable sense-making agency. This universe is mysterious, less because it is assumed to have an unfathomable meaning than because the category of meaning itself appears in doubt. As Hollander's reading of Nimrod's words reminds us, Dante's world is one in which freedom from this doubt (or confusion) is a fundamental imperative, as well as a precondition for any true understanding. The birdlike spirits who appear to Dante in *Par.* 18 write the significance of their appearance (and of the universe that he and they inhabit) into the sky, resolving themselves first into the Latin characters of the first verse of the Book of Wisdom, then into the shape of the Imperial Eagle (*Par.* 18.73–108). Whatever confusion may prevail in the minds and languages of those on earth or in hell, this universe itself bears the unmistakable imprint of divine justice.[14] By contrast, if Leopardi's creatures speak nonsense, nothing in the texts that present them points unambiguously to a more enlightened source of cosmological interpretation. And if indeed there is anything like an overarching order or law, it is one that is strikingly unreassuring. This becomes evident in the comparisons Leopardi draws between cosmographic unintelligibility and the disorder of human history and politics. Closely following the sketches of the dialogue between the Horse and the Bull, the "Dialogue of an Imp and a Gnome" underscores the fallacy of conflating human history and "world" history, sociopolitical upheavals and the revolutions of planet earth (*PP* 2:36; *ME* 60). Here, whatever the rules informing human life, they are apparently unrelated to those structuring the physical universe. A text such as the "Apocryphal Fragment of Strato of Lampsacus" reframes and generalizes this distinction as one between the histories of the component parts of the universe, and the fundamental ahistoricity of this universe itself. In calling attention to the latter frame, however, it hardly provides a promising ground for the construction of meaning: the historicity of human action—and indeed any perception of time—is ultimately irrelevant in view of the sheer permanence of matter.

This withdrawal of a cosmic ground for interpretation is reflected in the ambiguous status of the "Apocryphal Fragment" itself. The text, some five pages long, begins with a "Preamble," followed by a section "Concerning the Origin of the World" and a second section entitled "Of the end of the World." As in the *operetta* that directly precedes it, the "Canticle of the Wild Cock," an opening paragraph (the Preamble) tells of the text's origins:

> Questo Frammento, che io per passatempo ho recato dal greco in volgare, è tratto da un codice a penna che trovatasi alcuni anni sono, e forse ancora si trova, nella libreria dei monaci del monte Athos. Lo intitolo *Frammento apocrifo* perché, come ognuno può vedere, le cose che si leggono nel capitolo *della fine del mondo*, non possono essere state scritte se non poco tempo addietro; laddove Stratone da Lampsaco, filosofo peripatetico, detto il fisico, visse da trecento anni avanti l'era cristiana.

[This Fragment, which for a pastime I have translated from the
Greek into the vulgar tongue, is taken from a handwritten codex
which was to be found some years ago, and perhaps still is, in the
library of the monks of Mount Athos. I entitle it *Apocryphal
Fragment* because, as anyone can see, the things to be read in the
chapter *concerning the end of the world* can have been written
but a short while ago; whereas Strato of Lampsacus, a peripatetic
philosopher, known as the Physicist, lived about three hundred
years before the Christian era.]

(*PP* 2:166; *ME* 175)

If the immediate textual source for the "translation" is less obscure than that of the "Canticle," we are nonetheless told that its
authorship remains unclear. The first section accords with what is
known of Strato's writing, the translator explains; but he reminds
us that relatively little is known of Strato's work, and that this
knowledge comes to us by way of other writers. What earns the
piece its designation as "apocryphal" is the fact that the second
half seems to have been conceived centuries after the first. The
text's genesis is accordingly informed by a historical interruption,
one that is reflected in its structure. In its headings, the "Apocryphal Fragment" announces something like the minimum requirements of a plot: it tells, at least, of a beginning and an end. It
does not, however, present an Aristotelian whole in the sense of
connecting these two components with a middle peripety. The
piece remains disunited, a "Fragment," and it does so not least by
explicitly failing—or refusing—to connect its elements in narrative form.[15]

Indeed, the section titles are interesting because they seem to
promise a basic narrative development that will in fact be contra-
dicted by the theories that the text presents. The first section begins: "Le cose materiali, siccome elle periscono tutte ed hanno
fine, così tutte ebbero incominciamento. Ma la materia stessa
niuno incominciamento ebbe, cioè a dire che ella è per sua propria
forza ab eterno" (*PP* 2:166; Material things, just as they all perish
and have an end, so they all had a commencement. But matter itself had no commencement, that is to say it has existed *ab eterno*
by virtue of its own force [*ME* 175]). Matter takes on forms that
have beginnings as they have ends, and each of these could presumably be made into the subject of narrative. Matter itself, however, is unending and, from the point of view of its infinite dura-

tion, unnarratable. This idea is underscored by the fact that the section "Concerning the Origin of the World" does not in fact recount a story of origination, but instead lays out a pair of universal principles, asserting the eternity of matter, and the presence of a material "force" that perpetually leads matter to take on new and transient forms. This story of an "origin" in fact says no more about a particular origin than it does about a particular end; it merely establishes an overarching law of invariance within which all change is subsumed.

The second section does begin with a story—one that is announced in its title: the centrifugal force of the earth's revolutions on its own axis will lead to the planet's becoming gradually flatter and then annular before its matter fragments completely and falls into the sun. The latter half of the section, however, returns to the principles of the first part of the "Apocryphal Fragment." In a shift in perspective, we are told that this process of dissolution is common to all planets and stars, but that since matter itself will endure, infinite new creatures, species, and worlds will come about (*PP* 2:171; *ME* 178). This closely echoes the conclusion to the first section, in which we learn that just as an individual creature may die yet its species survive, so may a species die out without the natural order that contains it being destroyed (*PP* 2:168; *ME* 176). By extension, every particular being, class of beings or "world" may disappear, yet matter continues to take on new forms ad infinitum. To each level of particularity implicitly belong stories of commencement and ending; but all of these accounts lose significance in view of the fact of matter's duration. Read in this light, the "Apocryphal Fragment" provides a commentary on both the exchange between the Horse and Bull, and the "Dialogue of an Imp and a Gnome." The displacement of humankind announced in these texts underscores a more general law of ephemerality that pertains to all material forms.[16]

The second section of the text repeats the principles outlined in the first; and like the first section, it neither contains nor completes a narrative development. The "Apocryphal Fragment" is really made up of two fragments that present the same fundamental principles of existence and are closely related in their logic and vocabulary, but that do not lead from one section to the other in elaborating a narrative plot. Analogously, the supposed origin of these text-halves in widely separate historical periods does not re-

flect a development in intellectual history so much as it underscores the timelessness of the ideas they elaborate. What is striking about the second section is not just that it echoes the modern
thinking of Bayle, Fontenelle, and d'Holbach—echoes that render
the text's alleged antiquity suspect—but that its Enlightenment
materialism should in fact be so closely mirrored in the portion of
the text ascribed to Strato. The juxtaposition of the two parts situ-
ates Leopardi's conclusions outside of history. The eternity of
matter is a universal truth; and to recognize this truth as the defining principle of existence is also to give up narrative as a privileged
medium for the communication of truth. Leopardi's miniature
story of genesis and apocalypse foregoes these narrative markers,
and with them abandons the basic cosmological plot that its structural divisions appear to signal.

Permutations are inscribed in matter by a force or forces inherent within matter itself; nothing in the "Apocryphal Fragment"
alludes to a transcendent principle or intention guiding this force,
any more than the world regarded by the Imp and Gnome is
shaped by the volition of human beings. Instead, we are referred
back to the forms that matter takes—along that spatiotemporal
scale that extends from the short-lived individual organism to the
progressively longer lasting "species" and "genera," and from
these to the inorganic bodies of planets and stars (*PP* 2:168, 171;
*ME* 176, 178). This is true even when the latter are anthropomor-
phized and their relations given social form, as in the dialogue between Copernicus and the Sun. Until now, we learn in that Dialogue, "pareva che l'universo fosse a somiglianza di una corte;
nella quale la Terra sedesse come in un trono; e gli altri globi din-
torno, in modo di cortigiani, di guardie, di servitori, attendessero
chi ad un ministero e chi a un altro" (*PP* 2:189) [it seemed that the
universe was of the nature of a court; in which the Earth sat as on
a throne; and the other globes around, in the manner of courtiers,
guards and servants, attended some to one office and some to another (*ME* 196)]. Copernicus warns that if the Earth is made to give
up its position at the center of this universe, other planets will no
longer be willing to accord it such other privileges as its natural
landscapes and its human and animal inhabitants. Should the Sun
enthrone itself at the universe's center, therefore, this would en-
tail a general process of fragmentation, an explosion of life forms
and new, smaller centers of power: "Ed eccovi un altro rivolgi-

mento grandissimo nel mondo; e una infinità di famiglie e di popo-
lazioni nuove, che in un momento si vedranno venir su da tutte le
bande, come funghi. . . . [Le stelle] vorranno avere i loro pianeti,
come avrete voi; ciascuna i suoi propri. I quali pianeti nuovi, con-
verrà che sieno anche abitati e adorni come è la Terra" (*PP* 2:191)
[And so behold another vast upheaval in the universe; and an in-
finity of new families and populations, that in an instant we shall
see spring up on all sides like mushrooms. . . . [The stars] will want
to have their planets, as you have, each of them his own. And
these new planets will have to be inhabited and adorned, as the
Earth is (*ME* 197)]. Transformation of the cosmos here appears as a
frightening, Malthusian expansion of the universe's organic and
planetary populations—a vision that prompts the Sun to guarantee that resources will indeed be available for the survival of all.

On the one hand, then, these metaphors humanize the universe. Yet the core joke of the dialogue derives from the point that
the cosmos is in fact not historical in the way that human sociopolitical developments are. It experiences no crisis; the historical change in question pertains rather to a shift in perspective that
Copernicus initiates with his heliocentric theory among humankind. The *operetta* remains close to the "Apocryphal Fragment" and the "Dialogue of an Imp and a Gnome" in underscoring
the irrelevance of human life and thought to the workings of the
universe itself; and in its portrayal of the cosmos as a set of social
systems, it foregrounds by ironic contrast the inapplicability to it
of social and historical models.

The same is true of the "Canticle," which, of the *operette* I
have discussed, comes closest to telling a story in the sense of describing a process of cosmic development. The crowing Cock recalls humanity from its slumbers to a renewed consciousness of
the demise that informs all existence. Every life is a process directed toward death; and if the universe as a whole seems structured by such cyclical patterns as those of the seasons, it too is
nonetheless caught up in a process of aging until it, and nature,
will be "extinguished," *spenta*. Just as the greatest kingdoms and
empires have vanished without a trace, the world and all "cose
create" (created things) will disappear and leave only "silence"
(*PP* 2:164–65; *ME* 173). If, in the Dialogue cited above, Copernicus
warns that the Earth's abdication will give rise to frenzied competition for authority among myriad planets and stars, the "Canti-

cle" terminates instead in the inert silence of a kind of absolute zero. The Sun promises Copernicus benignly that its energy will suffice for all; however many the new populations, "la mia luce e il calore basterà per tutte, senza che io cresca la spesa però; e il mondo avrà di che cibarle, vestirle, alloggiarle, trattarle larga- mente, senza far debito" (PP 2:191; my light and heat will suffice for all, without my spending any more on that account; and the universe will have the wherewithal to feed them, clothe them, house them, and be generous with them, without getting into debt [ME 197]). In contrast to the Wild Cock's prophecy of a uni- verse reduced to empty, silent space, the Sun predicts an ever more crowded hubbub. However, it is worth noting the Sun's eco- nomic conservatism: it will "spend" no more than it has; it will avoid going into "debt." With the Sun deciding to stop moving and instead take a seat (another metaphor that recurs within the text), the total amount of energy in this universe will remain the same.

And what about that universe recklessly extinguished and "spent" in the "Canticle"? The profligacy of the Wild Cock's pro- nouncements is in a different way checked. A footnote that Leop- ardi appends to the text cautions: "Questa è conclusione poetica, non filosofica. Parlando filosoficamente, l'esistenza, che mai non è cominciata, non avrà mai fine" (PP 2:227 n. 56) [This is a poetic, not a philosophical conclusion. Philosophically speaking exis- tence, which never began, will never end (ME 258 n. 12)]. The two texts poetically historicize the universe in opposite ways, and to- gether may be said to cancel out this narrative divergence: the universe's death is as much a poetic conceit as is the notion that it might be caught up in a planetary population explosion. Individu- ally as well, the texts undermine the idea that the universe is sub- ject to any kind of overall progression, whether conceived posi- tively or negatively. Such notions of development belong to the category of what Leopardi terms "illusion," or what the footnote to the "Canticle" calls a "poetic" conclusion. This warning is- sued in the name of philosophy echoes the cautionary observa- tions presented by the philologist and translator at the beginning of the text itself. The Wild Cock is not to be trusted. Perhaps this creature is no more than a kind of trained parrot whose words originate elsewhere. Indeed, as the same sentence in the opening paragraph tells us, the creature is itself a product of writing—

transmitted in an indefinable language and from an unknowable source. The concluding footnote returns us to this textual frame, and to an awareness of the unreliability of the Wild Cock's prophecy as it is presented within this frame.

ॐ ॐ ॐ

The problem of framing is a dominant concern of the text to which I now turn in the remaining pages—a text that originates in a very different poetic sensibility and national culture, but that likewise brings both optimistic and skeptical traditions of Enlightenment thought into sharp relief. From a concise first draft written in the 1770s, Goethe's *Faust* evolved over the following sixty years into a work both longer and far more complex than its original conception. This complexity is in part related to the drama's reflection on its own status—and that of the figures who appear within it—as representation. This self-reflection begins with the Dedication, written in 1797, in which the poet, returning to the *Faust*-material after a long interruption, addresses the "schwankende Gestalten" (uncertain forms; l. 1)[17] that return with his memories of the past; and it becomes particularly obvious in the sequence of the following two scenes. First, in a "Prelude on the Stage," a small theater group convenes to discuss the play it is about to mount. This scene concludes with the Director exhorting his Poet and Clown to spare no effort in recreating creation itself within the bounds of the theater:

> Gebraucht das groß' und kleine Himmelslicht,
> Die Sterne dürfet ihr verschwenden;
> An Wasser, Feuer, Felsenwänden,
> An Tier und Vögeln fehlt es nicht.
> So schreitet in dem engen Bretterhaus
> Den ganzen Kreis der Schöpfung aus,
> Und wandelt mit bedächt'ger Schnelle
> Vom Himmel durch die Welt zur Hölle.

> [Use the sunshine and moonshine lights,
> Use starlight—we have stars galore,
> Water and fire and rocky heights,
> And birds and animals by the score!
> Thus on these narrow boards you'll seem

To explore the entire creation's scheme—
And with swift steps, yet wise and slow
From heaven, through the world, right down to hell you'll go!]
                                                    (l. 235–42)

So different is the tone of the succeeding Prologue in Heaven that the latter's readers sometimes forget that both the Prologue and the following action have been thus framed. If we believe the Director of the Prelude, the play that he and his partners throw together will invert Dante's journey. And if this play begins—as the Prologue does—with an encompassing, Miltonic vision of the sun, stars, and natural world, we may expect to be left either with a vision of hell, or worse, perhaps, with the knowledge that that heaven and earth into which the play lures us over the next twelve thousand lines are finally nothing more than dubious stage props. Mephistopheles will consistently remind us of this possibility, for instance in a particularly Brechtian moment in which he appears on the proscenium at the end of act 3, removes his buskins, mask and veil, and prepares to "comment on" (*kommentieren*) the play "as necessary" in an epilogue (stage directions following l. 10,038); or in a burlesque passage from act 5, in which he adopts a role analogous to the Director's as he vainly orders that a great hell mouth be erected in order to convince his modern viewers that what they are witnessing is something more than "Lug und Trug und Traum" (lies and trickery and dreams; l. 11,655).

I cite these passages to recall ways in which Goethe's *Faust* complicates the relation between audience and dramatic representation; for as this relation becomes problematic, so too does the relation between the story of Faust's career with Mephistopheles, and the frame theodicy that contains this story.[18] The Prologue in Heaven establishes this frame, citing from the Book of Job the idea of a wager made between Lord and devil over the fate of an individual human being. The Lord indicates that Faust will in any event be saved, his erring reconciled as part of the greater perfection of the Lord's universe.[19] The notion that evil is integrated within the harmony of the cosmos is anticipated in the opening stanzas of the scene. The Archangel Raphael describes the sun's path through the heavens:

Die Sonne tönt nach alter Weise
In Brudersphären Wettgesang,
Und ihre vorgeschrieb'ne Reise
Vollendet sie mit Donnergang.

[The sun proclaims its old devotion
In rival song with brother spheres,
And still completes in thunderous motion
The circuits of its destined years.]

(243–46)

The harmony of the spheres expresses a state of unchanging perfection that is itself *vorgeschrieben*, "prescribed" in the sense of being both ordained, and written in advance. Both this stanza, and the joint commentary of the three Archangels three stanzas later, conclude by reaffirming the point that this state of perfection has never varied: it is "herrlich wie am ersten Tag" [glorious as upon the first day] (l. 250; 270). Subsumed within this greater order is the apparent chaos of terrestrial existence:

Und Stürme brausen um die Wette,
Vom Meer auf's Land, vom Land auf's Meer,
Und bilden wütend eine Kette
Der tiefsten Wirkung rings umher.

[And turn by turn the tempests raging
From sea to land, from land to sea,
Build up, in passion unassuaging,
Their chain of furious energy.]

(l. 259–62)

The harmonious *Wettgesang* ("rival song") of the spheres in the first stanza is here contrasted with the chaos of a contention among storms whose outcome, as implied by the idiomatic phrase "um die Wette," initially remains open. This contrast is heightened in the preceding stanza (l. 251–58) by the opposition between the light of heaven and the dark of the world, between the raging of the waters below and the steady rotations of the spheres above. Yet harmony reasserts itself. The *Wette* ["bet"] of l. 259 is linked by rhyme to the *Kette* ["chain"] of l. 261; the seeming chaos of the tempest in fact reveals what l. 262, translated literally, describes

as a "chain of deepest effect all around." The Archangels are justified in asserting that the universe is "glorious as upon the first
day" since its every element is connected by a logic of cause and
effect to the visible order of the whole. This suggests that those
bets that Mephistopheles proposes to the Lord in the Prologue (l.
312, 331) and to Faust in the latter's study (l. 1698), and that structure the drama as a whole, may likewise be subordinate to an overarching divine order that is, like the orbits of the planets and stars,
preordained. The Lord confirms the stability of this overarching
order in stating at the outset that he will lead Faust "in die Klarheit" ["into clarity" (l. 309)], whatever his errors; and in proclaiming Mephistopheles to be one of his instruments, one who usefully
provokes human beings into activity (l. 340–43). If Mephistopheles is the child of "Chaos" (l. 1384), his actions nonetheless re-
dound to the greater perfection of the Lord's universe.

Yet to pursue the logic of this framing is also to reveal this universe's ambiguous status. The Prelude on the Stage encourages
the thought that Lord and devil, like the sun and the moon and
all of creation, are themselves theatrical improvisations. If Raphael admires the Sun's passage along its eternal, "prescribed" or-
bit, the production of which he forms a part is apparently cobbled
together with an expectant audience already waiting in its seats
(l. 41–42). In the Prelude on the Stage, the Poet accuses his companions of *Pfuscherei*, ["bungling" (l. 106)], announcing instead
that he would dedicate himself to verses that gradually achieve
perfection in the course of "years" (l. 71–72). The task of a poet, he
says, is to create unity from disunity, to tame the chaos of existence rhythmically and harmonically, to draw individual elements together into "herrlich[e] Akkorden" [magnificent chords
(l. 140–49)]—to create something, in short, that resembles that
harmony of the spheres subsequently depicted in the opening lines
of the Prologue. The Director instead urges that the group do its
work quickly—"Was heute nicht geschieht, ist morgen nicht
getan" [What's not begun / Today will still be left undone / To-
morrow (l. 225)]—and not bother about creating a unified whole:
"Gebt ihr ein Stück, so gebt es gleich in Stücken! [If you'll present
a piece, present it in pieces! (l. 99)]. That writing that subsequently takes place, we may infer, will struggle to keep pace with
a production already underway.

If the tension between chaos and order in *Faust* is interesting, however, it is so because it finds no simple resolution. The very premise of the Prelude—the notion that a play is here being produced in the course of its very performance—works against the notion that this scene might offer a privileged perspective from which to survey the succeeding action. Its questionable authority as a frame to the drama as a whole is further illuminated by its concluding words. Contrary to the Director's final injunction (l. 241–42), and despite Mephistopheles' vigorous efforts at the end, the drama will not finally lead us down to hell. Goethe's drama neither confirms unambiguously that cosmic harmony described in the Prologue, nor does it conclude with a Leopardian vision of cosmic entropy. As in the *operette* discussed above, however, Goethe's play does recast the question of cosmic order and disorder as the problem of reading a Book of Nature whose code is no longer unambiguously clear, nor even clearly meaningful.

This is perhaps best illustrated by the scene "Witch's Kitchen," which Goethe composed in 1787 or 1788, and in which a family of apes presents a burlesque, chaotic inversion of that cosmic system that the Archangels admire in the Prologue in Heaven. Mephistopheles takes Faust to the Witch in order that his charge be made younger by thirty years. They arrive while she is out, and an amused Mephistopheles and a revolted Faust look on as the kitchen's simian residents stir the contents of a cauldron. One monkey approaches Mephisto and asks for a dice throw that would make him rich: "wär' ich bei Geld, / So wär' ich bei Sinnen" [And if I had money / My head would stop spinning! (l. 2398–99)]. A stroke of fortune would bring him both wealth and understanding, he says. He then raises a "large ball" brought to him by his offspring:

> Das ist die Welt;
> Sie steigt und fällt
> Und rollt beständig;
> Sie klingt wie Glas:
> Wie bald bricht das?
> [ . . . ]
> Sie ist von Ton,
> Es gibt Scherben.

[The world is this ball:
See it rise and fall
And roll round and round!
It's glass, it will break,
[ . . . ]
It's made of clay;
Clay gets broken, they say.]
                    (l. 2402–15)

Like the cash that the monkey imagines receiving by a stroke of
luck, the world itself is subject to the vagaries of fortune, its rising and falling at any moment liable to end in shards. The monkeys force Mephisto to a chair, on which he seats himself "wie
der König auf dem Throne" [like a king enthroned in state (l.
2448)]. They also bring him a crown, but in doing so break it in
two:

Nun ist es geschehn!
Wir reden und sehn,
Wir hören und reimen;
[ . . . ]
Und wenn es uns glückt,
Und wenn es sich schickt,
So sind es Gedanken!

[Now it's done! It falls down!—
We can talk, see and hear,
We can rhyme loud and clear!
[ . . . ]
And if we're in luck,
And if it works out,
Why then we'll have thoughts!]
                    (l. 2453–60)

The scene depicts allegorically a physical cosmos in disarray, a political universe in turmoil, an economic system subject to wild
oscillations and sudden collapse (anticipating the fiscal turmoil
caused in act 1 of part 2 by the invention of paper money), and the
very possibility of thinking and speaking coherently. The monkeys' chorus is here marked by one of the abrupt transitions typical of the scene, with a reference to the broken crown being

followed immediately by a comment on the apparently arbitrary connection between "thoughts," and the monkeys' words. If the monkeys keep chattering, they may seem to make sense now and then, but this is purely a matter of chance. What they say about their own language in fact confirms what Mephisto claims elsewhere about the arbitrary relation between words and meanings in general (ll. 1995; 2564); but nowhere else in Goethe's drama is language as ruthlessly and explicitly degraded to nonsense as in the mouths of the Witch's babbling monkeys.

As I have argued elsewhere, in the final version of Goethe's *Faust* completed in 1832, this scene serves as a kind of anti-Prologue.[20] In the Prologue, chaos is integrated into a larger order that is said to be as perfect as at the beginning of creation. Here, order (or sense) appears, if at all, by chance, and independently of authorial intention. In place of the drama's frame theodicy, the cosmic and metaphysical condition represented in the Witch's Kitchen is cheerfully stochastic. Now the silliness of this scene can be understood within the larger order that that earlier scene proclaims. On the other hand, the sequence with the monkeys reminds us of a point that the drama makes throughout, namely that what we see is always a representation, and as such also a reading. As they roll forth the sphere, the monkeys admire its glassy surface and peer into its hollow interior (l. 2407) as though it were a crystal ball. But if the orbits of the planets in the Prologue are prescribed by (or permanently *in*scribed within) the matter of the universe, here no such revelatory and determining scripture becomes visible. In short, it is not just that the Witch's Kitchen presents a scene of chaos that stands in opposition to the order of the Prologue, but that the scene reminds us that both chaotic and ordered visions are themselves just that: representations. Whether the cosmos is staged by a family of apes or by a harried theater company, as long as we remain in the field of representation there is no definitive frame that would offer a reliable standpoint from which to make sense of it all.

This hermeneutic relativity, I suspect, is what links the apes of Goethe's Witch's Kitchen and the fabulous creatures of Leopardi's *Operette morali*. The Sun of Leopardi's "Copernicus" invokes the principle of the Archimedean lever to suggest that Copernicus should indeed be able to force the Earth into motion (*PP* 2:188; *ME*

195); but just as the Sun, at the beginning of their exchange, has been unable to offer Copernicus a seat, the dialogue will show that the new universe in fact lacks any fixed point of reference lying outside the motions of the planets and stars. Goethe's monkeys and Leopardi's assorted creatures illustrate this cosmological relativity, for instance when the Wild Cock speaks of the Earth's eventual disappearance, or when the monkeys of *Faust* produce a fragile world that oscillates and rolls. In addition, however, these figures also illustrate the more frightening possibility of a world in which human reason either plays no role, or survives only in the traces of its demise. For while the "two great luminaries" of Galileo's *Dialogue* present a mathematical reading that would account for the order of the post-Copernican universe in the simplest and most lucid terms, Goethe's and Leopardi's creatures instead present cosmologies that lack both a stable physical center, and a hermeneutic standpoint from which this universe might be coherently read. In contrast with his Prologue in Heaven, Goethe's Witch's Kitchen not only displays a physical universe whose motions are unpredictable, but also a hit-or-miss cosmology marked by the failure or absence of human sense. And like the Imp and the Gnome, Leopardi's Horse and Bull comment on the stupidity of the human species; to the extent that they themselves replicate it, it is in failing to transcend its errors. Similarly, the pronouncements of the Wild Cock are marked by the possibility that this creature itself only repeats its words like a parrot, without comprehension. In Goethe's *Faust*, the simian cosmologists of the Witch's Kitchen gaze into the world, and in doing so they rhyme, but without reason.

When Goethe and Leopardi put such creatures in charge of interpreting the Book of Nature, the effect is not to reaffirm by contrast the epistemological authority of human readings and rhymings. Goethe's monkeys belong to low comedy; Leopardi's creatures are products of the more serene wit of eighteenth-century fable. Yet the laughter that accompanies both groups of figures has its apocalyptic ring. Their judgments are spoken from a world that resists structuring either by a transcendent intention or by human reason. In openly displaying their nonsense, these creatures may be "aufrichtige Poeten" [honest poets (l. 2464)], as Mephisto says of the monkeys. They, like the crowing parrot cock, may occasionally even appear to make sense, reproducing as they do the elements of human speech. Yet in so doing, these writer-hermeneuts of the post-Enlightenment universe also enact what Freud will term the cosmological and biological blows to human narcissism. As a result, they not only raise the question of the universe's structure and humanity's position within it. These figures reassert the universe's status as a text, but as one whose writers and readers lack the authority or comprehension to endow this text with stable meaning. Goethe's and Leopardi's idiot oracles thus refer us back to the problems of reading and evaluating words, of which they are both products and producers.

## NOTES

1. Galileo Galilei, *Il saggiatore*, ed. Ferdinando Flora (Turin: Einaudi, 1977) 33. *Discoveries and Opinions of Galileo*, trans. and ed. Stillman Drake (Garden City, NY: Doubleday, 1957), 238.

2. Galileo Galilei, *Dialogue Concerning the Two Chief World Systems*, trans. Stillman Drake (New York: Modern Library, 2001), 137.

3. Ibid., 7.

4. Ibid., 6.

5. Galileo, *Discoveries*, 238.

6. John Milton, *Complete Poems and Major Prose*, ed. Merritt Y. Hughes (New York: Macmillan, 1957).

7. There is no indication that Goethe was ever aware of Leopardi. For his part, Leopardi refers in his correspondence and his *Zibaldone* to Goethe's 1774 novel *Werther*, and in his letters comments on Goethe's autobiographical writings. He mentions *Faust* only once, and in passing, in a comment on the decadence of the modern age: "basta appena a far impressione poetica tutta la novità e l'ardire che è nel Fausto o nel Manfredo" (all the novelty and daring that appear in *Faust* or *Manfred* barely suffice to make a poetic impression). Giacomo Leopardi, *Zibaldone*, ed. Rolando Damiani, 3 vols. (Milan: Mondadori, 1997), 2:3036 (entry from April 1, 1829; p. 4479 in Leopardi's pagination). Part 2 of Goethe's play had not yet appeared at the time of this note. It remains unclear what direct knowledge Leopardi had of those parts of the play that had at that time been published in German and, by Gérard de Nerval in 1828, in French translation. Regarding his knowledge of the play, see Sergio Solmi, *Studi e nuovi studi leopardiani* (Milan: Riccardo Ricciardi, 1975), 150–52.

8. Sigmund Freud, "A Difficulty in the Path of Psycho-Analysis," *Standard Edition of the Complete Psychological Works of Sigmund Freud* vol. 17, trans. James Strachey (London: Hogarth, 1964), 136–44, here 140–41. Freud defines

the three successive blows to human narcissism as "cosmological," "biological," and "psychological."

9. A few of the *Operette* had appeared in 1826. Other editions were published, during Leopardi's lifetime, in 1834 and 1835. For a history of the work's publication, see pp. 1271–72 of the Damiani edition (*Poesie e prose* II) cited in the following note.

10. Parenthetical references to Leopardi's work indicate volume and page numbers in *Poesie e prose* (*PP*), ed. Rolando Damiani, 2 vols. (Milan: Mondadori, 1988); and page numbers in *The Moral Essays—Operette Morali* (*ME*), trans. Patrick Creagh (New York: Columbia University Press, 1983). (I have myself translated from the sketch of the dialogue between the horse and the bull, which does not appear in Creagh's edition.) In a footnote to the Canticle, Leopardi quotes as a source for the image of the Wild Cock Johann Buxtorf's *Lexicon Hebraicum et Chaldaicum*, which includes passages from the Targums (*PP* 2:227, 1345).

11. "Dialogo della natura e di un islandese" (*PP* 2:76–83; "The Dialogue of Nature and an Icelander" [*ME* 98–104]); "Il Copernico, dialogo" (*PP* 182–93; "Copernicus" [*ME* 189–99]).

12. "Nature, and Nature's Laws lay hid in Night. / God said, *Let Newton be!* and All was *Light.*" *The Poems of Alexander Pope*, ed. John Butt (New Haven: Yale University Press, 1963), 808.

13. Robert Hollander, *Dante and Paul's Five Words with Understanding*, Occasional Papers no. 1, Center for Medieval and Early Renaissance Studies (Binghamton, NY: Medieval and Renaissance Texts and Studies, 1992), here 17–18, 20.

14. Hollander, 40.

15. For further elaboration of the question of narrative development in Leopardi's prose, see the chapters "Copernicus, or the Problem of Revolution" and "Telling Time: Columbus' Hesitation and the History of the Human Race" in my *Speculating on the Moment: The Poetics of Time and Recurrence in Goethe, Leopardi, and Nietzsche* (*Münchener Komparatistische Studien*), ed. Hendrik Birus and Erika Greber (Göttingen: Wallstein, 2005).

16. The Horse and the Imp note, for instance, that humans are hardly the first species to become extinct (*PP* 2:237, 34).

17. I cite *Faust* by line number only, referring to: Johann Wolfgang von Goethe, *Faust Dichtungen*, 3 vols., ed. Ulrich Gaier (Stuttgart: Reclam, 1999). Translations are based on *Faust* I and II, 2 vols., trans. David Luke (Oxford: Oxford University Press, 1987). I have departed from this excellent translation where doing so seemed helpful for the sake of literal clarity.

18. I refer to the distinction, made over half a century ago by Benno von Wiese, between the drama's frame theodicy and internal plot. *Die deutsche Tragödie von Lessing bis Hebbel* (Hamburg: Hoffmann und Campe, 1948), 143–201.

19. "Wenn er mir jetzt auch nur verworren dient; / So werd' ich ihn bald in die Klarheit führen" (Though he still only serves me in confusion, / I will soon lead him into clarity [l. 308–9]); "Ein guter Mensch in seinem dunkeln Drange

/ Ist sich des rechten Weges wohl bewußt" (A good man, in his dark, bewildered stress, / Well knows the path from which he should not stray [l. 328–29]).

20. See my reading of the "Witch's Kitchen" as a parody of the opening vision of the Prologue, in the chapter "The Aleatory Moment: Goethe Between Pascal and Mallarmé" in my *Speculating on the Moment*. In that chapter I also discuss Goethe's abhorrence of chaos and disorder, in particular as he saw it represented in the events leading up to and following from the French Revolution.

# Contributors

**Jamie Claire Fumo** holds a PhD from Princeton University and is currently an Assistant Professor in the Department of English at McGill University in Montreal. Specializing in medieval English literature, she has published articles on Chaucer and his literary influences in *Studies in Philology, Chaucer Review, Mediaevalia*, and *Neophilologus*. Her current research focuses on medieval classicism and mythography, and she is at work on a book on the literary history of the god Apollo in the Middle Ages.

**Suzanne Hagedorn** earned her AB at Princeton University, where she studied Dante with Professor Robert Hollander. After earning her doctorate in Medieval Studies at Cornell University, she taught at the University of Arizona and the College of William and Mary, where she is now Associate Professor of English. She is the author of *Abandoned Women: Rewriting the Classics in Dante, Boccaccio and Chaucer* (2004).

**Jessica Levenstein** is an independent scholar. She received her PhD in Comparative Literature from Princeton University, where her work focused on the classical tradition in the Italian Middle Ages and Renaissance. She has published essays in *Dante Studies* and *Italica*, and is a contributor to the *Dante Encyclopedia, Medieval Italy: An Encyclopedia*, and the collection *Dante for the New Millennium*.

**Simone Marchesi** studied with Robert Hollander between 1997 and 2001, writing under his direction a dissertation on Dante's poetics in the transition from *De vulgari eloquentia* to the *Commedia*. He is currently Assistant Professor of French and Italian at Princeton University. His special interest is in the influence of classical and late-antique Latin works on Italian medieval writers, in particular Dante and Boccaccio. Published work includes *Stratigrafie decameroniane* (2004), articles on Dante, Boccaccio, Petrarch, and Giovanni della Casa, as well as on the tradition of the twentieth-century novel and contemporary Italian cinema.

**James McGregor** is Professor and Co-Head of the Department of Comparative Literature at the University of Georgia. He is the author of two books and several articles on Boccaccio's opere minori; editor of *Approaches to Teaching Boccaccio's Decameron*; translator of Luigi Guicciardini, *The Sack of Rome*, and author of *Rome from the Ground Up* (2005).

**Nicholas Rennie** is an Associate Professor of German and affiliate faculty of Comparative Literature at Rutgers University, where he teaches courses on the Age of Goethe, eighteenth-century aesthetics, literary theory and the Frankfurt School. He has published articles on Lessing, Goethe, Nietzsche, and Benjamin. His book *Speculating on the Moment: The Poetics of Time and Recurrence in Goethe, Leopardi, and Nietzsche* appeared in the series *Münchener Komparatistische Studien* (ed. Hendrik Birus and Erika Greber in 2005). He is currently working on a study on the relation between word and image in G. E. Lessing and Sigmund Freud.

**Earl Jeffrey Richards** (Princeton, AB, 1974, PhD, 1978) has been Professor of Romance Literatures at the University of Wuppertal since 1995. Prior to this he taught at Tulane University, The University of North Carolina at Chapel Hill, and the University of Münster. Robert Hollander was the co-director of his dissertation on Dante and the *Romance of the Rose*, later published in revised form in 1981. He has published extensively on Christine de Pizan, Ernst Robert Curtius, literary nationalism, and the survival of Nazi thought in literary criticism after the Second War.

**Albert J. Rivero**, Professor of English at Marquette University, has published articles and books on eighteenth-century British literature. Editor of the annual, *The Eighteenth-Century Novel*, and a member of the Editorial Board of *The Works of Tobias Smollett*, he has edited the new Norton Critical Editions of *Gulliver's Travels* and *Moll Flanders*. He is writing a book, tentatively titled *Duplicitous Representations: Samuel Richardson, Henry Fielding, and the History of Women's Fiction*, as well as editing both parts of *Pamela* for the Cambridge edition of Richardson's works and complete correspondence.

**William Robins** is Associate Professor of English and Medieval Studies at the University of Toronto, where he also directs the Program in Editing Medieval Texts. He has published many articles on romance fiction in the Middle Ages, especially on the story of Apollonius of Tyre. He is currently completing a book on the fourteenth-century Italian poet

Antonio Pucci, as well as an edition of Pucci's *Cantari della Reina d'Oriente*.

**Lauren Scancarelli Seem** was a Hollander student both as an undergraduate and as a graduate student. She has published articles on Virgil, Dante, and Tasso. Since the inception of the Princeton Dante Project (PDP), she has worked with Robert Hollander first on its development and then on its implementation; currently she continues to work for the PDP.

**Janet Levarie Smarr** wrote her dissertation under Robert Hollander's direction. She taught for twenty years in the Comparative Literature Program at the University of Illinois in Urbana-Champaign, and is now a professor in the Theatre Department and Italian Studies Program at the University of California in San Diego. Her books include *Italian Renaissance Tales, Boccaccio and Fiammetta: The Narrator as Lover, Boccaccio's Eclogues, Joining the Conversation: Dialogues by Renaissance Women*, and edited volumes on *Historical Criticism and the Challenge of Theory* and (coedited with Daria Valentini) *Italian Women and the City*.

**Macklin Smith**, now professor of English at the University of Michigan, read Dante's *Commedia* with Robert Hollander while an undergraduate. After sojourns at Harvard and in the US Army, he returned to Princeton, writing his doctorate dissertation in Comparative Literature on "*Piers Plowman* and late medieval lives of Christ." There he worked with Hollander on the history and theory of allegory: a seminar essay on Prudentius and Virgil eventually was expanded, with Bob's encouragement, into *Prudentius' Psychomachia: A Reexamination*. Later publications include articles on Chaucer, a book on composition pedagogy entitled *Teaching Writing That Works*, and poetry, most recently *Transplant*. He is currently completing an introduction-to-poetry textbook, and is writing a comprehensive study of Langland's alliterative long line.

# Index

251

# *Commedia* Index

255